PRE-COURSE ASSESSMENT

This self-assessment will help you and your instructor see how you perceive your college success skills as you begin this course. Be honest and take your time. There are no wrong answers, and this is not a test! For each question, rate yourself according to the following scale:

1	**2**	**3**	**4**	**5**
Definitely Like Me	Somewhat Like Me	Not Sure	Somewhat Unlike Me	Not At All Like Me

Please circle the number which best represents your answer:

1. I believe this course will help me build skills for college success.	1	2	3	4	5
2. I know how to find the people and resources that can help me make the transition to college.	1	2	3	4	5
3. I understand how habits can affect my ability to succeed.	1	2	3	4	5
4. I am aware of my learning styles and preferences.	1	2	3	4	5
5. I make choices in school and out based on how I learn.	1	2	3	4	5
6. I am effective at planning and managing my schedule.	1	2	3	4	5
7. I manage my finances actively and budget well.	1	2	3	4	5
8. I know exactly what goals I want to achieve in college.	1	2	3	4	5
9. I am effective at managing stress.	1	2	3	4	5
10. I take steps to keep my mind and body as healthy as possible.	1	2	3	4	5
11. I am comfortable with students who are different than me.	1	2	3	4	5
12. I work well in groups and teams.	1	2	3	4	5
13. I ask questions and think critically about what I hear and read.	1	2	3	4	5
14. I solve problems effectively.	1	2	3	4	5
15. I have strong memory and recall abilities.	1	2	3	4	5
16. I feel prepared to handle the reading in my college courses.	1	2	3	4	5
17. I use particular techniques to read textbooks in different academic areas.	1	2	3	4	5
18. I take comprehensive and clear notes.	1	2	3	4	5
19. I have excellent test-taking skills for college courses.	1	2	3	4	5
20. I manage test anxiety well.	1	2	3	4	5
21. I know how to work with a group on a presentation.	1	2	3	4	5
22. I am confident that I will succeed in college.	1	2	3	4	5

POST-COURSE ASSESSMENT

This self-assessment will help you and your instructor see how you developed skills during this course. Please be honest, take your time, and answer each question in terms of your experience in this course. For each question, rate yourself according to the following scale:

1	2	3	4	5
Definitely Like Me	Somewhat Like Me	Not Sure	Somewhat Unlike Me	Not At All Like Me

Please circle the number which best represents your answer:

1. This course helped me build skills for college success.   1 2 3 4 5

2. I know how to find the people and resources that can help me complete a successful transition to college.   1 2 3 4 5

3. I understand how habits can affect my ability to succeed.   1 2 3 4 5

4. I am aware of my learning styles and preferences.   1 2 3 4 5

5. I make choices in school and out based on how I learn.   1 2 3 4 5

6. I am effective at planning and managing my schedule.   1 2 3 4 5

7. I manage my finances actively and budget well.   1 2 3 4 5

8. I know exactly what goals I want to achieve in college.   1 2 3 4 5

9. I am effective at managing stress.   1 2 3 4 5

10. I take steps to keep my mind and body as healthy as possible.   1 2 3 4 5

11. I am comfortable with students who are different than me.   1 2 3 4 5

12. I work well in groups and teams.   1 2 3 4 5

13. I ask questions and think critically about what I hear and read.   1 2 3 4 5

14. I solve problems effectively.   1 2 3 4 5

15. I have strong memory and recall abilities.   1 2 3 4 5

16. I feel prepared to handle the reading in my college courses.   1 2 3 4 5

17. I use particular techniques to read textbooks in different academic areas.   1 2 3 4 5

18. I take comprehensive and clear notes.   1 2 3 4 5

19. I have excellent test-taking skills for college courses.   1 2 3 4 5

20. I manage test anxiety well.   1 2 3 4 5

21. I know how to work with a group on a presentation.   1 2 3 4 5

22. I am confident that I will succeed in college.   1 2 3 4 5

Sixth Edition

Keys to Effective Learning

Study Skills and Habits for Success

Carol Carter

Joyce Bishop

Sarah Lyman Kravits

Boston   Columbus   Indianapolis   New York   San Francisco   Upper Saddle River
Amsterdam   Cape Town   Dubai   London   Madrid   Milan   Munich   Paris   Montreal   Toronto
Delhi   Mexico City   Sao Paulo   Sydney   Hong Kong   Seoul   Singapore   Taipei   Tokyo

Executive Editor: Sande Johnson
Series Editorial Assistant: Clara Ciminelli
Development Editor: Charlotte Morrissey
Vice President, Director of Marketing: Quinn Perkson
Executive Marketing Manager: Amy Judd
Production Editor: Gregory Erb

Editorial Production Service: Elm Street Publishing Services
Manufacturing Buyer: Megan Cochran
Electronic Composition: Integra Software Services Pvt. Ltd.
Interior Design: Deborah Schneck
Photo Researcher: Annie Pickert
Cover Designer: Linda Knowles

For related titles and support materials, visit our online catalog at www.pearsonhighered.com.

Between the time website information is gathered and then published, it is not unusual for some sites to have closed. Also, the transcription of URLs can result in typographical errors. The publisher would appreciate notification where these errors occur so that they may be corrected in subsequent editions.

Photo credits: Background banners in "Real People" features; "silhouettes"; photos accompanying multiple intelligence tables; apple "habit" photos in Chapters 1–3, 6–9, and 11; and photos in quotation boxes on pp. 5, 21, 29, 52, 61, 85, 97, 119, 129, 152, 163, 181, 211, 223, 242, 251, 271, 283, 302, 311, and 326: © iStockphoto.com. Apple "habit" photos for Chapters 4–5 and 10, and photos in quotation boxes on pp. 197, 334, 349: © Shutterstock. All individual photos in the "Real People" and "Inside Tips" features provided by the photo subjects.

Library of Congress Cataloging-in-Publication Data
Carter, Carol.
Keys to effective learning: study skills and habits for success / Carol Carter, Joyce Bishop, Sarah Lyman Kravits.—6th ed.
    p.   cm.
Includes bibliographical references and index.
ISBN 978-0-13-700750-9 (alk. paper)
1. Study skills.   2. Adult learning.   I. Bishop, Joyce (Joyce L.), 1950-   II. Kravits, Sarah Lyman.   III. Title.
LB2395.C267 2011
378.1'70281—dc22

                                        2009032454

Printed in the United States of America
10 9 8 7 6 5 4 3 2 1   WEB 14 13 12 11 10

www.pearsonhighered.com

ISBN-13: 978-0-13-700035-7
ISBN-10:   0-13-700035-9

Brief Contents

Contents

Contents

Contents

Preface

If you're using this text, you are working with students heading (or returning) to school in search of new and better skills, knowledge, and experiences. Each chapter of *Keys to Effective Learning* will help them plan and reach their learning destination, whatever it might be. How? By offering practical, updated academic skills coverage that will help them succeed in any college course; thorough self-management and thinking skills coverage so they can stay accountable and on track with goals; and a proven "habits for success" theme that builds lifelong learning skills.

- **Practical academic skills coverage**—more comprehensive than in any previous edition—allows students to personalize, practice, and master abilities needed to succeed in college.

- Essential **self-management and thinking skills** threaded through the book enable students to make the crucial shift from passive to active learning. They'll discover ways to take more initiative, make better decisions, stay motivated, and experience less stress. In-chapter assessments, an end-of-chapter exercise, and activities at the end of every third chapter focus on self-discovery and keeping them accountable as they develop self-management skills.

- **Habits for Success** coverage in each chapter helps develop habits that research proves are the hallmark of successful students and lifelong problem solvers.

What's New in This Edition?

Before we started this revision we conducted extensive market research and sought extensive instructor and student feedback to study changes in higher education, student and instructor expectations, and the work world. This information helped us shape this revision to meet your needs more effectively and to focus on the biggest challenges in this course—making the best use of your time, and helping students develop essential academic skills in a motivating way. Here are the key content changes.

A shorter text. We streamlined our coverage to give you what you need in fewer pages.

More extensive reading, memory, and test coverage.

- **New! Two reading chapters** provide the tools to tackle any type of text from science to literature to print or electronic. The first chapter covers reading comprehension, reading strategies (SQ3R), reading print and online materials, and taking efficient notes on text reading. The second chapter focuses on reading in different disciplines.

- **New! A full chapter on memory**, with expanded coverage of how memory works and how it relates to test preparation. Students will be better equipped to remember information that is important to them after reading this chapter.
- **New! Two test-taking chapters** thoroughly cover test preparation, objective and subjective test-taking strategies, and how to make the grade on group projects.
- **Revised! More learning styles integration and application**. The learning styles chapter has been moved forward to Chapter 2 and is exclusively focused on how students learn, how to make the most of strengths, and how to face challenges. Once-per-chapter grids showing how to apply Multiple Intelligence strategies to chapter material now begin with Chapter 3 and extend through Chapter 11.

Improved, and more integrated, theme.   To help students jump start their college career, we incorporated a set of lifelong learning skills, or "Habits for Success," which strengthen the ability to manage time, relate with others, think critically, and take responsibility for learning. Based on reviewer and student feedback, we've made the Habits for Success in this edition more accessible, applied, and integrated.

- **New! A walk-through of the habit-building process** in Chapter 1.
- **New! Chapter 12 is a focused wrap-up**, entirely devoted to revisiting the Habits and taking them into the future.
- **New! Habit-building exercises** after every third chapter ask students to practice putting a habit to use and then assess habit-building progress over the term.
- **New! A habits-based self-assessment** opens the text so you and your students can gauge how well they developed the habits over the term.

Life skills are now covered in the context of academic skills.

- **New! Chapter 3 now pairs time and money management,** two crucial resources students need to stay in college. Research shows poor time and money management skills are the top two reasons students "stop out" or leave college altogether.
- **Revised! Chapter 4**, on goal setting and achievement, now covers group goals. The importance of **teamwork, cross-cultural,** and **communication skills** are discussed in that context instead of being treated separately in a late chapter in the text.

New appendices.   Easy-to-use reference materials on quantitative learning, writing, and research now appear in three separate appendices. The segments focus on the essentials of each topic.

New Features and Exercises Help Students Reflect, Assess, and Build Skills

The features and exercises in this sixth edition of *Keys to Effective Learning* give students better opportunities to reflect on and apply what they learn.

POWERFUL QUESTIONS

It is now common to have more than one career, and perhaps several, over your lifetime. Whether you change careers because you don't like what you're doing or because you lose your job in an economic downturn, you may have to return to school to learn new skills. Imagine yourself back in school several years after finishing college as you answer these questions:

What would your attitude be if you had to further your education? What are you willing to do now to acquire the "keep learning" Habit for Success so that you can weather the ups and downs of life and work?

Revised! Powerful Questions. Once per chapter, a Powerful Question gives students an opportunity to think or journal about a chapter topic and connect it to their own lives.

New! Real People. This critical-thinking feature is a case based on a real person who has put the chapter's Habit for Success to use. Thought questions encourage students to think more deeply and critically about the situation and relate it to themselves.

New! By the way…
Several times in each chapter, we "interrupt" to bring students an interesting fact about college and student life. Facts like these can wake up the brain as they read, improving learning and memory.

By the way . . .

according to a 2007 survey, nearly 50% of college freshmen add a job to their scheduled weekly responsibilities in order to earn money to pay for tuition.[3]

New! Inside Tips. Coaching questions are a great way to turn thought into action. New to this edition, each chapter features an "Inside Tip" with coaching questions from one of the three authors. Carol will focus on careers, Joyce on technology, and Sarah on self-management.

New! "Test Prep: Start It Now" exercise. In addition to the end-of-chapter critical-thinking and teamwork exercises, we've included this exercise to build the success habits involved with test preparation skills. Students will find out how preparing for tests starts on the first day of class.

New! Self-assessments. These self-assessments appear once or twice per chapter, within the chapter text—giving students a chance to build self-awareness about the chapter topic and learn more about how they think.

Revised! Take Action. As with the previous edition, these in-text exercises allow students to apply learning immediately. They have been revised to reach different types of learners. Each exercise has students use at least two types of intelligences.

Revised! Note the Important Points. The chapter summary is a set of guided notes with questions that hit on high points of each of the chapter topics. This exercise builds the ability to summarize text information.

Keys to Effective Learning Builds Habits for Life

Just as scientists discovered that the habit of eating "an apple a day" can improve physical health enough to "keep the doctor away," academic researchers have discovered that the lifelong learning habits addressed in this text, used consistently, will help students learn more effectively in college and life. As they work to build these habits, they will be better equipped to face academic (and life) challenges and acquire new knowledge and skills:

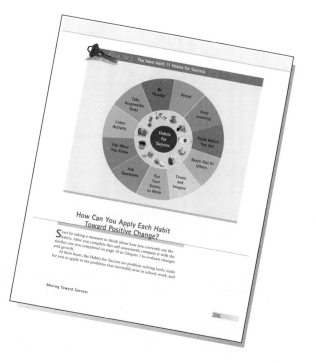

- Persist
- Keep learning
- Think before you act
- Reach out to others
- Create and imagine
- Put your senses to work
- Ask questions
- Use what you know
- Listen actively
- Take responsible risks
- Be flexible

Put these Habits for Success to work. And watch them work for you and your students as they pursue and achieve their most significant goals.

Many of our best suggestions come from you. Send your questions, comments, and ideas about *Keys to Effective Learning* to Carol Carter at caroljcarter@lifebound.com. We look forward to hearing from you, and we are grateful for the opportunity to work with you.

Acknowledgments

This significant revision has been produced through the efforts of an extraordinary team. Many thanks to:

- Our reviewers, for their responsiveness and invaluable input: Andrew T. Alexson, Tennessee Temple University; Arne J. Anderson, College of DuPage; Dede deLaughter, Gainesville State College; Jennifer Hodges, University of Akron; Jeremy Jones, Lee College; Deborah Maness, Wake Technical Community College; Rhonella Owens, City College of San Francisco; Terri Provost, Utica College; Paige Sindt, Arizona State University; Fatina Taylor, Prince George's Community College; Karla Thompson, New Mexico State University; Michael Young, Valdosta Technical College

- Previous edition reviewers: Erskine P. Ausbrooks III, Dyersburg State Community College; Glenda Belote, Florida International University; John Bennett, Jr., University of Connecticut; Ann Bingham-Newman, California State University–LA; Mary Bixby, University of Missouri–Columbia; Linda Blair, Pellissippi State Technical Community College; Barbara Blandford, Education Enhancement Center at Lawrenceville, NJ; Jerry Bouchie, St. Cloud State University; Rhonda Carroll, Pulaski Technical College; Mona Casady, SW Missouri State University; Janet Cutshall, Sussex County Community College; Marie Davis-Heim, Mississippi Gulf Coast Community College; Valerie DeAngelis, Miami-Dade Community College; Rita Delude, NH Community Technical College; Judy Elsley, Weber State University in Utah; Katherine Erdman, South Dakota State University; Jo Ella Fields, Oklahoma State University, Oklahoma City; Carlesa Ramere Finney, Anne Arundel Community College; Shirley Flor, San Diego Mesa College; Sue Halter, Delgado Community College in Louisiana; Vesna Hampel, University of Minnesota, Twin Cities; Suzy Hampton, University of Montana; Maureen Hurley, University of Missouri–Kansas City; Karen Iversen, Heald Colleges; Gary G. John, Richland College; Ken Jones, Metro Community College, Omaha; Kathryn K. Kelly, St. Cloud State University; Deborah Kimbrough-Lowe, Nassau Community College; Heidi Koring, Lynchburg College; Nancy Kosmicke, Mesa State College in Colorado; Christine Laursen, Westwood College; Polly Livingston, Portland State University; Jeanine Long, Southwest Georgia Tech; Frank T. Lyman, Jr., University of Maryland; Jo McEwan, Fayetteville Technical Community College; Barnette Miller Moore, Indian River Community College in Florida; Kathie Morris, Edison Community College; Rebecca Munro, Gonzaga University in Washington; Maria Parnell, Brevard County Community College; Virginia Phares, DeVry of Atlanta; Brenda Prinzavalli, Beloit College in Wisconsin; Linda Qualia, Colin County Community College; Laura Reynolds, Fayetteville Technical Community College; Mary Rider, Grossmont College; Tina Royal, Fayetteville Technical Community College; Maria D. Salinas, Del Mar College; Jacqueline Simon, Education Enhancement Center at Lawrenceville, NJ; Carolyn Smith, University of Southern Indiana; Joan Stottlemyer, Carroll College in Montana; Karla Thompson, New Mexico State University, Carlsbad; Thomas Tyson, SUNY Stony Brook; Lisa Taylor-Galizia, Carteret Community College; Karen N. Valencia, South Texas Community College;

Mary Walkz-Chojnacki, University of Wisconsin at Milwaukee; Peggy Walton, Howard Community College; Mary Walz-Chojnacki, University of Wisconsin-Milwaukee; Rose Wassman, DeAnza College in California; Michelle G. Wolf, Florida Southern College; Helen Woodman, Ferris State University in Michigan; Patricia Wright, Lenoir Community College; and Leesa Young, Asheville Buncombe Technical Community College.

- Art Costa, for his work that led to the development of the Habits of Mind, his generosity in permitting us to use the Habits as a framework for this text, and his valuable insights about our evolving approach to the Habits.

- Debbie Maness and Martha Martin, for their collaborative work with the authors on the Instructor's Manual and MyStudentSuccessLab, and Karla Thompson, for her contributions. Special thanks to Carol Howard, Karyn Schulz, and Cheri Tillman for their worthwhile feedback and enthusiastic support of this and other *Keys* books.

- Our student editors Heather Brown, Chelsey Emmelhainz, Kara Kiehle, and Brandon Mayberry for their insightful comments and hard work.

- Our editor, Sande Johnson; developmental editor, Charlotte Morrissey; and editorial assistants Lynda Cramer and Clara Ciminelli for their dedication, vision, and efforts.

- Our production team for their patience, flexibility, and attention to detail, especially production editor Greg Erb, director of production Elaine Ober, book designer Deborah Schneck, cover designer Linda Knowles, and Amanda Zagnoli and the team at Elm Street Publishing Services.

- Our marketing gurus, especially Amy Judd, Executive Marketing Manager; Quinn Perkson, Vice President, Director of Marketing; and our Sales Director Team: Connie James, Director of Sales Programs; Deb Wilson, Senior Sales Director; and Sean Wittmann, Missy Bittner, Lynda Sax, Chris Cardona, and Hector Amaya, Sales Directors.

- President of Pearson Teacher Education and Student Success, Nancy Forsyth; CEO of Teacher Education & Development, Susan Badger; and Prentice Hall President, Tim Bozik; for their interest in the *Keys* series.

- The Pearson representatives and the management team led by Brian Kibby, Senior Vice President Sales/Marketing.

- The staff at LifeBound: Heather Brown, Kelly Carson, Kara Kiehle, and Cynthia Nordberg.

- Our families and friends, who have encouraged us and put up with our commitments.

- We extend a very special thanks to Judy Block, whose research, writing, and editing work was essential and invaluable.

Finally, for their ideas, opinions, and stories, we would like to thank all of the students and professors with whom we work. Joyce in particular would like to thank the thousands of students who have allowed her, as their professor, the privilege of sharing part of their journey through college. We appreciate that, through reading this book, you give us the opportunity to learn and discover with you—in your classroom, at home, on a bus or train, and wherever else learning takes place.

Acknowledgments

Supplemental Resources for *Keys to Effective Learning*

Instructor Resources

Book-Specific Print Resources

Instructor's Manual with Test Bank. ISBN: 0-13-700739-6. *Keys to Effective Learning* provides instructor support to minimize your prep work, whether it's your first time teaching or you're simply looking for new ideas to bring to the classroom. We designed the manual to improve your students' experience and enhance your teaching. The manual is organized by chapter. Highlights of each chapter's material include:

Brief Chapter Overview and Chapter Outline.

Chapter Walk-through. Includes icebreakers, in-class activities, teaching tips, and supplements integration.

Exercise Recommendations.

- **Guided Notes handout** for each chapter
- **Tips on how to use chapter exercises** in class and for homework
- **Additional exercises**
- **Photocopy-ready handouts** to enhance chapter concepts or support exercises

Vocabulary Quiz. Consists of ten matching questions.

Test Item File. This rich test bank of quality-tested questions includes nearly 500 test items, with a balance of multiple choice, true/false, fill-in-the-blank, short answer, and essay. *Each test item is linked to a learning objective* so you can create tests that match your learning outcomes. In addition, the Pre- and Post-Course Assessment in the student version of the text is also available in the instructor's manual in photocopy-ready form, accompanied by a brief discussion of how to use the assessment.

Book-Specific Online Resources

PowerPoints. ISBN: 0-13-700738-8. *Keys to Effective Learning* offers you a full set of PowerPoint slides per chapter, downloadable from the Instructor's Resource Center and modifiable so you can use and customize them. Each chapter provides a guided lecture

outline, chapter objectives, key points, quotes, thought questions, and key text visuals. A separate set of "clicker question" slides that allow you to use PowerPoint technology to quiz your students is also available.

MyTest. This Pearson computerized testing system allows you to easily modify, re-order, and add to the test questions offered in the text-specific test bank. This technologically-reliable, secure testing system also gives you the ability to organize test questions by learning objective and offer feedback, and has a wide range of test types to suit any teaching and testing style.

PEARSON mystudentsuccesslab Are you teaching online, in a hybrid setting, or looking to infuse exciting technology into your classroom? Then be sure to refer to the MyStudentSuccessLab section on pages xxi–xxii to learn more.

Other Resources

"Easy access to online, book-specific teaching support is now just a click away!"

Instructor Resource Center: Register. Redeem. Login. Three easy steps that open the door to a variety of print and media resources in downloadable, digital format, available to instructors exclusively through the Pearson IRC.
www.pearsonhighered.com/irc

"Choose from a wide range of Video resources for the classroom!"

Prentice Hall Reference Library: Life Skills Pack: ISBN: 0-13-127079-6 contains all 4 videos, or they may be requested individually as follows:

- Learning Styles and Self-Awareness, 0-13-028502-1
- Critical and Creative Thinking, 0-13-028504-8
- Relating to Others, 0-13-028511-0
- Personal Wellness, 0-13-028514-5

Prentice Hall Reference Library: Study Skills Pack: ISBN: 0-13-127080-X contains all 6 videos, or they may be requested individually as follows:

- Reading Effectively, 0-13-028505-6
- Listening and Memory, 0-13-028506-4
- Note Taking and Research, 0-13-028508-0
- Writing Effectively, 0-13-028509-9
- Effective Test Taking, 0-13-028500-5
- Goal Setting and Time Management, 0-13-028503-X

Prentice Hall Reference Library: Career Skills Pack: ISBN: 0-13-118529-2 contains all 3 videos, or they may be requested individually as follows:

- Skills for the 21st Century—Technology, 0-13-028512-9
- Skills for the 21st Century—Math and Science, 0-13-028513-7
- Managing Career and Money, 0-13-028516-1

Complete Reference Library—Life/Study Skills/Career Video Pack on DVD: ISBN: 0-13-501095-0.

- Our Reference Library of thirteen popular video resources has now been digitized onto one DVD so students and instructors alike can benefit from the array of video clips. Featuring Life Skills, Study Skills, and Career Skills, they help to reinforce the course content in a more interactive way.

Faculty Video Resources:

- Teacher Training Video 1: Critical Thinking, 0-13-099432-4
- Teacher Training Video 2: Stress Management & Communication, 0-13-099578-9
- Teacher Training Video 3: Classroom Tips, 0-13-917205-X
- Student Advice Video, 0-13-233206-X
- Study Skills Video, 0-13-096095-0
- Faculty Development Workshop (DVD) 0-13-227192-3

Current Issues Videos:

- ABC News Video Series: Student Success 2/E, 0-13-031901-5
- ABC News Video Series: Student Success 3/E, 0-13-152865-3

MyStudentSuccessLab PH Videos on DVD: ISBN: 0-13-514249-0.

- Our six most popular video resources have been digitized onto one DVD so students and instructors alike can benefit from the array of video clips. Featuring Technology, Math and Science, Managing Money and Career, Learning Styles and Self-Awareness, Study Skills, and Peer Advice, they help to reinforce the course content in a more interactive way.
- Also accessible through our MyStudentSuccessLab and course management offerings and available on VHS.

"Through partnership opportunities, we offer a variety of assessment options!"

LASSI: The LASSI is a 10-scale, 80-item assessment of students' awareness about and use of learning and study strategies. Addressing skill, will and self-regulation, the focus is on both covert and overt thoughts, behaviors, attitudes and beliefs that relate to successful learning and that can be altered through educational interventions. Available in two formats: Paper ISBN: 0-13-172315-4 or Online ISBN: 0-13-172316-2 (Access Card).

Noel Levitz/RMS: This retention tool measures Academic Motivation, General Coping Ability, Receptivity to Support Services, PLUS Social Motivation. It helps identify at-risk

Supplemental Resources for *Keys to Effective Learning*

students, the areas with which they struggle, and their receptiveness to support. Available in Paper or Online formats, as well as Short and Long versions. PAPER Long Form A: #0-13-512066-7; PAPER Short Form B: #0-13-512065-9; Online Forms A,B & C: #0-13-098158-3.

Robbins Self Assessment Library: This compilation teaches students to create a portfolio of skills. S.A.L. is a self-contained, interactive, library of 49 behavioral questionnaires that help students discover new ideas about themselves, their attitudes, and their personal strengths and weaknesses. Available in paper, CD-Rom, and online (access card) formats.

Readiness for Education at a Distance Indicator (READI): READI is a web-based tool that assesses the overall likelihood for online learning success. READI generates an immediate score and a diagnostic interpretation of results, including recommendations for successful participation in online courses and potential remediation sources. Please visit www.readi.info for additional information. ISBN: 0-13-188967-2.

Pathway to Student Success CD-ROM: ISBN: 0-13-239314-X. The CD is divided into several categories, each of which focuses on a specific topic that relates to students and provides them with the context, tools and strategies to enhance their educational experience.

Student Resources

Tools to help make the grade now, and excel in school later.

"Today's students are more inclined than ever to use technology to enhance their learning."

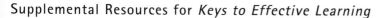

PEARSON
mystudentsuccesslab

Be sure to refer to the MyStudentSuccessLab section on pages xxi–xxii to learn more about this revolutionary resource (www.mystudentsuccesslab.com).

"Time management is the #1 challenge students face. We can help."

Prentice Hall Planner: A basic planner that includes a monthly & daily calendar plus other materials to facilitate organization. 8.5 x 11.

Premier Annual Planner: This specially designed, annual 4-color collegiate planner includes an academic planning/resources section, monthly planning section (2 pages/month), weekly planning section (48 weeks; July start date), which facilitate short-term as well as long-term planning. Spiral bound, 6 x 9. Customization is available.

"Journaling activities promote self-discovery and self-awareness."

Student Reflection Journal: Through this vehicle, students are encouraged to track their progress and share their insights, thoughts, and concerns. 8.5 x 11. 90 pages.

"The Student Orientation Series includes short booklets on specialized topics that facilitate greater student understanding."

S.O.S. Guides help students understand what these opportunities are, how to take advantage of them, and how to learn from their peers while doing so. They include:

- Connolly: Learning Communities 0-13-232243-9
- Hoffman: Stop Procrastination Now! 10 Simple and SUCCESSFUL Steps for Student Success, 0-13-513056-5
- Watts: Service Learning 0-13-232201-3
- Jabr: English Language Learners 0-13-232242-0

PEARSON

mystudentsuccesslab™

Succeed in college and beyond!
Connect, practice, and personalize with MyStudentSuccessLab.

www.mystudentsuccesslab.com

MyStudentSuccessLab is an online solution designed to help instructors engage their students in the course content, provide practice on skill development, and assess mastery. Additional resources, including sample syllabi, guide, assignments, and rubrics are included.

MyStudentSuccessLab saves class prep time and supports implementation:
Instructor Tools/Support –

• **Sample syllabus** – provided to ensure easy implementation.

• **Instructor's guide** - includes information that describes each activity, the skills each addresses, an estimated student time on task for each exercise, and a grading rubric for the final Apply activity.

• **Additional Assignments** - Extra suggested activities to use with each topic:
  1. General activity related to an important objective for each topic.
  2. Internet use Assignment (e.g. Google "You Tube" video on topic) to find a video on key strategies and write a critique and present it to the class.
  3. Student Resource tool usage – ie. Read and take online notes on the main points of the Understanding Plagiarism guide.

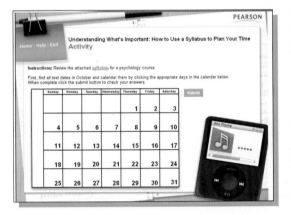

MyStudentSuccessLab is easy to use and assign.
Support is available in the following ways:

• Visit **www.mystudentsuccesslab.com** under "Tours and Training" and "Support."

• Contact your local sales professional.

• Send an inquiry to **Student.Success@pearson.com** for additional support.

• Join one of our weekly WebEx training sessions.

• Request on-campus training with a Faculty Advocate for qualified adoptions.

• Access technical support 24 hours a day, seven days a week, at **http://247pearsoned.custhelp.com**.

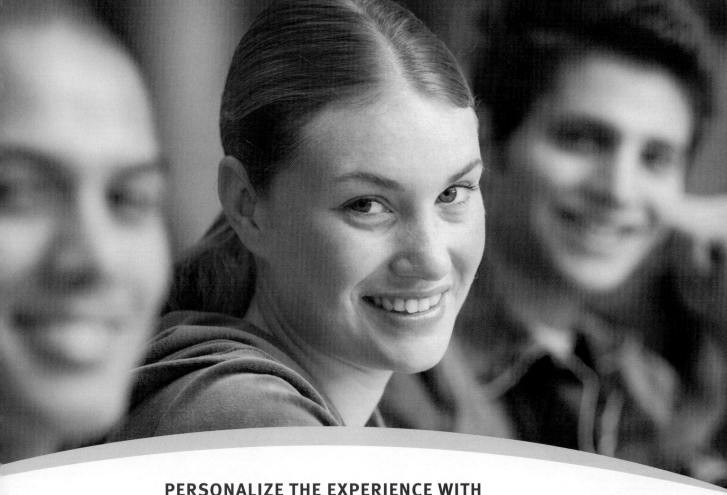

PERSONALIZE THE EXPERIENCE WITH

EARSON LEARNING SOLUTIONS

FOR STUDENT SUCCESS AND CAREER DEVELOPMENT

Pearson Custom Library Catalog

earson Custom Library, you can create a custom book cting content from our course-specific collections. The ons consist of chapters from Pearson titles like this one, refully selected, copyright cleared, third-party content, edagogy. The finished product is a print-on-demand book that students can purchase in the same way they se other course materials.

om Media

n Learning Solutions works with you to create a ized technology solution specific to your course ments and needs. We specialize in a number of best es including custom websites and portals, animation nulations, and content conversions and customizations.

Custom Publications

We can develop your original material and create a textbook that meets your course goals. Pearson Learning Solutions works with you on your original manuscript to help refine and strengthen it, ensuring that it meets and exceeds market standards. Pearson Learning Solutions will work with you to select already published content and sequence it to follow your course goals.

Online Education

Pearson Learning Solutions offers customizable online course content for your distance learning classes, hybrid courses, or to enhance the learning experience of your traditional in-classroom students. Courses include a fully developed syllabus, media-rich lecture presentations, audio lectures, a wide variety of assessments, discussion board questions, and a strong instructor resource package.

e end, the finished product reflects your insight into what your students to succeed, and puts it into practice. Visit us on the web to learn more at pearsoncustom.com/studentsuccess or call us at 800-777-6872

habits for success

reality check

alan does his best to stay on top of his assignments, but when he feels burned out he tends to avoid schoolwork completely. Last night, instead of reading the chapter assigned for today, he watched some TV and then got caught up on his favorite leisure-time activity—instant messaging with some friends. Before he knew it, the clock read 1:00 A.M. He planned to get up early to read. Instead, he woke up late. He made it to class on time, but he is totally unprepared to participate or even grasp what the teacher is talking about. He sits in his chair not asking questions and not interacting with his classmates, trying to quietly get through the class period.

In this chapter . . .

you explore answers to the following questions:

© Shutterstock

Habit for Success

persist

Keep moving ahead no matter the obstacles to get what you want from school and life.

Where Are You Headed, and How Will College Get You There?

Start by congratulating yourself, because your persistence has paid off. You may have just completed high school or its equivalent. You may be returning after staying at home with young children. You may have worked in one or more jobs or served in the armed forces or any combination of possibilities. Whatever your situation, you have been building life skills from experience. Now you have enrolled in college, found a way to pay for it, signed up for courses, and shown up for class. And, in deciding to pursue a degree, you chose to believe you can accomplish important goals. You have earned this opportunity to be a college student.

Focus for a moment on Alan, the student you read about on the opening page of this chapter. Ask yourself these questions:

- If you were Alan's teacher, what credit would you give him for class participation? For preparation? What would you say if he asked you to write a job recommendation?
- If you were in a study group with Alan after class and were depending on his contribution, what would you say to him if he showed up empty-handed?
- What do Alan's actions say about his approach toward college?
- If you were a business owner, would you be likely to hire someone like Alan?

Alan may have a tough time passing courses and earning a degree if he doesn't make some adjustments. Although you are not Alan, you may be making one or more similar choices. Now is the time to consider what these behaviors and attitudes mean for you and—more importantly—what you plan to do about them.

We can do anything we want to if we stick to it long enough.

Helen Keller, blind and deaf author and activist

To make the most of your college opportunities, take your coursework seriously and work hard to prepare for the future.

Think of college as a training ground in which you acquire skills that will enable you to compete in the global marketplace, where workers in the United States are on a level playing field with workers in other parts of the world. Thomas Friedman, author of *The World Is Flat*, explains how the **digital revolution** has transformed the working environment you will enter after college:

> It is now possible for more people than ever to collaborate and compete in real time with more other people on more different kinds of work from more different corners of the planet and on a more equal footing than at any previous time in the history of the world—using computers, e-mail, fiber-optic networks, teleconferencing, and dynamic new software.[1]

These developments in communication, combined with an enormous increase in **knowledge work** such as Internet technology and decrease in labor-based work such as factory jobs, mean that you may compete for information-based jobs with highly trained and motivated people from around the globe. To achieve your goals in this new "flat" world, you will need to acquire solid skills, commit to lifelong learning, persevere despite obstacles, perform high-quality work consistently, and embrace change as a way of life. If you gather and hone your tools in college, you will receive the maximum benefit and be a ready-for-hire package when you graduate.

Now think about yourself *right now*. Complete the short self-assessment at the top of the next page. Then consider: Would you hire yourself? If you answered no, all is not lost. The work you do in this course will prepare you to succeed in college and get the job you want after graduation. If you answered yes, this course will help you get even better. As you think about the value of your work in this course, look at Key 1.1, which shows what employers look for in new employees.

Back to Alan: If you see yourself in him, you may have some behaviors that are leading you away from, rather than toward, success. The good news is that you are on your way to identifying and changing these behaviors. First, look at the transition to college-level work and how this text will help you through it.

Digital Revolution
the change in how people communicate, brought on by developments in computer systems.

Knowledge Work
work that is primarily concerned with information rather than manual labor.

If you were a hiring manager and could only hire one person in your small company this year, what qualities would you most want in that employee? For example, would you require strong communication skills, a self-starter personality, or a good attitude about teamwork? Write your top five qualities in the spaces that follow and rank their levels of importance from 1 to 5, with 1 being the highest and 5 the lowest.

Quality   Ranking

_____   _____

_____   _____

_____   _____

_____   _____

_____   _____

Compare your list with one or more classmates. Ask the following questions: What qualities from other lists would you include on your own? Would you change your rankings?

How Can You
Transition to College-Level Work?

The "typical" path of the student—graduating from high school at 18, attending college for two to four years, and then finding a job right after graduation—is no longer typical. Today students follow different paths and different time schedules to reach their goals. However, whether high school graduation was last year, 10 years ago, or achieved by working toward a GED, every student faces the challenge of transitioning to college-level work.

It takes time to adjust to a college classroom experience. Pay close attention to your instructor and syllabus so you know what to expect.

Knowing what to expect will enable you to prepare your attitude and skills. As the saying goes, "forewarned is forearmed." Here are some general differences everyone will face (spend some time with your college's student handbook to get informed about details specific to your school).

More independence and responsibility.
Perhaps the single most significant difference between high school and college is the extent to which you are responsible for your actions. Your college instructors will not provide the level of guidance and support that you had in high

© Annette Brieger/Goldpitt/PH College/Pearson Education

Chapter 1

 **Employers rate the importance of candidate qualities and skills**

Items ranked on a 5-point scale, where 1 = not at all important and 5 = extremely important.

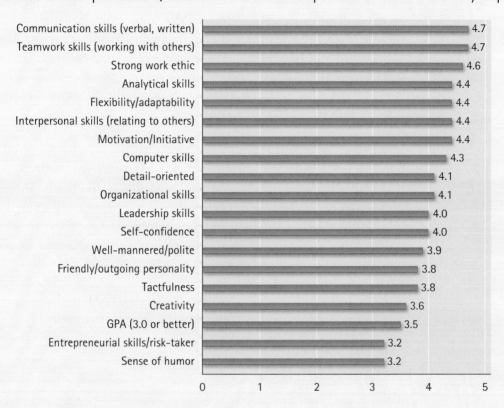

Communication skills (verbal, written)	4.7
Teamwork skills (working with others)	4.7
Strong work ethic	4.6
Analytical skills	4.4
Flexibility/adaptability	4.4
Interpersonal skills (relating to others)	4.4
Motivation/Initiative	4.4
Computer skills	4.3
Detail-oriented	4.1
Organizational skills	4.1
Leadership skills	4.0
Self-confidence	4.0
Well-mannered/polite	3.9
Friendly/outgoing personality	3.8
Tactfulness	3.8
Creativity	3.6
GPA (3.0 or better)	3.5
Entrepreneurial skills/risk-taker	3.2
Sense of humor	3.2

Source: NACE Research: Job Outlook 2006, p.18

school. You will be expected to make the following—and more—happen on your own:

- Buy books and other assigned materials for your courses.
- Use your syllabi to set up your schedule for the term.
- Keep on top of deadlines and important dates so you can turn in projects on time and be prepared for exams.
- Get help when you need it.
- Complete assigned coursework.
- Set up study group meetings.
- Get to class and everywhere else on time and with the stuff you need.

Increased workload. College means more work per course. You will be required to read more material in your textbooks and other resources than you did in high school and to move faster through those materials. This workload and the speed at which courses move demand more study time. A rule of thumb is to study at least two hours for each hour spent in class, meaning that if you are in class for 9 hours a week, you need to schedule at least 18 hours of studying through the week, every week.

More challenging work. Your work will be more challenging on every level. Reading will be more difficult, assignments will be more involved, and your brain will consistently have to go beyond simple recall into higher levels of thinking—analyzing, comparing and contrasting materials to what you know, evaluating, generating new ideas. (Chapter 5 will focus on the different thinking skills that foster college success.)

More out-of-class time to manage. Whereas a high school day generally keeps you in the building all day five days a week, college courses meet fewer times per week and are each scheduled individually. You might have days when your classes end at noon or don't begin until 2:00 in the afternoon or don't meet at all. It will be up to you to use these blocks of free time effectively as you juggle your other responsibilities, including perhaps a job and family.

You are not alone as you face these challenges. Look to the people around you, the technology available to you, and this book for support.

People Can Help

Faculty and staff are among the most valuable—but underused—sources of help. A recent survey of college freshmen indicated that only 25% of students asked a teacher for advice after class throughout the term, and only 8% considered seeking counseling.[3] That means that 75% would not ask their instructor for help, and 92% would never seek counseling, no matter the need.

Don't let these important sources of support go untapped. Make it a point to connect with instructors, teaching assistants, advisors, tutoring centers, and counselors throughout your college career.

Instructors and Teaching Assistants

You have the greatest contact with instructors, whom you may see in class from one to five times a week. Instructors and the teaching assistants who support them see your work, and, if your class size is small, they may get to know you quite well. Consult them to:

- Clarify material presented in class
- Help with homework
- Find out how to prepare for a test
- Ask about a paper while you are working on it

By the way . . .

out of all the factors linked to a long and healthy life, education is the one that helps the most.[2]

- Find out why you received a particular grade on a test or assignment
- Get advice about the department—courses, majoring—or related career areas

Before or after class works well for a quick question. When you want to speak personally with an instructor for longer than a minute or two, make an appointment during office hours, send e-mail, or leave voice-mail messages.

Office hours. Instructors' regular office hours appear on your syllabi, on office doors, and on instructors' or departmental Web pages. Always make an appointment for a conference. Face-to-face conferences are ideal for working through ideas and problems or asking for advice.

E-mail. Instructors' e-mail addresses are generally posted on the first day of class and on your syllabus. Use e-mail to clarify assignments and assignment deadlines, to ask questions about lectures or readings, and to clarify what will be covered on a test.

Voice mail. If something comes up at the last minute, you can leave a message in your instructor's voice mailbox. Make your message short and specific. Avoid calling instructors at home unless they give specific permission to do so.

Academic Advisors

In most colleges, every student is assigned an advisor who is the student's personal connection with the college. (At some schools, students receive help at an advising center.) Your advisor will help you choose courses every term, plan your overall academic program, and understand college regulations, including graduation requirements. You may be required to meet with your advisor once each term. However, don't hesitate to schedule additional meetings if and when you need your advisor.

Tutors and Academic Centers

Tutors can give you valuable and detailed help on specific academic subjects. Most campuses have private tutoring available, and many schools offer free peer tutoring. If you feel you could benefit from the kind of one-on-one work a tutor can give, ask your instructor or your academic advisor to recommend a tutor. If your school has one or more academic centers, you may be able to find a tutor there. *Academic centers*, including reading, writing, math, and study-skills centers, offer consultations and tutoring to help students improve skills at all levels.

Counseling

College counseling services can help you address academic problems, stress, and psychological problems. As stated on one school's counseling services Web site, "counseling services are designed to assist students with addressing the difficulties that they encounter during these years and to promote greater overall wellness within the student population."[4]

Counseling is confidential, focused on your particular needs, and directed toward helping you handle what is bothering you. In most cases it is not ongoing and ends when you have achieved the goals that you and your counselor have defined. Whatever type of problem you encounter in college, a counselor can help you get through it.

Knowing How to Use Technology Can Help

Transitioning to college requires that you become comfortable with technology. In a given day you might access a syllabus online, e-mail a student, use the Internet to tap into a library database, draft an assignment on a computer, and e-mail a paper to an instructor. Most dorm rooms are wired for computers, and an increasing number of campuses have wireless networks. Some schools are even moving to a "paperless" system where all student notifications are sent via e-mail, requiring every student to activate an e-mail account and check it regularly. Here are some suggestions for using technology to ease your transition into college:

© Patrick White/Merrill Education

Working in a computer lab is a great way to learn software and equipment, because there is usually a trained lab technician available to answer questions.

Get trained. Register for an e-mail account at your school and connect to the college network. Learn how to work in a course management system, such as Blackboard, if your school uses one. Register your cell phone number with the school so you can get emergency alerts.

Use computers to find information. Frequent the college Web site, and use library databases. If they are available, download podcasts of lectures.

Be a cautious user. Save your work periodically onto a primary or backup hard drive, CD, or flash drive. In addition, install an antivirus program and update it regularly.

Stay on task. During study time, try to limit Internet surfing, instant messaging, visiting Facebook pages, and playing computer games.

Follow guidelines when contacting instructors via e-mail. When you submit assignments, take exams, or ask questions electronically, rules of etiquette promote civility and respect. Try these suggestions the next time you e-mail an instructor:

- **Use your school account.** Instructors may delete unfamiliar e-mails. "Helen_Miller@yourschool.edu" will get read, but "disastergirl@yahoo.com" may not.

- **Don't ask for information you can find on your own.** Flooding your instructor with unnecessary e-mails may work against you when you really need help.

- **Write a clear subject line.** State exactly what the e-mail is about.

- **Address the instructor by name and use his or her title.** "Hello, Professor Smith," or "Hi, Dr. Reynolds," is better than "Hey."

- **Be clear and comprehensive.** First, state your question or problem and what you want to achieve. Next, if necessary, support your position, using bullet points if you have a number of statements. Finally, end by thanking the instructor and signing your full name.

- **Use complete sentences, correct punctuation, and capitalization.** Avoid abbreviations and acronyms. Write as though you were crafting a business letter, not a text message to a friend.

- **Give the instructor time to respond.** Don't expect a reply within two hours. If you hear nothing after a couple of days, send a follow-up note that contains the full text of your first message.

This Book Can Help

This book is designed to give you a set of skills with which you can manage the challenges of the college transition. Here's what your reading and work will build:

- **A sense of how you learn.** Chapter 2 helps you discover your learning styles, and the following chapters invite you to look at how to use those styles to make your best study and life choices.

- **Critical thinking and problem-solving skills.** If you can analyze information, come up with new ideas, and work through problems effectively, you will be ready for any challenge. Chapter 5, as well as exercises in every chapter, will help you in this area.

- **Self-management and resource management.** Planning your time, making sure you can pay tuition and expenses, setting goals, and handling stress are basics no college student can do without. Chapters 3 and 4 get you off on the right foot.

- **Solid academic skills.** The bulk of this text—Chapters 6 through 11—is devoted to all kinds of ways for you to become a better reader, note taker, test taker, listener, team member, and project manager.

In the theme of this book—the Habits for Success—is one final important tool for you: the ability to build positive habits that will help you achieve your goals in college and beyond. First, take a look at how habits affect your life and what you can do to improve them.

How Can Habits
Change Your Life for the Better?

Habits form much of your day-to-day life including what you eat, what you wear, what you do and when, where you put things, and much more. People perform habits over and over again without really thinking about what they are doing.

Habit

a regular pattern of behavior that has become almost involuntary.

Bad and Good Habits

What makes a habit "bad" or "good"? *Bad habits* have negative effects. Some, like alcohol and drug abuse, are destructive to your health and well-being. Other bad habits prevent you from reaching important goals. A common example: Leaving studying until late in the evening after classes, your work shift, and social time may leave you with almost no energy to do schoolwork well or on time. *Good habits*, in contrast, have positive effects. If you are in the habit of keeping your books with you throughout the day and taking them out whenever you have a block of time, you'll be more able to stay on top of your assignments.

Alan probably came to college equipped with a set of habits that he has had for years, including doing no schoolwork at all when he's feeling overloaded, letting his social time online run too long, and so on. Alan's challenge is to break these habits and replace them with a set of positive habits that foster success (tackling challenging assignments one small concrete step at a time, putting a time limit on instant messaging).

How to Change Habits

Changing habits is a challenge for anyone, but determination combined with self-knowledge can bring change. In fact, recent brain research shows that when people work to change old habits and solidify new habits, they actually create new brain cells and new neural pathways that move currents from cell to cell.[6] There are two ways to adjust your habits:

Replace or change an existing habit. When an existing habit has negative effects, it is not enough to just ditch it. You have to substitute something in its place, says Scott H. Young, a student who is a habits expert: "If you opened up your computer and started removing hardware, what would happen? Chances are your computer wouldn't work. Similarly, you can't just pull out habits without replacing the needs they fulfill. Giving up television might mean you need to find a new way to relax, socialize or get information."[7]

Begin a new habit. When you create a new habit, you are starting from the ground up, deciding on the specific nature of the habit as well as when, where, and how to use it.

Whether you are replacing or generating a habit, use the following steps to make the change:[8]

1. **Identify what you want to change and why.** Get specific. What do you want to accomplish? Would it require changing an existing habit or beginning a new habit? Make the goal concrete by writing it down. Use positive terms: "I will use my time between classes to study" is more motivating than "I need to stop wasting time between classes."

2. **Name specific, short-term actions related to this habit change.** For example, if you aim to use between-class time to study, specific behaviors might be "Bring my psychology book on Tuesdays so I can study between algebra and lunch" or "Head to the library after psych class on Wednesdays."

3. **Set up support.** You are more likely to succeed if your friends or family help you stay on track. Start by letting them know what you are trying to do. Then set up a progress-report plan. Maybe you'll post a note on an online networking site, like Facebook, or call once a week. You can also ask them to leave encouraging messages on your phone or e-mail.

4. **Get started, and keep it up for at least 21 days—maybe 30.** Habits experts note that it takes at least 21 days of consistently performing a new or changed habit to get it to stick. Personal development expert Steve Pavlina, noting how software companies give consumers 30 days to try out a new product, recommends that you follow that lead and beef up your "trial period" to 30 days.

5. **Be accountable as you go.** Note your actions and your progress in writing, to yourself as well as to your supporters. Use whatever works for you—your planner, a separate notebook, e-mails, a computer document.

6. **Evaluate your progress.** Step back and evaluate how the process is going, and ask your support person or people to give you feedback if possible.

7. **If necessary, switch gears.** If a new habit isn't sticking or your attempts to change are making you so miserable that you want to give up, go back to the beginning of this process and adjust your habit goal. For example, although some people respond well to a "cold turkey" approach, a student who has always pulled all-nighters before exams might not be able to cut out *all* late-night cramming. Instead, she could build in three hours of study time the night before the exam as part of a week-long study schedule. Over time and through trial and error, you will find what works for you.

As you work to establish new habits, remember to keep it simple. Work on only one or maybe two habits at a time. If you attempt more, you run the risk of overloading and not successfully changing any of them.

TAKE ACTION
Prepare to Change a Habit

Think of a habit that gets in the way of your ability to succeed in college—one that you would call a bad habit (in Chapter 2, you'll learn that you are using your intrapersonal intelligence as you do this). Write it here: _____

_____

Why do you want to change this habit—in other words, what negative effect does it have on your academic performance? _____

_____

Describe the new or changed habit you would like to adopt. _____

_____

Name two specific, short-term actions you will take to create this habit.

1. _____

2. _____

Name someone who will support your efforts. _____

Finally, describe how you will track your progress.

_____

_____

Hold this plan in your mind—you will revisit it in one of the Time for a Change exercises at the end of Chapters 3, 6, and 9.

Now that you know more about habits, you are ready to consider the set of habits that forms the backbone of this book. You will explore them throughout your reading and work in this course. Any of them that you make your own will benefit you throughout your life.

real people

persist

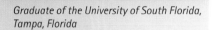

Yvette Gomez

Graduate of the University of South Florida, Tampa, Florida

Growing up with two loving, dedicated but uneducated parents, Yvette Gomez learned some important life lessons early on.

"My parents never stopped reminding me of how crucial an education is to a stable future by telling me how difficult it was for them to get where they are now," says Yvette. Without a solid knowledge of English or a high school diploma, it was difficult for her parents to realize their potential in the working world. Because they did not want their daughter to experience the same hardships, they encouraged her to do whatever it took to get through high school and then go to college.

Stop and Think

Like Yvette, you can benefit from the support of people who care about you. With whom in your life do you share basic values that will help you persist?

Despite her determination, Yvette found that it was tough to succeed in high school. She had doubts about her abilities, and initially her motivation was dampened by seeing many friends lose steam and even drop out. Not wanting to give up made her feel like an "oddball."

The turning point for Yvette came when her best friend, then 16 years old,

became pregnant and subsequently left school. Yvette watched as her friend became a mother and struggled to earn money to support her child. She saw similarities between her friend and her parents, and realized that this friend would have to make familiar sacrifices on the road ahead. She became determined that she would do whatever it took to get through high school and continue on to college.

Stop and Think

Yvette found out how tough it can be to make different choices from those close friends have made. Is there a path you want to follow that would take you away from friends or family? If so, what is it, and what difference would it make in your life?

Yvette shifted away from the friends she was hanging out with and focused her energy on her studies, facing academic roadblocks with a positive attitude. "I always kept my head up to the sky, even if things weren't looking too good," she says. "I knew that if I didn't [keep myself strong], I would be the person to be affected by the consequences."

Yvette's work paid off. Her high school grades were good enough for her

to enter the University of South Florida, where she earned a B.A. in public relations and political science. Her advice to students everywhere struggling to persist: "Never give up. Education is the key to a successful future. Learn not to follow others because your future only depends on yourself. Stay strong and focus, and soon you will reap the benefits of the hard work that you put in."

Think about Yvette and Think about Yourself

- Yvette had strong images of what would happen if she stuck to her goal— and what would happen if she didn't. Why are you more likely to persist when you know what you will gain from your hard work or what you will lose if you give up?

- Her parents' experience, and the choices her friends made, motivated Yvette to stay strong toward her goal. What experience or knowledge might motivate you to persist in your education?

Source: USF Latino Scholarship & Community/ Mental Health Counseling Program (adapted with permission from original story, ©2003, online at http://www.coedu.usf.edu/zalaquett/ls/lsiv.html).

Oprah Winfrey's life is a study in persistence. From a childhood marked by abuse and difficulty, she forged a career in journalism, acting, and television that has enabled her to help people around the globe. When abuse surfaced in the staff of the school for girls she had opened in South Africa, she persisted in making improvements and keeping the dream of education alive for the students.

© Chris Pizzello/AP Images

persist

What Habits Fuel College Success?

Problems of all sorts are a fact of life. Being able to solve them effectively is a key ingredient of academic, career, and life success. Art Costa, professor emeritus of education at California State University, Sacramento, and co-director of the Institute for Intelligent Behavior in El Dorado Hills, California, studied how students respond to problems, looking specifically at what they did when faced with unfamiliar information and situations. He found that successful students tend to rely on a certain group of positive habits to think through and solve problems. Like the "apple a day" that (as the saying goes) keeps you healthy, these habits promote success when used regularly and consistently.

The Habits for Success

To help you solve problems successfully and achieve your college and life goals, *Keys to Effective Learning* features 11 Habits for Success based on Costa's work. Key 1.2 describes the habits and some ways in which you might use them. Start now to practice these habits so you can:

- Get the grades you want this term and from now on
- Manage yourself—your time, money, and responsibilities—effectively
- Maximize your learning potential
- Work well with others at school and elsewhere
- Succeed in your coursework for your major
- Graduate and get a job that suits you and fulfills you

The chapters of *Keys to Effective Learning* introduce you to these habits and give you opportunities to explore them. In each chapter, you will find:

- An introduction to the chapter's featured habit
- Features and exercises that incorporate the habit, both within the chapter and at the end (see the bulleted list next to the habit introduction for page numbers)
- A visual organizer to close the chapter, showing ways to put the habit into action
- An apple image representing the habit, used throughout the chapter wherever the habit appears

Finally, in the last chapter, you will have the opportunity to revisit all 11 habits—to apply each, evaluate your development, and plan how to make progress in the future.

You may already use some of the Habits for Success comfortably and successfully. Keep in mind that trying to acquire too many new habits at once can

HABIT	CORRESPONDING CHAPTER	APPLY IT TO THE CHAPTER...	APPLY IT TO LIFE...
PERSIST. Stick to whatever you are doing until you complete it. Keep moving ahead.	*Chapter 1 Habits for Success*	Stick to your goal of earning a college degree.	Persist in working on a relationship that means a lot to you.
KEEP LEARNING. Be a lifelong learner, always seeking to know more. See problems and circumstances as valuable opportunities to learn and grow.	*Chapter 2 Learning Styles*	As your strengths and challenges change over time, lifelong learning allows you to respond to those changes.	Be ready to learn new skills and knowledge to stay employable in an era of rapid workplace change.
THINK BEFORE YOU ACT. Manage impulsive behavior by creating a plan of action and defining your specific goals before beginning.	*Chapter 3 Time and Money*	Plan out your class meetings, work times, and other responsibilities at the beginning of each week.	Before rushing into a big purchase such as a car, research what will get you the most bang for your buck.
REACH OUT TO OTHERS. Learn to ask for help and give help when you can. Experience the power of achieving a goal as part of a team.	*Chapter 4 Setting and Reaching Goals*	Friends and classmates can help hold you accountable for steps toward an important goal.	Ask for ideas about how others manage stress through food and exercise choices.
CREATE AND IMAGINE. Come up with new, original, and clever ideas, solutions, and techniques.	*Chapter 5 Critical and Creative Thinking*	Brainstorm possible ways to get the courses you need to fulfill requirements.	Risk trying out a new idea in your home life, and let it be okay if you make a mistake.
PUT YOUR SENSES TO WORK. Note—and then look past—what you see and hear. Open your sensory pathways up to all kinds of information you can use in your life.	*Chapter 6 Memory*	Use senses-based mnemonic devices to remember science and math facts.	Engage your vision, hearing, and other senses to strengthen your ability to remember procedures and people's names on the job.

(continued)

HABIT	CORRESPONDING CHAPTER	APPLY IT TO THE CHAPTER...	APPLY IT TO LIFE...
ASK QUESTIONS. Use questions to fill in the gaps between what is known and what is not. Use questions to identify problems before they stop you in your tracks.	*Chapter 7 Reading and Studying*	Ask questions before reading (while skimming material) or during reading (in margins) in order to maximize your understanding of what you read.	In any conversation, take time to ask questions that help you understand the situation and the person better.
USE WHAT YOU KNOW. Build on your past knowledge and experiences to learn new materials and solve problems.	*Chapter 8 Reading Across the Disciplines*	Concepts in one course can apply to another; for example, you can use psychology ideas when analyzing a character in a book.	When you are stopped short by a problem, recall and use how you've approached similar problems in the past.
LISTEN ACTIVELY. Consider what others have to say, and work to understand perspectives that differ from yours. Consider new ideas.	*Chapter 9 Active Listening and Note Taking*	When classmates speak up in class, listen to and consider their questions and ideas as you would those of your instructor.	Let coworkers have a say when a situation comes up, and consider their ideas carefully.
TAKE RESPONSIBLE RISKS. Challenge your limits, but do it wisely. When you have thought through a risk and the likelihood of success is strong, dive in.	*Chapter 10 Test Taking I: Test Preparation and Objective Tests*	Use test preparation strategies to make the risk of test taking a responsible one, with a strong likelihood of success.	Before making a drastic life change, consider whether your chances of success are good enough for you to take the plunge.
BE FLEXIBLE. Be ready and able to adjust your actions and change your mind to fit a changing situation.	*Chapter 11 Test Taking II: Getting Results on Essay Tests and Graded Projects*	When you encounter a tricky essay question, a flexible mind will help you approach it comprehensively.	When a health problem throws you a curve ball, think flexibly to come up with a new course of action.

Source: Adapted with permission from *Discovering & Exploring Habits of Mind* (pp. 22–37), by Arthur L. Costa and Bena Kallick. Alexandria, VA: ASCD. © 2000 by ASCD. Learn more about ASCD at www.ascd.org.

Here is a list of the Habits for Success. First, rate each based on how much you think you have and use that habit right now—from 1 (I don't have it at all) to 10 (I live this habit).

_____Persist   _____Ask questions

_____Keep learning   _____Use what you know

_____Think before you act   _____Listen actively

_____Reach out to others   _____Take responsible risks

_____Create and imagine   _____Be flexible

_____Put your senses to work

Next, underline what you consider to be your three strongest habits. Then, circle what you consider the three habits that need the most work.

Finally, look at the Take Action exercise on page 14 in which you were trying to change a negative habit. What is the relationship between this habit and a Habit for Success you want to develop? Describe the connection here. (Example: Alan's time-wasting habit of IMing his friends instead of studying is linked to his need to develop the habit of thinking before he acts.)

_____

_____

As you learn about each habit through your work in this book, consider the following: How have your three strongest habits improved your life? How would your life change if you developed your three weakest habits? Remember, with work you can improve and strengthen your habits. You will have a chance to revisit this assessment in the last chapter and measure your progress.

work against you. To succeed, you need to keep your focus narrow and your persistence strong. Two in-text tools will help you to:

- **make each habit specific and concrete.** At the end of each chapter, a Habit Summary puts the habit into action and gives you an opportunity to fill in three examples that apply to you.

- **Explore in depth a few habits that need your special attention.** Three times in the text—at the end of Chapters 3, 6, and 9—you will have the chance to create an in-depth plan for building a habit.

POWERFUL
QUESTIONS

People attend college for technical training, for the sake of learning, for increased earning power, and for many other reasons. Ask yourself:

What are your reasons for attending college? Consider the Habit for Success that opened this chapter: Which of the reasons you have for attending college seem most likely to help you persist, and why?

persist

You can use one or more of the Habits for Success to confront academic challenges you will face in college—from learning to understand difficult texts to listening from the perspective of your instructor. In many cases you will use more than one habit at a time. For example, when brainstorming a problem with a study group, you may reach out to others, listen to other perspectives, and communicate clearly. With more practice, the habits will become simpler to apply no matter what the situation and will become an essential part of how you operate in school, in the workplace, and in your personal life.

Inside Tips from the Authors

As you build knowledge, skills, and the Habits for Success throughout the term, the authors stand ready to support you in ways that match their areas of expertise. Look in each chapter for a tip from one of the three. Related podcasts are available at www.mystudentsuccesslab.com. Besides providing helpful tips, these podcasts are a great tool for students who tend to learn best by listening.

Carol Carter is the career coach.   Carol was a vice president in the corporate world and now is president of her own company. She has hired hundreds of graduates and has worked with many interns throughout her 25-year career. She will give you the inside story on what employers look for in people they hire.

Dr. Joyce Bishop is the technology coach.   Joyce teaches student success both in person and online. If working with online course components is unfamiliar territory, Joyce's tips can help you manage the ways your courses may require you to use e-mail, book and course Web sites, and Internet research. If you are comfortable with technology, what she has to say can help you become even more tech savvy.

Sarah Lyman Kravits is the self-management coach.   Sarah thrived as a student and attributes a large portion of her academic success to her ability to self-manage. She has ideas about how to solidify the self-management skills you have, improve the ones you struggle with, and use these skills to improve your academic performance.

Remember, you have to want to succeed badly enough to rid yourself of habits that limit you and to develop habits that empower you. Think for a moment about your level of motivation to succeed in college. On a scale of 1–10, how badly do you want to get the most out of your education and graduate? If your answer was 7 or higher, fasten your seat belt; you are about to change your

My motto was always to keep swinging. Whether I was in a slump or feeling badly or having trouble off the field, the only thing to do was keep swinging.

Hank Aaron, baseball champion

world. If your answer was less than 7, ask yourself why you might not be willing to persist toward a better future. Whether you have spent years struggling academically or not, this book and course will give you the chance to change your reality, opening doors and creating opportunities for the rest of your life.

Habit for Success

persist

Below are examples of how you can put this habit into action in different situations. Use the three spaces to add your own ideas for actions you can accomplish now or in the future. Be specific, and be real.

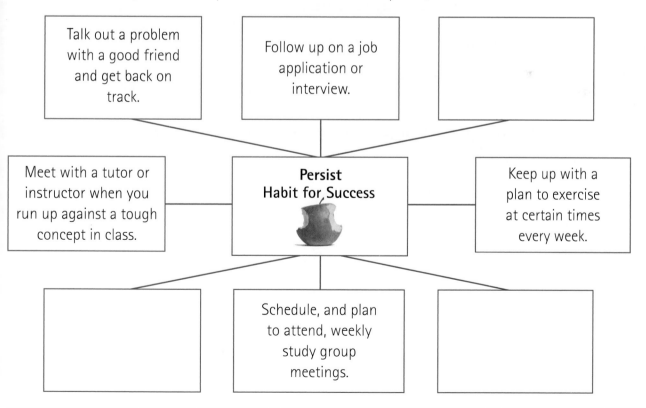

Talk out a problem with a good friend and get back on track.	Follow up on a job application or interview.	
Meet with a tutor or instructor when you run up against a tough concept in class.	**Persist Habit for Success**	Keep up with a plan to exercise at certain times every week.
	Schedule, and plan to attend, weekly study group meetings.	

Building Skills

Note the Important Points

Where are you headed, and how will college get you there?

Describe an important goal that you believe college will help you achieve.

_____

_____

How can you transition to college-level work?

Name the top two challenges you face in dealing with the difference between college and high school.

_____

How can habits change your life for the better?

How does a bad habit differ from a good habit?

_____

Name two strategies you would use to change or replace a habit that holds you back.

_____

_____

What habits fuel college success?

What do the Habits for Success help people to do, specifically?

_____

Name the three Habits for Success that you feel you most need to work on.

_____

_____

Critical Thinking

Target Challenges at the Start

Ponder these two points:[9]

- Instructors note that many students, all over the country, lack academic preparation in reading, writing, and math.
- Students note that the amount of work they had to do in high school often does not prepare them for how hard and how much they need to study in college.

FIRST, ASK QUESTIONS THAT GATHER INFORMATION. What are your day-to-day classroom experiences? Do you feel that you lack skill in reading, writing, math, or any other area? How well do you think your high school experience prepared you for the amount of work necessary in college?

NEXT, BRAINSTORM. On a separate piece of paper, generate ideas about how you have addressed academic or workload challenges in the past. What has worked, and what has not? Flip through the text and find chapters and sections that might help you in your particular area of challenge. What catches your eye?

FINALLY, GET MOVING. Make a plan to address a specific challenge. Commit to two strategies from the book, and include page numbers where you can explore them. Look at the syllabus for this course to see when you will cover those topics. Finally, locate one campus resource that can help you and indicate when you will contact them and what you plan to gain. Then, put your plan to work starting <u>now</u>.

Your challenge: _____

Book strategy #1 _____ on page _____

Book strategy #2 _____ on page _____

Syllabus dates/weeks to watch: _____ and _____

Campus resource: _____

Location: _____ Phone/e-mail:_____

Contact resource by: _____ Goal of contact: _____

Team Building

Shifting to College-Level Work

Gather in a group of three to five students. Together, brainstorm some challenges of transitioning to college-level work—challenges that prevent students from performing well in the classroom or getting work done outside of it. When you have as many challenges as you have group members, each person should choose one and write it at the top of a blank sheet of paper.

Look at the challenge on your page. Under it, write one practical idea about how to overcome it. When everyone is finished, pass the pages one person to the left. Then write an idea about the new challenge at the top of the page you've received. If you can't think of anything, pass the page as is. Continue this way until your original page comes back to you. Then discuss the ideas as a group, analyzing which ideas might work better than others. Add other ideas to the lists if you think of them.

The last step: On your own, keeping in mind your group discussion, list something about the transition that you personally find challenging. Then, name two specific actions that you commit to taking in order to face that challenge.

Challenge: _____

_____

1. _____

_____

2. _____

_____

Test Prep: Start It Now

persist

Persistence Is a Test Preparation Tool

The preparation for tests scheduled at any time in the term starts on the first day of class. Why? Because everything you do for a course—every fact and idea you hear in class, every concept you read, all the work you generate for your assignments, and everything you talk about with classmates—builds your knowledge, preparing you to show what you know on test day. In addition, the syllabus you receive on the first day gives you the information you need to plan your time.

Make a plan to persist toward test success starting now. Looking at the syllabi for the courses you are taking this semester, determine which test is coming up first. Fill in the following in relation to this test:

Course: _____

Test date and time (note this in your planner): _____

From what you can tell from the syllabus, topic(s) covered on the test: _____

_____

Time each week you will study for this test (for example, every Thursday from 3:00 to 4:30):
_____ (put this in your planner as well)

Office hours for the instructor who teaches this course: _____

Use this information to prepare—honor your weekly study times, consult with your instructor, and stay aware of the test date. After the test, evaluate whether organizing your study time, defining your study topics, and knowing how to contact your instructor with questions helped you persist and succeed. Write your evaluation here:

_____

_____

_____

_____

_____

_____

learning styles
building and using self-knowledge

merlette perceives herself as more of a words person than a numbers person. From middle school on, she has had more trouble in math and science classes than in English and social studies. However, her experience during the first term of college has left her confused about what she does well. In her algebra class, which had a group-study focus that was new to her, she kept her head above water. On the other hand, in her lecture-based history and freshman composition courses, she struggled. She isn't sure what to make of it all—and how to improve.

In this chapter . . . .

you explore answers to the following questions:

WHY understand how you learn?   p. 28

WHAT can assessments teach you about yourself?   p. 29

HOW can you use your self-knowledge? p. 36

HOW can you identify and manage learning disabilities?   p. 49

Habit for Success

keep learning

Always strive to know more, to understand something new and different about the world, yourself, and others. Explore how you learn so you can get the most from college.

Why Understand How You Learn?

As a college student, you invest valuable resources—time, effort, and money—in your education. Getting a good return on that investment depends in part on how well you understand yourself as a learner and how you use that self-knowledge to make specific decisions about how to approach your studies.

The way you think about yourself—your strengths and challenges—comes from many different sources and starts in childhood. Maybe your mother thinks you are "the funny one" or "the quiet one." Merlette, the student you just read about, considers herself a "words person" based on her school experiences. These labels—from yourself and others—influence your day-to-day decisions and long-term goals. However, the danger in accepting a label as truth is that it can shut down the potential for growth.

Your Abilities Can Change and Develop

Learning Style
a particular way in which the mind receives and processes information.

Every person has a unique **learning style**. You are also born with particular levels of ability and potential in different areas. However, you are not simply stuck with what you've been given. Studies support the idea that intelligence can grow over time no matter your starting point, if you start with solid knowledge of where you are and work to keep learning.[1]

Picture a bag of rubber bands of different sizes. Some are thick, and some are thin; some are long, and some are short—*but all of them can stretch.* A small rubber band, stretched out, can reach the length of a larger one that lies unstretched. In other words, with effort and focus, you can grow to some extent whatever raw material you have at the start. To begin thinking about

> # Be yourself. Everyone else is already taken.
>
> Oscar Wilde, author and playwright

where you can go, ask yourself: Who am I right now? Where would I like to be in five years? In 10 years?

Self-Knowledge Gives You the Power of Choice

There is much about yourself, your surroundings, and your experiences that you cannot control. However, self-knowledge gives you tools to choose how you *respond* to circumstances. Merlette, like nearly all students, cannot control the courses she's required to take or the way her instructors teach. But she can manage how she responds in each situation.

Understanding yourself as a learner will also help you choose how to respond to others in a group situation. In a study group, classroom, or workplace, each person takes in material in a unique way. You can use what you know about how others learn to improve communication and teamwork.

The two assessments in this chapter—Multiple Pathways to Learning and the Personality Spectrum—will give you greater insight into your strengths and weaknesses. This knowledge will help you make specific choices about what you do in class and during study time.

What Can Assessments Teach You about Yourself?

Unlike the dozens of tests you will take in college, self-assessments have no right or wrong answers. Rather, they are a snapshot of who you are at a given moment. Completed honestly, they have the potential to guide your future. As you respond to the assessment questions in this chapter, it might help you to compare the experience to trying on new glasses to correct blurred vision. The glasses will not create new paths and possibilities, but they will enable you to see more clearly the ones that are right in front of you.

The two assessments in this chapter have different objectives. Multiple Pathways to Learning is inner-directed as it focuses on eight unique learning styles. In contrast, the Personality Spectrum is outer-directed as it helps you evaluate how you react to people and situations.

A strong visual-spatial intelligence may have helped this film and television production student find his area of interest.

Following each assessment is information about the typical traits of each **intelligence** or personality spectrum dimension. As you will see from your scores, you have abilities in all areas, though some are more developed than others.

Assess Your Multiple Intelligences with Pathways to Learning

In 1983, Howard Gardner changed the way people perceived intelligence and learning with his theory of Multiple Intelligences. Gardner believes that the traditional view of intelligence—based on mathematical, logical, and verbal measurements comprising an "intelligence quotient," or IQ—does not reflect the spectrum of human ability. He focuses on the idea that humans possess a number of different areas of natural ability and potential.

The Theory of Multiple Intelligences

Gardner's research led him to believe that there are eight unique "intelligences," or areas of ability. These include the areas traditionally associated with the term "intelligence"—logic and verbal skills—but go beyond, to encompass a range of human ability. These intelligences almost never function in isolation. You will almost always use several at a time for any significant task.[3]

Look at Key 2.1 for descriptions of each intelligence along with examples of people who have unusually high levels of ability in each intelligence. Although few people will have the verbal-linguistic intelligence of William Shakespeare or the interpersonal intelligence of Oprah Winfrey, everyone has some level of ability in each intelligence. Your goal is to identify what your levels are and to work your strongest intelligences to your advantage.

Different cultures value different abilities and therefore place a premium on different intelligences. In Tibet, mountain dwellers prize the bodily-kinesthetic ability of a top-notch Himalayan mountain guide. In Detroit, auto makers appreciate the visual-spatial talents of a master car designer.

Your Own Eight Intelligences

Gardner believes that all people possess some capacity in each of the eight intelligences and that every person has developed some intelligences more fully than others. When you find a task or subject easy, you are probably using a more fully developed intelligence. When you have trouble, you may be using a less developed intelligence.[4]

Furthermore, Gardner believes your levels of development in the eight intelligences can grow or recede throughout your life, depending on your

Intelligence
as defined by H. Gardner, an ability to solve problems or create products that are of value in a culture.

By the way . . .
nearly half of all U.S. adults are involved in some formal type of lifelong learning.[2]

INTELLIGENCE	DESCRIPTION	HIGH-ACHIEVING EXAMPLE
Verbal–Linguistic	Ability to communicate through language; listening, reading, writing, speaking	Playwright William Shakespeare
Logical–Mathematical	Ability to understand logical reasoning and problem solving; math, science, patterns, sequences	Microsoft founder Bill Gates
Bodily–Kinesthetic	Ability to use the physical body skillfully and to take in knowledge through bodily sensation; coordination, working with hands	Olympic swimmer Dara Torres
Visual–Spatial	Ability to understand spatial relationships and to perceive and create images; visual art, graphic design, charts and maps	Architect Maya Lin
Interpersonal	Ability to relate to others, noticing their moods, motivations, and feelings; social activity, cooperative learning, teamwork	Telejournalist Oprah Winfrey
Intrapersonal	Ability to understand one's own behavior and feelings; self-awareness, independence, time spent alone	Tenzin Gyatso, the Dalai Lama
Musical	Ability to comprehend and create meaningful sound; sensitivity to music and musical patterns	Singer and musician Alicia Keys
Naturalist	Ability to identify, distinguish, categorize, and classify species or items, often incorporating high interest in elements of the natural environment	Conservationist Steve Irwin

efforts and experiences. Although Merlette might never become a world-class mathematician, she can grow her ability with focus and work. Conversely, even a highly talented numbers person will lose ability without practice. This reflects how the brain grows with learning and becomes sluggish without it.

A related self-assessment that you may have heard of, or have already taken, is the VAK or VARK questionnaire. VAK/VARK assesses learning preferences in three (or four) areas: Visual, Auditory, (Read/Write), and Kinesthetic. The Multiple Intelligences (MI) assessment is this book's choice because it incorporates the elements of VAK/VARK and expands upon them, giving you a more comprehensive picture of your abilities. If you would like further information about VARK, go to www.vark-learn.com.

A note about auditory learners who learn and remember best through listening: Auditory learning is part of two MI dimensions.

- Many auditory learners have strong <u>verbal intelligence</u> but prefer to hear words (in a lecture or discussion or on a recording) instead of reading them.
- Many auditory learners have strong <u>musical intelligence</u> and remember and retain information based on sounds and rhythms.

If you tend to absorb information better through listening, try study suggestions for these two intelligences. Podcasts are especially helpful to auditory learners, and an increasing number of instructors are converting their lectures into digital format for downloading. Check out the podcasts for this textbook at www.mystudentsuccesslab.com.

Use the Multiple Pathways to Learning assessment to determine where you are right now in the eight intelligence areas. Then look at Key 2.2, immediately following the assessment, to identify specific skills associated with the each area. Finally, the Multiple Intelligence Strategies grids in Chapters 3 through 12 will help you apply different learning styles in an effort to solve a chapter-specific problem.

Assess Your Style of Interaction with the Personality Spectrum

Personality assessments help you understand how you respond to the world around you, including people, work, and school. They also can help guide you as you explore majors and careers.

The concept of dividing human beings into four basic "personality types" goes as far back as Aristotle and Hippocrates, ancient Greek philosophers. Psychologist and philosopher Carl Jung, working early in the 20th century, focused on personality **typology**. He defined the following:[5]

Typology
a systematic classification or study of types.

- **An individual's preferred "world."** Jung said that *extroverts* tend to prefer the outside world of people and activities, while *introverts* tend to prefer the inner world of thoughts, feelings, and fantasies.
- **Different ways of dealing with the world.** Jung defined four distinct interaction dimensions, which are used to different degrees: *sensing* (learning through what your senses take in), *thinking* (evaluating information rationally), *intuiting* (learning through an instinct that comes from many integrated sources of information), and *feeling* (evaluating information through emotional response).

Katharine Briggs and her daughter, Isabel Briggs Myers, developed an assessment based on Jung's typology, called the Myers-Briggs Type Inventory, or MBTI (information is available online at www.myersbriggs.org). One of the most widely used personality inventories in the world, it creates 16 possible types from four dimensions. A comprehensive inventory, it is also quite

Multiple Pathways to Learning

Each intelligence has a set of numbered statements. Consider each statement on its own. Then, on a scale from 1 (lowest) to 4 (highest), rate how closely it matches who you are right now and write that number on the line next to the statement. Finally, total each set of six questions.

1. rarely   2. sometimes   3. usually   4. always

---

1. _____ I enjoy physical activities.
2. _____ I am uncomfortable sitting still.
3. _____ I prefer to learn through doing.
4. _____ When sitting I move my legs or hands.
5. _____ I enjoy working with my hands.
6. _____ I like to pace when I'm thinking or studying.
_____ TOTAL for **BODILY–KINESTHETIC**

1. _____ I enjoy telling stories.
2. _____ I like to write.
3. _____ I like to read.
4. _____ I express myself clearly.
5. _____ I am good at negotiating.
6. _____ I like to discuss topics that interest me.
_____ TOTAL for **VERBAL–LINGUISTIC**

---

1. _____ I use maps easily.
2. _____ I draw pictures/diagrams when explaining ideas.
3. _____ I can assemble items easily from diagrams.
4. _____ I enjoy drawing or photography.
5. _____ I do not like to read long paragraphs.
6. _____ I prefer a drawn map over written directions.
_____ TOTAL for **VISUAL–SPATIAL**

1. _____ I like math in school.
2. _____ I like science.
3. _____ I problem-solve well.
4. _____ I question how things work.
5. _____ I enjoy planning or designing something new.
6. _____ I am able to fix things.
_____ TOTAL for **LOGICAL–MATHEMATICAL**

---

1. _____ I listen to music.
2. _____ I move my fingers or feet when I hear music.
3. _____ I have good rhythm.
4. _____ I like to sing along with music.
5. _____ People have said I have musical talent.
6. _____ I like to express my ideas through music.
_____ TOTAL for **MUSICAL**

1. _____ I need quiet time to think.
2. _____ I think about issues before I want to talk.
3. _____ I am interested in self-improvement.
4. _____ I understand my thoughts and feelings.
5. _____ I know what I want out of life.
6. _____ I prefer to work on projects alone.
_____ TOTAL for **INTRAPERSONAL**

---

1. _____ I like doing a project with other people.
2. _____ People come to me to help settle conflicts.
3. _____ I like to spend time with friends.
4. _____ I am good at understanding people.
5. _____ I am good at making people feel comfortable.
6. _____ I enjoy helping others.
_____ TOTAL for **INTERPERSONAL**

1. _____ I like to think about how things, ideas, or people fit into categories.
2. _____ I enjoy studying plants, animals, or oceans.
3. _____ I tend to see how things relate to, or are distinct from, one another.
4. _____ I think about having a career in the natural sciences.
5. _____ As a child I often played with bugs and leaves.
6. _____ I like to investigate the natural world around me.
_____ TOTAL for **NATURALISTIC**

Source: Developed by Joyce Bishop, Ph.D., Golden West College, Huntington Beach, CA. Based on Howard Gardner, *Frames of Mind: The Theory of Mulitple Intelligences*, New York: Harper Collins, 1993.

Multiple Pathways to Learning

For each intelligence, shade the box in the row that corresponds with the range where your score falls. For example, if you scored 17 in Bodily–Kinesthetic intelligence, you would shade the middle box in that row; if you scored a 13 in Visual–Spatial, you would shade the last box in that row. When you have shaded one box for each row, you will see a "map" of your range of development at a glance.

A score of 20–24 indicates a high level of development in that particular type of intelligence, 14–19 a moderate level, and below 14 an underdeveloped intelligence.

	20–24 (Highly Developed)	14–19 (Moderately Developed)	Below 14 (Underdeveloped)
Bodily-Kinesthetic			
Visual-Spatial			
Verbal-Linguistic			
Logical-Mathematical			
Musical			
Interpersonal			
Intrapersonal			
Naturalistic			

Verbal–Linguistic
- Analyzing own use of language
- Remembering terms easily
- Explaining, teaching, learning, using humor
- Understanding syntax and word meaning
- Using writing or speech to convince someone to do or believe something

Musical–Rhythmic
- Sensing tonal qualities
- Creating/enjoying rhythms, melodies
- Being sensitive to sounds and rhythms
- Using an understanding of musical patterns to hear music
- Understanding the symbols and structure of music

Logical–Mathematical
- Recognizing abstract patterns
- Using facts to support an idea, and generating ideas based on evidence
- Discerning relationships and connections
- Performing complex calculations
- Reasoning scientifically (formulating and testing a hypothesis)

Visual–Spatial
- Perceiving and forming objects accurately
- Recognizing relationships between objects
- Representing something graphically
- Manipulating images
- Finding one's way in space

Bodily–Kinesthetic
- Strong mind–body connection
- Controlling and coordinating body movement
- Improving body functions
- Expanding body awareness to all senses
- Using the body to create products or express emotion

Intrapersonal
- Accessing one's internal emotions
- Understanding feelings and using them to guide behavior
- Evaluating own thinking
- Understanding self in relation to others
- Forming a comprehensive self-concept

Interpersonal
- Seeing things from others' perspectives
- Noticing moods, intentions, and temperaments of others
- Cooperating within a group
- Communicating verbally and nonverbally
- Creating and maintaining relationships

Naturalistic
- Ability to categorize something as a member of a group or species
- Ability to distinguish items in a group from one another
- Understanding of relationships among natural organisms
- Appreciation of the delicate balance in nature
- Deep comfort with, and respect for, the natural world

Source: Adapted from David Lazear, *Seven Pathways of Learning,* Tucson: Zephyr, 1994.

complex. David Keirsey and Marilyn Bates later condensed the MBTI types into four temperaments, creating the Keirsey Sorter (found at www.keirsey.com).

When author Joyce Bishop developed the Personality Spectrum assessment in this chapter, she adapted and simplified the Keirsey Sorter and MBTI material into four personality types—Thinker, Organizer, Giver, and Adventurer. Like the assessments on which it is based, the Personality Spectrum helps you identify the kinds of interactions that are most, and least, comfortable for you. As with the Multiple Intelligences, these results may change over time as you experience new things, change, and continue to learn. Key 2.3, on page 39, shows skills characteristic of each personality type.

How Can You Use Your Self-Knowledge?

In completing the Multiple Pathways to Learning and Personality Spectrum assessments, you developed a clearer picture of who you are and how you interact with others. Now focus on how you can use this new picture to choose effective strategies inside the classroom, during study time, relating to your career, and relating to technology.

Classroom Choices

Most students have to complete a set of "core curriculum" courses, as well as whatever courses their majors require. Additionally, busy students don't have a lot of flexibility when it comes to choosing particular sections of courses—you usually sign up for what fits best into your jam-packed weekly schedule and generally don't know what to expect in terms of your instructors and their styles. You may be asking: Where are the choices in this situation? Merlette, the student from the beginning of the chapter, is probably asking the same question about the trouble she is having in the classes that she thought would be easiest for her.

Here's the answer for you and for Merlette: The opportunity for choice lies in how you interact with your instructor and function in the classroom. It is impossible for instructors to tailor classroom presentation to 15, 40, or 300 unique learners—especially since they operate according to their own teaching styles. As a result, you may find yourself in a great learning situation with one teacher and in a complete mismatch with another. Sometimes, the way the class is structured can have more of an effect on your success than the subject matter, which may be why Merlette can stay on her feet in a course she expected would cause trouble for her.

After several class meetings, you should be able to assess each instructor's dominant teaching styles (see Key 2.4) and figure out how to maximize your learning.

Although presentation styles vary, the standard lecture is still the norm in most classrooms. For this reason, the traditional college classroom is generally

Personality Spectrum

1. I like instructors who
   a. ☐ tell me exactly what is expected of me.
   b. ☐ make learning active and exciting.
   c. ☐ maintain a safe and supportive classroom.
   d. ☐ challenge me to think at higher levels.

2. I learn best when the material is
   a. ☐ well organized.
   b. ☐ something I can do hands-on.
   c. ☐ about understanding and improving the human condition.
   d. ☐ intellectually challenging.

3. A high priority in my life is to
   a. ☐ keep my commitments.
   b. ☐ experience as much of life as possible.
   c. ☐ make a difference in the lives of others.
   d. ☐ understand how things work.

4. Other people think of me as
   a. ☐ dependable and loyal.
   b. ☐ dynamic and creative.
   c. ☐ caring and honest.
   d. ☐ intelligent and inventive.

5. When I experience stress I would most likely
   a. ☐ do something to help me feel more in control of my life.
   b. ☐ do something physical and daring.
   c. ☐ talk with a friend.
   d. ☐ go off by myself and think about my situation.

6. I would probably not be close friends with someone who is
   a. ☐ irresponsible.
   b. ☐ unwilling to try new things.
   c. ☐ selfish and unkind to others.
   d. ☐ an illogical thinker.

7. My vacations could be described as
   a. ☐ traditional.
   b. ☐ adventuresome.
   c. ☐ pleasing to others.
   d. ☐ a new learning experience.

8. One word that best describes me is
   a. ☐ sensible.
   b. ☐ spontaneous.
   c. ☐ giving.
   d. ☐ analytical.

STEP 2 Add up the total points for each letter.

TOTAL FOR   a. ☐ Organizer   b. ☐ Adventurer   c. ☐ Giver   d. ☐ Thinker

STEP 3 Plot these numbers on the brain diagram on page 38.

Personality Spectrum

scoring diagram for personality spectrum

Write your scores from page 37 in the four squares just outside the brain diagram—Thinker score at top left, Giver score at top right, Organizer score at bottom left, and Adventurer score at bottom right.

Each square has a line of numbers that go from the square to the center of the diagram. For each of your four scores, place a dot on the appropriate number in the line near that square. For example, if you scored 15 in the Giver spectrum, you would place a dot between the 14 and 16 in the upper right-hand line of numbers. If you scored a 26 in the Organizer spectrum, you would place a dot on the 26 in the lower left-hand line of numbers.

THINKER

Technical
Scientific
Mathematical
Dispassionate
Rational
Analytical
Logical
Problem Solving
Theoretical
Intellectual
Objective
Quantitative
Explicit
Realistic
Literal
Precise
Formal

ORGANIZER

Tactical
Planning
Detailed
Practical
Confident
Predictable
Controlled
Dependable
Systematic
Sequential
Structured
Administrative
Procedural
Organized
Conservative
Safekeeping
Disciplined

GIVER

Interpersonal
Emotional
Caring
Sociable
Giving
Spiritual
Musical
Romantic
Feeling
Peacemaker
Trusting
Adaptable
Passionate
Harmonious
Idealistic
Talkative
Honest

ADVENTURER

Active
Visual
Risking
Original
Artistic
Spatial
Skillful
Impulsive
Metaphoric
Experimental
Divergent
Fast-paced
Simultaneous
Competitive
Imaginative
Open-minded
Adventuresome

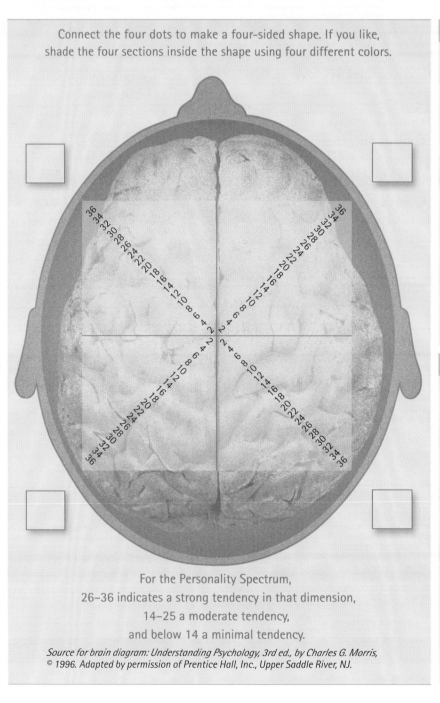

Connect the four dots to make a four-sided shape. If you like, shade the four sections inside the shape using four different colors.

For the Personality Spectrum,
26–36 indicates a strong tendency in that dimension,
14–25 a moderate tendency,
and below 14 a minimal tendency.

Source for brain diagram: Understanding Psychology, 3rd ed., by Charles G. Morris,
© 1996. Adapted by permission of Prentice Hall, Inc., Upper Saddle River, NJ.

Thinker

- Solving problems
- Developing models and systems
- Analytical and abstract thinking
- Exploring ideas and potentials
- Ingenuity
- Going beyond established boundaries
- Global thinking—seeking universal truth

Organizer

- Responsibility, reliability
- Operating successfully within social structures
- Sense of history, culture, and dignity
- Neatness and organization
- Loyalty
- Orientation to detail
- Comprehensive follow-through on tasks
- Efficiency
- Helping others

Giver

- Honesty, authenticity
- Successful, close relationships
- Making a difference in the world
- Cultivating potential of self and others
- Negotiation; promoting peace
- Openness
- Helping others

Adventurer

- High ability in a variety of fields
- Courage and daring
- Hands-on problem solving
- Living in the present
- Spontaneity and action
- Ability to negotiate
- Nontraditional style
- Flexibility
- Zest for life

Source: © 2001, Joyce Bishop, in *Keys to Success,* 3rd ed., Upper Saddle River, NJ: Pearson Prentice Hall, 2001.

Dr. Joyce Bishop

Professor of Psychology, Golden West College, Huntington Beach, California

I have a learning disability that causes problems with understanding words I hear, which made listening to lectures in college very hard. No one, including me, knew I had this difficulty because I learned how to compensate for it. In fact, I didn't know it myself until years after I graduated.

College was confusing for me. I did well in some classes and felt totally lost in others. The hardest were the lecture-based classes. When I wasn't familiar with the information or the words, I couldn't make sense of what I was hearing. If I read the material ahead of time and looked up concepts, the lectures made more sense. Also, I bargained with my classmates to borrow their notes in exchange for typing their term papers. Typing is bodily-kinesthetic and helped me to internalize what I was learning.

Stop and Think

Like Joyce, every student faces learning challenges. What are yours?

My strengths in logical-mathematical and visual intelligence helped me get by. Science classes were easiest for me because they are more visual. I switched from sociology to biology my freshman year; it was easier for me to remember the visual biology material as opposed to the more verbal liberal arts classes. Without my commitment to my education and my will to learn, I probably would not have graduated.

Determined to get back up on the horse and keep learning, I pursued my master's in public health 12 years later. My graduate classes were much more hands-on, but there was still a great deal of reading. One day my eye doctor expressed concern about the stress my schoolwork was causing my eyes and suggested that I get tested for a learning problem. He sent me to a center that usually tests small children for learning disabilities. The therapist giving the test said words, and I was to spell out the words with blocks. I consistently confused words with close sounds. It was determined that I processed language on a fourth-grade level, a condition that has not changed in my adult life.

Stop and Think

Joyce found out key information about herself through her determination to continue learning. What has your own determination to come to college taught you about yourself?

After the test, the therapist asked me, "How far did you go through school?" I asked her, "How far do you think I went?" She guessed that I had not made it past the tenth grade. I shared that I was just completing my master's degree. Her eyes got big, and she said, "You work really hard in school, don't you?" At that moment my head flooded with memories of report cards saying "doesn't pay attention in class" and "isn't working up to potential." I started to cry. An explanation for what had brought years of pain and struggle had finally surfaced.

Now that I know what the problem is, I can continue to learn, choosing strategies that work best for me. We all have our strengths and weaknesses; the way we work to manage those weaknesses while maximizing our strengths makes all the difference.

Think about Joyce and Think about Yourself

- What have the assessments in this chapter taught you about how you can strengthen your learning?
- Which of your personal goals are you likely to reach through lifelong learning?

Tiki Barber emerged from a college career at the University of Virginia to become a star running back with the New York Giants. To the shock of many, Barber retired at the peak of his football career, determined to keep learning about more than football. He now works as a television correspondent as well as a writer.

ke
lea

TEACHING STYLE	WHAT TO EXPECT IN CLASS
Lecture, verbal focus	Instructor speaks to the class for the entire period, with little class interaction. Lesson is taught primarily through words, either spoken or written on the board, overhead projector, handouts, or text.
Lecture with group discussion	Instructor presents material but encourages class discussion.
Small groups	Instructor presents material and then breaks class into small groups for discussion or project work.
Visual focus	Instructor uses visual elements such as PowerPoint slides, diagrams, photographs, drawings, transparencies, and videos.
Logical presentation	Instructor organizes material in a logical sequence, such as by steps, time, or importance.
Random presentation	Instructor tackles topics in no particular order and may jump around a lot or digress.
Conceptual presentation	Instructor spends the majority of time on the big picture, focusing on abstract concepts and umbrella ideas.
Detailed presentation	Instructor spends the majority of time, after introducing ideas, on the details and facts that underlie them.
Experience-based presentation	Instructor uses demonstrations, experiments, props, and class activities to show key points.

a happy home for the verbal or logical learner and the Thinker and Organizer. However, many students learn best when interacting with other students more than a traditional lecture allows. What can you do when your preferences don't match up with how your instructor teaches? Here are three suggestions:

Play to your strengths.   For example, if you are a musical learner who easily picks up information through listening, with an instructor who has a random delivery style, you might record and listen to the lecture several times on your MP3 player (get permission from your instructor before you record). Likewise, if you are a Giver with an instructor who delivers straight lectures, you should consider setting up a study group to go over details and fill in factual gaps.

Work to strengthen weaker areas.   As a visual learner reviews notes from a structured lecture, he could use logical-mathematical strategies such as outlining notes or thinking about cause-and-effect relationships within the material. An Organizer, studying for a test from notes delivered by an

These students find that sitting in a circle and taking turns sharing ideas works for their group study session. An off-duty classroom serves as a useful location.

© Spencer Grant/PhotoEdit

instructor with a random presentation, could organize the material in different formats, including tables and timelines.

Ask your instructor for additional help. If you are having trouble with coursework, take the initiative to communicate with your instructor or teaching assistant through e-mail or during office hours. This is especially important in large lectures where you are anonymous unless you speak up. A visual learner, for example, might ask the instructor to recommend graphs, figures, or videos that illustrate the lecture.

Merlette will be able to improve her classroom experience after taking the assessments. If she shows strengths in interpersonal and verbal-linguistic intelligences as well as Giver and Organizer dimensions, she might begin to understand why the group-study focus helped her even in an area that she considers difficult. She can then organize and run study groups for other courses or look for courses that feature discussion sections or small-group work.

No instructor can completely mesh with how you learn, so don't expect it. Instead, adapt by finding a way to apply what you do well to the situation. This kind of flexibility will serve you well in your career and life. Just as you can't handpick your instructors, you will rarely, if ever, be able to choose your work colleagues or their work styles.

A final point: Some students try to find out more about an instructor by asking students who have already taken the course or looking up comments that appear online. Be careful with investigations like this. You may not know or be able to trust an anonymous poster who comments on an instructor, and even if you hear a review from a friend you do trust, every student-instructor relationship is unique. An instructor your friend loved may turn out to be a bad match for you, or vice versa. Prioritize taking the courses that you need, and know that you will find a way to make the most of what your instructors offer, no matter who they are.

Study Choices

Start now to use what you have learned about yourself to choose the best study techniques. For example, if you tend to learn successfully from a linear, logical presentation, you can look for order (for example, a *chronology*—information organized sequentially according to event dates—or a problem–solution structure) as you review notes. If you are strong in interpersonal intelligence, you should try to work in study groups whenever possible or learn dry facts in the context of stories.

TAKE ACTION
Link How You Learn to Coursework and Major

First, on paper or on a computer, summarize yourself as a learner in a paragraph or two. Focus on what you learned about yourself from the chapter assessments. Done? Check here. _____

Next, schedule a meeting with your academic advisor (use your interpersonal intelligence).

Name of advisor: _____

Time/date of meeting: _____

Give the advisor an overview of your learning strengths and challenges, based on your summary. Ask for advice about courses that might interest you and majors that might suit you. Take notes.

Indicate two courses to consider in the next year:

1. _____

2. _____

Indicate two possible majors:

1. _____

2. _____

Finally, create a separate to-do list of how you plan to explore one course offering and one major. Set a deadline for each task.

When faced with a task that challenges your weaknesses, use strategies that boost your ability. For example, if you are an Adventurer who does *not* respond well to linear information, you can apply your strengths to the material—for example, through a hands-on approach. Or you can focus on developing your area of weakness by using study skills that work well for Thinker-dominant learners.

When you study with others, you and the entire group will be more successful if you understand the different learning styles in the group. For example:

- An Interpersonal learner could take the lead in teaching material to others.
- An Organizer could coordinate the group schedule.
- A Naturalistic learner might organize facts into categories that solidify concepts.

Key 2.5 shows study strategies that suit each intelligence, and Key 2.6 shows study strategies that suit each Personality Spectrum dimension. Because you have some level of ability in each area, and because there will be times that you need to boost your ability in a weaker area, you may find useful suggestions under any of the headings. Try different techniques, analyze how effective they are, and use what works best for you.

Technology Choices

Technology is everywhere these days. You see it in social settings, as people communicate using e-mail, text messaging, and social networking sites on the Internet. It also plays a significant role in academic settings, where you may encounter:

- Instructors who require students to communicate via e-mail
- Courses that have their own Web sites where you can access the syllabus and connect with resources and classmates
- Textbooks that have corresponding Web sites that you can, or are required to, use to complete assignments and e-mail them to your instructor

For some with extensive know-how, technology comes easily. For everyone else, knowing your strengths and challenges as a learner can help you make decisions about how to approach technology. Are you strong in the logical-mathematical intelligence or Thinker dimension? Working with an online tutorial may be a good choice. Are you an interpersonal learner? Find a tech-savvy classmate to help you get the hang of it. An Adventurer may want to just dive in and try out the features of a book or course Web site in a random way. Know yourself, and make choices that can best help you demystify technology and get you up to speed.

Inside Tips from Carol, Career Coach

Some students "fall in love" with a career by watching a TV show. However, if CSI is your favorite show, for example, it doesn't necessarily mean you would be well-suited to forensics. Are you good in math and science? Are you a strong detail person? Can you deal with the seamy and scary? Listen to who you are and what you are interested in, and try out the things you think you want to do. If you don't try out a field or profession, it is like marrying someone without ever dating. So, when you start to think about careers and fields, develop a list of places where you might intern or work to find out if the field and the job really make you tick.

Verbal–Linguistic 	■ Reading text; highlighting selectively ■ Using a computer to retype and summarize notes ■ Outlining chapters ■ Teaching someone else ■ Reciting information or writing scripts/debates
Musical–Rhythmic	■ Creating rhythms out of words ■ Beating out rhythms with hand or stick while reciting concepts ■ Writing songs/raps that help you learn concepts ■ Chanting or singing study material to a wordless tune ■ Taking music breaks
Logical–Mathematical	■ Organizing material logically; if it suits the topic, using a spreadsheet program ■ Explaining material sequentially to someone ■ Developing systems and finding patterns ■ Writing outlines ■ Analyzing and evaluating information
Visual–Spatial	■ Developing graphic organizers for new material ■ Drawing mind maps and think links ■ Using a computer to develop charts and tables ■ Using color in notes to organize ■ Linking material in your mind with items or places that you can visualize (method of loci)
Bodily–Kinesthetic	■ Moving while you learn; pacing and reciting ■ Using tangible items as memory devices ■ Rewriting or retyping notes to engage "muscle memory" ■ Designing and playing games to learn material ■ Acting out scripts of material
Intrapersonal 	■ Reflecting on personal meaning of information ■ Visualizing information ■ Keeping a journal ■ Studying in quiet areas ■ Imagining essays or experiments before beginning
Interpersonal	■ Studying in a group ■ As you study, discussing information over the phone or sending IMs ■ Using flash cards with others ■ Teaching someone else the material ■ Making time to discuss assignments and tests with your instructor
Naturalistic	■ Breaking down information into categories ■ Looking for ways that items fit or don't fit together ■ Looking for relationships among ideas, events, facts ■ Studying in a natural setting if it helps you to focus ■ Forming study groups of people with similar interests

Source: Adapted from David Lazear, *Seven Pathways of Learning,* Tucson: Zephyr, 1994.

Thinker

- Finding time to reflect independently on new information
- Learning through problem solving
- Designing new ways of approaching issues
- Converting material into logical charts, flow diagrams, and outlines
- Trying to minimize repetitive tasks
- Looking for opportunities to work independently

Organizer

- Defining tasks in concrete terms so that you know what is required
- Looking for a well-structured study environment
- Requesting feedback from instructors and classmates via e-mail or phone
- Using a planner or PDA to schedule tasks and dates
- Organizing material by rewriting and summarizing class and/or text notes
- Using flash cards
- Highlighting materials and notes carefully

Giver

- Studying with others in person, on the phone, or using instant messages
- Teaching material to others
- Seeking out tasks, groups, and subjects that involve helping people
- Expressing thoughts and feelings clearly and honestly
- Prioritizing your most important academic relationships

Adventurer

- Looking for environments/courses that encourage nontraditional approaches
- Finding hands-on ways to learn
- Seeking instructors and students whom you find stimulating
- Using or developing games and puzzles to help memorize terms
- Fighting boredom by asking to do something extra or performing a task in a more active way

Source: © 2001, Joyce Bishop, in *Keys to Success,* 3rd ed., Upper Saddle River, NJ: Pearson Prentice Hall, 2001.

Workplace Choices

The self-knowledge you build as you work through this chapter will help you work more effectively at any job, helping you to focus on what you do well and ask for help in areas that pose more of a challenge. It can also make you more successful in a team. Finally, it will help you plan your career.

Key 2.7 links majors and **internships** to the eight intelligences. This list represents only a fraction of the available opportunities. Use it to inspire thought and spur investigation. If something from this list or elsewhere interests you, consider looking for an opportunity to "shadow" someone (follow the person for a day to see what he or she does) to see if the more significant commitments of interships and majoring will make sense for you.

Internship
a temporary work program in which a student can gain supervised practical experience in a job and career area.

POWERFUL QUESTIONS

It is now common to have more than one career, and perhaps several, over your lifetime. Whether you change careers because you don't like what you're doing or because you lose your job in an economic downturn, you may have to return to school to learn new skills. Imagine yourself back in school several years after finishing college as you answer these questions:

What would your attitude be if you had to further your education? What are you willing to do now to acquire the "keep learning" Habit for Success so that you can weather the ups and downs of life and work?

keep learning

MULTIPLE INTELLIGENCE . . .	CONSIDER MAJORING IN . . .	THINK ABOUT AN INTERNSHIP AT A . . .
Bodily-Kinesthetic	Massage or physical therapy Kinesiology Construction engineering Sports medicine Dance or theater	Sports physician's office Physical or massage therapy center Construction company Dance studio or theater company Athletic club
Intrapersonal	Psychology Finance Computer science Biology Philosophy	Accounting firm Biology lab Pharmaceutical company Publishing house Computer or Internet company
Interpersonal	Education Public relations Nursing Business Hotel/restaurant management	Hotel or restaurant Social service agency Public relations firm Human resources department Charter school
Naturalistic	Geology Zoology Atmospheric sciences Agriculture Environmental law	Museum National park Environmental law firm Zoo Geological research firm
Musical	Music Music theory Voice Composition Performing arts	Performance hall Radio station Record label or recording studio Children's music camp Orchestra or opera company
Logical-Mathematical	Math Physics Economics Banking/finance Computer science	Law firm Consulting firm Bank Information technology company Research lab

Verbal–Linguistic	Communications Marketing English/literature Journalism Foreign languages	Newspaper or magazine PR/marketing firm Ad agency Publishing house Network TV affiliate
Visual–Spatial	Architecture Visual arts Multimedia design Photography Art history	Photo or art studio Multimedia design firm Architecture firm Interior design firm Art gallery

How Can You Identify and Manage Learning Disabilities?

Although all students have areas of strength and weakness, some challenges are more significant and are diagnosed as learning disabilities. These merit specific attention. Focused assistance can help students who are learning disabled manage their conditions and excel in school.

Identifying a Learning Disability

The National Center for Learning Disabilities (NCLD) defines learning disabilities as:[7]

- Neurological disorders that interfere with one's ability to store, process, and produce information

- Often running in families and being lifelong conditions, although learning-disabled people can use specific strategies to manage and even overcome areas of weakness

- Requiring a professional diagnosis in order for the disabled person to receive federally funded aid

- *Not* including mental retardation, autism, behavioral disorders, impaired vision, hearing loss, or other physical disabilities

- *Not* including attention deficit disorder and attention deficit hyperactivity disorder, although these problems may accompany learning disabilities[8]

How can you determine if you should be evaluated for a learning disability? According to the NCLD, persistent problems in any of the following areas may indicate a learning disability:[9]

- Reading or reading comprehension
- Math calculations, understanding language and concepts
- Social skills or interpreting social cues
- Following a schedule, being on time, meeting deadlines
- Reading or following maps
- Balancing a checkbook
- Following directions, especially on multistep tasks
- Writing, sentence structure, spelling, and organizing written work

Details on specific learning disabilities appear in Key 2.8. For an evaluation, contact your school's learning center or student health center for a referral to a licensed professional.

Key 2.8 What different learning disabilities are and how to recognize them

DISABILITY OR CONDITION	WHAT ARE THE SIGNS?
Dyslexia and related reading disorders	Problems with reading (spelling, word sequencing, comprehension) and processing (translating written language to thought or the reverse)
Dyscalculia (developmental arithmetic disorders)	Difficulties in recognizing numbers and symbols, memorizing facts, understanding abstract math concepts, and applying math to life skills (time management, handling money)
Developmental writing disorders	Difficulties in composing sentences, organizing a writing assignment, or translating thoughts coherently to the page
Handwriting disorders (dysgraphia)	Disorder characterized by writing disabilities, including distorted or incorrect language, inappropriately sized and spaced letters, or wrong or misspelled words
Speech and language disorders	Problems with producing speech sounds, using spoken language to communicate, and/or understanding what others say
LD-related social issues	Problems in recognizing facial or vocal cues from others, controlling verbal and physical impulsivity, and respecting others' personal space
LD-related organizational issues	Difficulties in scheduling and in organizing personal, academic, and work-related materials

Source: LD Online: LD Basics, http://www.ncld.org/content/view/445/389, © 2009.

Managing a Learning Disability

If you are diagnosed with a learning disability, take steps to manage it and maximize your ability to learn:

Be informed about your disability. Search the library and the Internet—try NCLD at www.ncld.org or LD Online at www.ldonline.org. Or call NCLD at 1-888-575-7373. If you have an Individualized Education Program (IEP)—a document describing your disability and recommended strategies—read it and make sure you understand it.

Seek assistance from your school. Speak with your advisor about getting a referral to the counselor who can help you get specific accommodations in your classes. Services mandated by law for students who are learning disabled include:

- Extended time on tests
- Note-taking assistance (for example, having a fellow student take notes for you)
- Assistive technology devices (MP3 players, tape recorders, laptop computers)
- Modified assignments
- Alternative assessments and test formats

Other services that may be offered include tutoring, study skills assistance, and counseling.

Be a dedicated student. Be on time and attend class. Read assignments before class. Sit where you can focus. Review notes soon after class. Spend extra time on assignments. Ask for help.

Build a positive attitude. See your accomplishments in light of how far you have come. Rely on support from others, knowing that it will give you the best possible chance to succeed.

> No two selves, no two consciousnesses, no two minds are exactly alike. Each of us is therefore situated to make a unique contribution to the world.

Howard Gardner, psychologist and educator

Habit for Success

keep learning

Below are examples of how you can put this habit into action in different situations. Use the three spaces to add your own ideas for actions you can accomplish now or in the future. Be specific and be realistic.

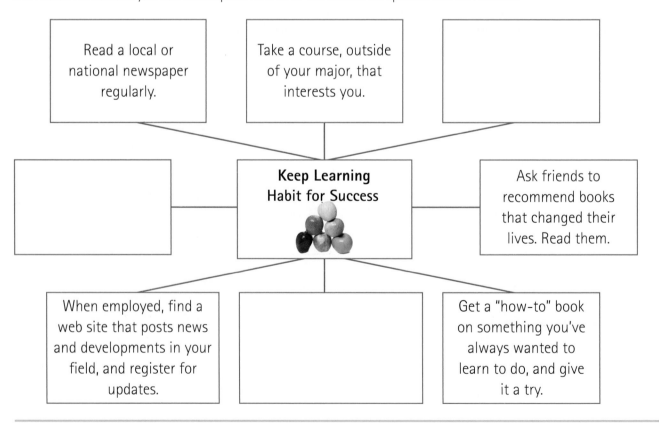

Read a local or national newspaper regularly.	Take a course, outside of your major, that interests you.

Keep Learning Habit for Success

Ask friends to recommend books that changed their lives. Read them.

When employed, find a web site that posts news and developments in your field, and register for updates.

Get a "how-to" book on something you've always wanted to learn to do, and give it a try.

Building Skills
for successful learning

Note the Important Points

Why understand how you learn?

How would you define the term "learning style"? _____

_____

Name two benefits of getting to know your unique way of learning and interacting._____

_____

What can assessments teach you about yourself?

Describe what the Multiple Intelligences assessment can help you discover. _____

_____

What are the four dimensions of the Personality Spectrum assessment? _____

_____

How can you use your self-knowledge?

Name one way to use your understanding of how you learn in . . .

. . . the classroom. _____

. . . your study time. _____

. . . the workplace. _____

How can you identify and manage learning disabilities?

Name a fact about learning disabilities. _____

Learning Styles

Critical Thinking

Maximize Your Classroom Experience

Consider first what you know about yourself as a learner. Then reflect on your instructors' teaching styles this term. Consider which instructors' styles mesh well with how you learn and which are not in sync. Make notes here about the situation that you think is the most challenging.

Course: _____ Instructor style: _____

Your view of the problem: _____

_____

_____

Next, brainstorm three ideas about actions you can take to improve the situation. Note the intelligence (or intelligences) on which each action is based (refer to Keys 2.5 and 2.6 for ideas):

1. _____

_____

2. _____

_____

3. _____

_____

Finally, choose one and put it to work. Briefly note what happened: Were there improvements as a result?

_____

_____

_____

_____

Team Building

Ideas About Personality Types

Divide into groups according to the four types of the Personality Spectrum—Thinker-dominant students in one group, Organizer-dominant students in another, Giver-dominant students in a third, and Adventurer-dominant students in the fourth. If you have scored the same in more than one of these types, join whatever group is smaller. With your group, brainstorm the following lists for your type:

1. The strengths of this type

2. The struggles, or things that cause stress, for this type

3. Career areas that tend to suit this type

4. Career areas that are a challenge for this type

5. Challenges for this type in relating to the other three Personality Spectrum types

If there is time, each group can present this information to the entire class; this will boost understanding and acceptance of diverse ways of relating to information and people.

Test Prep: Start It Now

Learn More About Your Test-Taking Self Using a Self-Portrait

Complete the following on separate sheets of paper or electronically (if you can use a graphics program).

Getting ready for tests means more than just learning your material—it also requires the kind of self-knowledge that helps you make the best study choices. You can build that self-knowledge by combining everything you have learned about yourself as a student into one comprehensive "self-portrait."

Design your portrait in "think-link" or mind-map style. A think link is a visual construction of related ideas, similar to a map or web, which represents your thought process. Ideas are written inside geometric shapes, often boxes or circles, and related ideas and facts are attached to those ideas by lines that connect the shapes (see the note-taking section in Chapter 7 for more about think links). Use the style shown in Key 2.9, or try something different like a treelike think link, a line of boxes with connecting thoughts, or another design that makes sense to you.

In your self-portrait, describe your dominant Multiple Intelligences, Personality Spectrum dimensions, preferred teaching styles and classroom settings, preferred study situations (times, locations, company), abilities and interests, and anything else relevant to who you are as a test-taker.

After creating and thinking about your self-portrait, make two NEW choices regarding how you will prepare for tests this term. Will you change your study location or time? Will you adjust your strategies to take advantage of a strength in a particular intelligence or Personality Spectrum dimension? Note the changes here.

1. _____

_____

2. _____

_____

You will change as you continue to learn. Revisit your self-portrait in the future—next term or even next year. Revise it to reflect what you've learned and how you've changed.

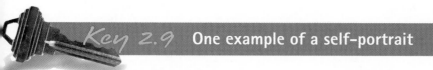

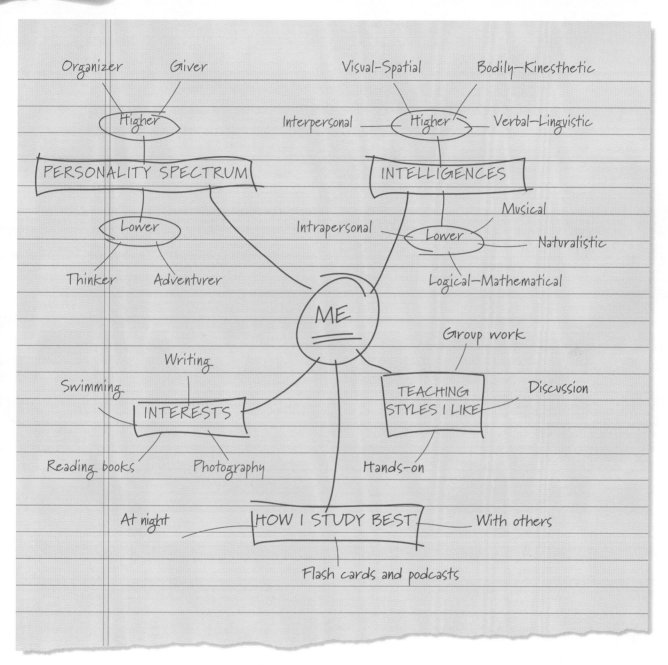

Organizer   Giver

Higher

PERSONALITY SPECTRUM

Lower

Thinker   Adventurer

Visual–Spatial   Bodily–Kinesthetic

Interpersonal —— Higher —— Verbal–Linguistic

INTELLIGENCES

Musical

Intrapersonal —— Lower —— Naturalistic

Logical–Mathematical

ME

Group work

Writing

Swimming

INTERESTS

TEACHING STYLES I LIKE   Discussion

Reading books   Photography

Hands-on

At night   HOW I STUDY BEST —— With others

Flash cards and podcasts

time and money
managing important resources

sajid was working one part-time job in the evenings, as an assistant manager at Radio Shack, and another on weekends, doing book-keeping at his cousin's auto body shop. The income from both jobs was enough for tuition, rent, food, and other expenses. However, the time commitment was too much. Without evening and weekend time to study, he couldn't keep up with the work in his 12 credits of classes, and his grades were suffering.

When Sajid lost his job in the electronics store, he considered it a mixed blessing. He knew he would have money problems. However, he also knew that he would have the time to catch up on his schoolwork. He feels like it is impossible to have both the time *and* the money he needs to get through school.

In this chapter . . .

you explore answers to the following questions:

© iStockphoto.com

Habit for Success

think before you act

Get the most out of your actions by starting with clear goals and a plan. Thinking ahead about your time and your budget will mean fewer obstacles in your path.

- Powerful Questions about Thinking Before You Act *p. 70*
- Real People Think Before They Act *p. 71*
- Habit Summary *p. 85*
- Test Prep: Start It Now *p. 93*

What Do Time and Money Have to Do with College Success?

A student like Sajid might have the skill and talent to succeed in school. He might have chosen the college and major that are a good fit. He might have a strong support system, an organized study area, top-notch computer equipment, and the best of intentions. However, if he doesn't have the time to study or the money to pay his tuition and expenses, he will face obstacles that are hard to overcome.

Time and money are valuable resources. You need time to attend classes, study, and work on projects and papers. You need money to pay for tuition, books, and other expenses. These resources are linked; for example, many students need time to work, so that they can earn the money to pay for expenses.

Making Money Costs You Time

Look at money and what you buy with it in terms of the time you spend earning it. For example, you are thinking about purchasing a new $200 cell phone. If you have a job that pays $10 an hour after taxes, you have to work 20 hours to buy that phone. Ask yourself: Is it worth it? If the answer is no, use the money for something that matters more to you.

Considering the time you have to spend earning money can hit home when you look at where your money goes from day to day. Cutting back on regular expenses can make a significant difference (see Key 3.1). If it takes you a month of work to earn $1,000 at your part-time job, you need to decide whether you would rather spend that money on coffee or put it toward next term's tuition.

> The bad news is time flies. The good news is you're the pilot.

Michael Altschuler, motivational speaker

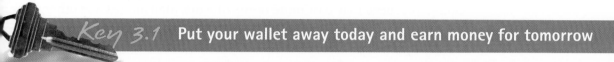

Key 3.1 Put your wallet away today and earn money for tomorrow

DAY-TO-DAY EXPENSE	APPROXIMATE COST	POTENTIAL SAVINGS IF INVESTED*
Gourmet coffee	$4 per day, 5 days a week, totals $20 per week	$80 per month; $1040 for the year. With interest from a savings account earning 3% would be $1, 071.
Cigarettes	$5 per day, 7 days a week (for a pack-a-day habit), totals $35 per week	$140 per month; $1,820 for the year. With interest from a savings account earning 3% would be $1,874.
Ordering in meals	$15 per meal, twice per week, totals $30 per week	$120 per month; $1,560 for the year. With interest from a savings account earning 3%, would be $1,606.

*Monthly cost = weekly cost × 4 weeks
Yearly cost = weekly cost × 52 weeks

Managing Time and Money May Mean Taking Longer to Graduate

Managing your key resources—time and money—is a crucial part of your job as a student. Time is a finite resource—everyone has the same 24 hours in a day, every day—and money is limited for nearly every student. The key is to make smart decisions about how you spend each of them. Such decisions may involve adjustments in when you take courses and for how long.

The reality for many college students is that they do not have enough money to go to college full time, straight through the two or four years it takes to graduate. For example, statistics show that public college students working toward a four-year degree take, on average, more than six years to finish.[1] Students like Sajid have a variety of choices, including:

- Going part time in order to maintain a work schedule while having enough time to study.

- Working full time over a summer—or, if necessary, while "stopping out" (leaving school temporarily) for a year—in order to put money away for tuition.

- Taking some or all courses online in order to have more flexibility with a work schedule.

- Transferring to a school with cheaper tuition or one that doesn't require living on campus.

Students all over the country are turning to solutions like these to afford college.

Going to college may cost more hours of work than almost any other purchase, and it takes hours away from your day that you might otherwise spend earning money. However, you are spending tuition and time in order to better your chances of long-term financial success. If you look at the statistics in Key 3.2, you will see that college graduates tend to earn more in the workplace than non-graduates. However long it takes you to attain your degree or certificate, you are making a sound investment in your future.

As you read through the rest of the chapter, remember that how you spend both time and money reflects what you value (see Chapter 4). Therefore, if

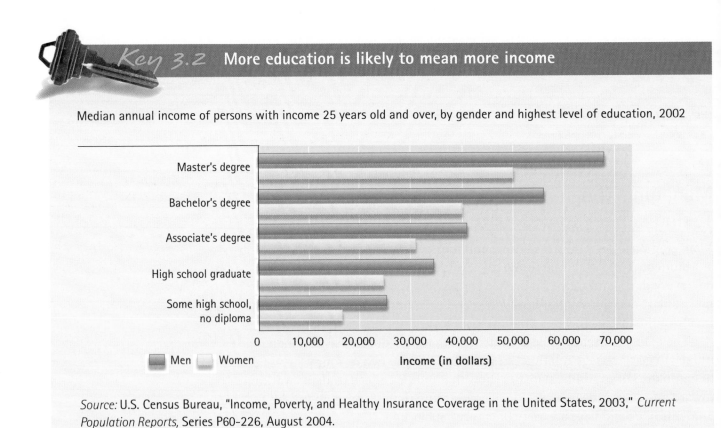

Key 3.2   More education is likely to mean more income

Median annual income of persons with income 25 years old and over, by gender and highest level of education, 2002

Source: U.S. Census Bureau, "Income, Poverty, and Healthy Insurance Coverage in the United States, 2003," *Current Population Reports,* Series P60-226, August 2004.

along the way you find that the way you use either or both of these precious resources is causing problems, look carefully at how you can adjust your choices to align with your most important values.

What Kind of Time and Money Manager Are You?

Successful time and money management is based on self-knowledge, so start by thinking about how you interact with these resources.

For each question, circle the number in the range that most applies to you.

My energy is best in the . . .	morning	1	2	3	4	5	evening
I tend to be . . .	always on time	1	2	3	4	5	always late
I focus best . . .	for long periods	1	2	3	4	5	for short periods
I'm most likely to . . .	save money	1	2	3	4	5	spend money
I put money toward . . .	things now	1	2	3	4	5	future needs
I would borrow money . . .	anytime	1	2	3	4	5	never

Identify Your Time-Related Needs and Preferences

Body rhythms and habits affect how each person deals with time. Some people are night owls; others are at their best in the morning. A mismatch between your habits and your schedule causes stress that may affect your grades. Take the following steps to identify how you can make time work for you rather than against you:

Create a personal time "profile." Ask yourself the following questions:

- At what time of day do I have the most energy? The least energy?
- Do I tend to be early, on time, or late?
- Do I focus well for long stretches or need regular breaks?

Consider your profile when creating a schedule. For example:

- Early birds may try to schedule early classes; people whose energy peaks later may look for classes in the afternoons or evenings.
- People who tend to be late might want to determine what situations contribute to this tendency (early classes, back-to-back classes, etc.) and try to avoid them.
- If you focus well for long stretches, you can handle classes back to back; if you tend to need breaks, try to set up a schedule with time between class meetings.

Note Your Unique Way of Managing Money

The way you interact with money is as unique as you are: You might be a spender or a saver. You might focus on money in the present tense, or you might look primarily to the future. You might charge everything, only purchase things that you can buy with cash, or do something in between. You might search actively for college loans or try to avoid borrowing altogether.

How you handle money and the level of importance it has for you affects your decisions about college, major, and career. Among the factors that influence you as a money manager are:

- **Your values.** You tend to spend money on what you think is most important.

- **Your personality.** Thinkers may focus on planning, Organizers may balance bank accounts down to the penny, Givers may prioritize spending money to help others, Adventurers may spend impulsively and deal with the consequences later.

- **Your culture.** Some cultures see money as a collective resource to be shared within families; others prize individual accumulation as a sign of independence. Some cultures tend to avoid borrowing; others use credit and loans freely.

- **Your family and peer group.** You tend to either follow or react against how your parents and immediate family handle money. Your friends also influence you.

Money coach Connie Kilmark notes that you cannot change how you handle money until you analyze your attitudes and behaviors. "If managing money was just about math and the numbers, everyone would know how to manage their finances sometime around the fifth grade," she says.[2] Once you take a hard look at your approach to money, you can make real-life money decisions based on what works best for you.

Now that you have a better idea of your tendencies, take a closer look at time, the resource accessible to everyone.

How Can You Manage Your Time?

Consider each day as a jigsaw puzzle: You have all the pieces (seconds, minutes, hours) in a pile, and your task is to form a picture of how you want your day to look. Start by building the schedule that works best for you.

Build a Schedule

Schedules help you gain control of your life in two ways: They provide segments of time for things you have to do, and they remind you of events, due dates, responsibilities, and deadlines. Start by recording your schedule in a planner.

Choose a Planner

Planners help you keep track of events, commitments, and tasks. You can choose a notebook planner (which devotes a page to each day or shows a week's schedule on a two-page spread) or an electronic planner or "smartphone" such as a BlackBerry or iPhone (which allows you to perform functions like scheduling events and due dates, making lists, and creating an address book). You might also consider online calendars, such as Google calendar, which can "communicate" with your phone or other electronic planning device.

Coordinating your schedule with classmates, work colleagues, and friends is a crucial task. These students use electronic devices to update contact information.

Though electronic devices are handy and have a large data capacity, they cost more than the paper versions, and their small size means they are easy to lose. Which tool should you choose? The one that you are most likely to use every day. An inexpensive notebook, used conscientiously, may work as well for some people as a top-of-the-line electronic device.

Schedule and Prioritize Tasks, Events, and Commitments

Everything that has a date, a time, or a deadline goes in your planner. However, not every item has the same level of importance, and you need to spend the bulk of your time on your **priorities**. As you get ready to enter items into your planner, think through your responsibilities using three priority levels:

Priorities
tasks or intentions that are more important than others.

Priority 1 items are the most crucial. They include:

- Class meeting times and dates
- Exam and quiz dates
- Due dates for papers, projects, lab assignments, and presentations
- Work shifts
- Child-care responsibilities (pickups, times during which you are responsible for children)

Priority 2 items are important but more flexible parts of your routine. These include:

- Blocks of study time
- Meetings for study groups, tutoring, discussion groups, clubs, support groups
- Steps that are part of a major task, such as dates you want to complete project research
- Personal needs (medical appointments, food shopping, cooking, workout time)

Priority 3 items are lowest in importance. These include:

- Social activities and events
- Leisure-time activities (downloading new tunes, getting in touch with a friend)
- Maintenance tasks (cleaning out a closet, organizing a room)

Next, use the following steps to lay everything out in your planner:

Put in Priority 1 items first.   Enter your class and work times for the entire term all at once. Your syllabus will tell you when readings and assignments are due and when quizzes and tests will take place (see the sample syllabus on page 101 in Chapter 4).

Next, schedule Priority 2 items around Priority 1 items.   Start by blocking out study time where available on your schedule, being sure to indicate the specific material you plan to study. According to one formula, you should spend at least two hours studying and working on assignments for every credit hour. That means that if you take 12 credits, you should study about 24 hours a week outside of class. Although this may not be easy, especially if you have a job, a family, or both, do whatever you can to put in the hours. After you schedule your study time, include other Priority 2 items.

Finally, insert Priority 3 items when you can.   You may not want to put these into your schedule ahead of time. One strategy is to keep a separate list of these tasks so that you can refer to it when free time pops up.

Once your schedule is filled out, decide on a visual way to indicate priority level. Some people use numbers or letters (A, B, C). Some write different priority items in different-colored pens (red for Priority 1, blue for Priority 2, etc.). Electronic planners may allow you to color-code or flag items according to priority.

Key 3.3 shows parts of a daily schedule and weekly schedule.

Make Your Schedule Work for You

Once your schedule is written, it's time to put it to use. These six strategies will help.

Plan regularly.   Set aside regular periods: each day to plan the next day and the weekend to plan the next week. Keep your planner with you at all times, and check it periodically.

Look at your term or semester all at once.   Don't be fooled—finals week is *not* the only busy week you'll face. If you map out your biggest responsibilities from the beginning to the end of the term, you can see where your work-heavy weeks will come up and can plan how to handle those ahead of time. For example, a student who has three tests and a presentation all in one week

Monday, March 14		
TIME	TASKS	PRIORITY
6:00 A.M.		
7:00		
8:00	Up at 8am — finish homew	
9:00		
10:00	Business Administration	
11:00	Renew driver's license @ D	
12:00 P.M.		
1:00	Lunch	
2:00	Writing Seminar (peer editi	
3:00	↓	
4:00	check on Ms. Schwartz's of	
5:00	5:30 work out	
6:00	↳6:30	
7:00	Dinner	
8:00	Read two chapters for	
9:00	Business Admin.	
10:00	↓	
11:00		
12:00		

Monday, March 28

8		Call: Mike Blair	1
9	BIO 212	Financial Aid Office	2
10		EMS 262 *Paramedic	3
11	CHEM 203	role-play*	4
12			5
Evening	6pm yoga class		

Tuesday, March 29

8	Finish reading assignment!	Work @ library	1
9			2
10	ENG 112	(study for quiz)	3
11	↓		4
12			5
Evening		↓ until 7pm	

Wednesday, March 30

8		Meet w/advisor	1
9	BIO 212		2
10		EMS 262	3
11	CHEM 203 *Quiz		4
12		Pick up photos	5
Evening	6pm Dinner w/study group		

in November may have to adjust a work schedule, arrange extra child care, or simply schedule extra blocks of study time to handle the load.

Make and use to-do lists.   Use a *to-do list* to record the things you want to accomplish on a busy day or for a particular challenge like exam week or a major project. Write items on separate paper, prioritize the list, and then transfer the items you plan to accomplish each day to open time slots in your planner.

Post monthly calendars at home.   Use a monthly wall calendar for an overview of your major commitments and upcoming events. If you live with family or friends, create a group calendar to stay on top of plans and avoid scheduling conflicts. Try having each person write commitments in a particular color.

Time and Money

Make a to-do list for your busiest day this week. Include all the tasks and events you know about, including attending class and study time, and the activities you would like to do (exercising, lunch with a friend) if you have extra time. Then use a coding system (and your naturalistic intelligence) to categorize your list according to priority.

Date: _____

1. _____   7. _____

2. _____   8. _____

3. _____   9. _____

4. _____   10. _____

5. _____   11. _____

6. _____   12. _____

After examining this list, record your daily schedule in your planner (if you have a busy day, you may want to list Priority 3 items separately to complete if time permits). At the end of the day, evaluate this system. Did the list help you to manage your time and tasks effectively? If you liked it, use a to-do list on a daily and weekly basis.

Schedule leisure time. Taking time off—to watch a show, chat online, get some exercise, take a nap—will refresh you and actually improve your productivity when you get back on task. Even small 10-minute breathers within study sessions can help, because you often can't concentrate well for extended periods of time without a break.

Avoid time traps. Carefully limit activities that take time that you need for study and work. Surfing the Internet, instant messaging, playing computer or video games, and talking with friends on your cell phone can eat up hours before you know it.

Fight Procrastination

It's human and common to leave difficult or undesirable tasks until later. Taken to the extreme, however, **procrastination** can develop into a habit that causes

Procrastination
the act of putting off a task until another time.

serious problems including stress from a buildup of responsibilities, work that is not up to par, and the disappointment of others counting on you.

Among the reasons people procrastinate are:

Inside Tips from Joyce, Technology Coach

Technology can save you a tremendous amount of time, but it can also be an enormous time drain, as when you start texting friends or surfing YouTube on a study break and look up to see that an hour has passed. Control your social tech time by scheduling it tightly. Assign yourself 25 minutes of reading and 5 minutes of computer time every half-hour, for example. Set an alarm so you know when to get back on task.

- **Perfectionism.** Habitual procrastinators often measure their value by their ability to achieve.[4] To the perfectionist procrastinator, a failed project equals a failed person. For that reason, not trying at all is better than an attempt that falls short of perfection.

- **Fear of limitations.** Procrastinators can blame a failure on waiting too long, not on any personal shortcoming. If you don't try, you don't have to face your limitations.

- **Being unsure of the next step.** If you get stuck and don't know what to do, sometimes it seems easier to procrastinate than to make the leap to the next level of your goal.

- **Facing an overwhelming task.** Some big projects can immobilize you. If a person facing such a task fears failure, she may procrastinate to avoid confronting the fear.

The following strategies will help you avoid procrastination:

- **Analyze its effects.** Ask yourself what is likely to happen if you put something off. Realizing that procrastination will hurt you more than help you is often the first step to facing your responsibilities.

- **Set reasonable goals.** Unreasonable goals can immobilize you. Set manageable goals, and allow enough time to complete them.

- **Break tasks into smaller parts.** If you concentrate on one small step at a time, the task may become less burdensome. Setting time limits for each task may help you feel more in control.

- **Get started whether or not you "feel like it. "** The motivation techniques from Chapter 1 might help you take the first step. Once you start, you may find it easier to continue.

- **Ask for help.** Once you identify what's holding you up, see who can help you face the task. Another person may come up with an innovative way to get you moving.

Think about what leads you to procrastinate—a particular kind of assignment, a certain course, instructions from a person you find difficult. What do you tend to do, and what happens because of it? Now think about how this chapter's Habit for Success can help you improve the situation.

How can thinking before you act—or fail to act—help you face your responsibilities? Name one upcoming task on which you commit to *not* procrastinating—and get on it.

- **Don't expect perfection—ever.** Most people learn by starting at the beginning, making mistakes, and learning from those mistakes. It's better to try your best than to do nothing at all.

- **Reward yourself.** When you accomplish a task, take a break, see a movie, and tell yourself that you are making progress.

Be Flexible

No matter how well you think ahead, sudden changes can up-end your plans if you are inflexible. Change is a fact of life, and although you can't always choose your circumstances, you can make decisions about how you handle them.

For changes that occur periodically—the need to work an hour overtime at your after-school job, a meeting that tends to run late—think through a backup plan ahead of time. For surprises, the best you can do is to be ready to brainstorm and rely on your internal and external resources. If you have to miss a class, for example, ask to see a classmate's notes. When change involves more serious problems—your car breaks down, a family member gets sick—use problem-solving skills to help you through (see Chapter 5). Your academic advisor, counselor, dean, financial aid advisor, and instructors may have ideas and assistance.

Change is a reality for money management as well as time management. Staying in control of your money will help you make adjustments when sudden expenses pop up.

How Can You Manage Your Money?

According to the American Psychological Association, nearly three out of four Americans cite money as the number one stressor in their lives.[5] Adding college expenses to the basic cost of living means that, for the vast

Thinking before taking action propelled these three friends from difficult circumstances to successful medical and dental careers—and to a lifelong quest to help others realize their dreams.

Doctor **Sampson Davis**
Doctor **Rameck Hunt**
Doctor **George Jenkins**

Graduates of Seton Hall University

Before they met as young teenagers, each had grown up in Newark, New Jersey, in struggling families.

George spent his early years living in and around the projects with his mother and brother. His father left when George was 2. From the age of 11, Sam, his five siblings, and his mother lived on welfare after Sam's father left. Rameck lived with his grandmother. His father was in and out of jail, and both of his parents were fighting drug addictions.

Stop and Think

George, Sam, and Rameck grew up facing enormous challenges. What difficulties have you faced that made it hard to focus on your schoolwork?

Because of their academic abilities, each boy caught the attention of teachers. Sam and George were tested and admitted in the seventh grade to University High School in Newark, a magnet school for high achievers in math and science. Rameck joined them in ninth grade.

When they were juniors, they went to a presentation about an opportunity at Seton Hall University called the Pre-Medical/Pre-Dental Plus Program, which provided

Source: The Three Doctors, LLC.

financial support to poor students who showed promise. Thinking about his childhood dream of becoming a dentist, George convinced his two friends to apply to the program, and they made a pact that they "would apply to Seton Hall, go to college together, then go to medical [and dental] school and stick with one another to the end . . . . We . . . headed back to class, without even a hint of how much our lives were about to change."

Stop and Think

Have you had a moment, like George, Sam, and Rameck, when something you heard or read opened you to new possibilities? What happened, and how did it change your attitude and goals?

Although all three got into the program, life continued to present challenges. Rameck and Sam both did time in juvenile detention after which they redoubled their efforts at school. Ultimately they attended Seton Hall University together.

Later, George was accepted into the University of Medicine and Dentistry, and Rameck and Sam were accepted into the Robert Wood Johnson Medical School. Through the next few years, they continued to keep one another focused

on the goal ahead. Sam failed his medical boards the first time out, but with his friends' support he passed with flying colors on his next attempt.

As they passed each hurdle, the men saw more and more how important their mutual support had been to their achievements. During their residencies, they created The Three Doctors Foundation, dedicated to exposing poor children to colleges, professional people, and the working world as well as providing financial assistance. Their pact to help one another has become a pact to help many more.

Think about George, Sam, and Rameck and Think about Yourself

■ Which of the actions of the three doctors was successful because they thought carefully before acting? Why is this habit so crucial when you are making a big move in your life?

■ First, think of a choice you made without thinking beforehand. What would you do differently now? Then, describe a choice you have coming up, and discuss how you plan to get the best results.

After graduating from college, **Andrea Jung** took a sales management job, figuring it would give her a strategic advantage when she went to law school. However, she thrived in the sales world. Thinking carefully, she shifted her course and stayed in sales, which led her up the ladder. She eventually became the first female CEO of Avon and has spearheaded a movement to address and combat violence against women around the world.

think
before
you act

majority of college students, money is tight. Soaring college costs far outpace the cost of living. From 1997 to 2007, the cost of living rose 24%. In contrast, college costs increased by more than 80%. This steep rise places a burden on students and their families to find a way to pay for college.[6]

Finances can be especially problematic for self-supporting students who may have to come up with funds for tuition, books, and other college fees. Additionally, many older students—and even a few traditional-aged ones—are responsible for living expenses and supporting children or other family members on top of school costs. The more complicated the situation, the more it can distract you from your work and your academic goals.

Your challenge is to come up with enough money to pay for college and expenses, without working so many hours that you have no time to study (remember Sajid?) or taking out so many loans that you can't dig out of debt for years. The answer may involve some combination of applying for financial aid, holding a job, effective budgeting, and avoiding credit card debt.

Explore and Apply for Financial Aid

Financing your education—alone or with the help of your family—involves gathering financial information and making decisions about what you can afford and how much help you need. Some roadblocks stand in the way of getting help. Your challenge is to find a way around them:

Students don't apply.   One recent report indicated that almost 40% of full-time community college students do not fill out a federal aid application, including 29% of students with incomes under $10,000 per year. These students may be intimidated by the application process or simply believe that they won't qualify for aid.[7]

The economy has an effect.   When the economy is struggling, private banks are less likely to grant loans, and federal programs like the Pell Grants (see Key 3.5) have less money. Also, in tough economic times, more students apply for grants like the Pell, with the result that more people will get smaller pieces of the pie.[8]

Colleges vary in what they offer.   State colleges provide fewer opportunities for aid when their funding is reduced. Additionally, concerned about students' ability to pay back loans, some smaller colleges stop offering federal loans to their students.[9]

Types of Aid

Aid comes in the form of student loans, grants, and scholarships. *Almost all students are eligible for some kind of need-based or merit-based financial assistance.*

Student loans.   Student loan recipients are responsible for paying back the amount borrowed, plus interest, according to a payment schedule that may stretch over a number of years. The federal government administers or

LOAN	DESCRIPTION
Perkins	Low, fixed rate of interest. Available to those with exceptional financial need (determined by a government formula). Issued by schools from their allotment of federal funds. Grace period of up to nine months after graduation before repayment, in monthly installments, must begin.
Stafford	Available to students enrolled at least half-time. Exceptional need not required, although students who prove need can qualify for a subsidized Stafford loan (the government pays interest until repayment begins). Two types of Staffords: the direct loan comes from federal funds, and the FFEL (Federal Family Education Loan) comes from a bank or credit union. Repayment begins six months after you graduate, leave school, or drop below half-time enrollment.
PLUS	Available to students enrolled at least half-time and claimed as dependents by their parents. Parents must undergo a credit check to be eligible, or may be sponsored through a relative or friend who passes the check. Loan comes from government or a bank or credit union. Sponsor must begin repayment 60 days after receiving the last loan payment.

oversees most student loans. To receive aid from a federal program, you must be a citizen or eligible non-citizen and be enrolled in a program that meets government requirements. Key 3.4 describes the main student loan programs to which you can apply.

Grants. Unlike student loans, grants do not require repayment. Grants, funded by federal, state, or local governments as well as private organizations, are awarded to students who show financial need. Key 3.5 describes federal grant programs. Additional information about both grants and loans is available in *The Student Guide to Financial Aid*, which you can find at your school's financial aid office, request by phone (800-433-3243), or access online at www.ed.gov/prog_info/SFA/StudentGuide/.

Scholarships. Scholarships are awarded to students who show talent or ability in specific areas (academic achievement, sports, the arts, citizenship, or leadership). They may be financed by government or private organizations, employers (yours or your parents'), schools, religious organizations, local and community groups, credit unions, or individuals.

Looking for Aid

Take the following five actions in your quest to pay for college.[10]

Ask, ask, ask. Visit the financial aid office more than once. Ask what you are eligible for. Alert the office to any money problems, such as a change in your

Time and Money

GRANT	DESCRIPTION
Pell	Need-based; the government evaluates your reported financial information and determines eligibility from that "score" (called an expected family contribution, or EFC). Available to undergraduates who have earned no other degrees. Amount varies according to education cost and EFC. Adding other aid sources is allowed.
Federal Supplemental Educational Opportunity (FSEOG)	Need-based; administered by the financial aid administrator at participating schools. Each participating school receives a limited amount of federal funds for FSEOGs and sets its own application deadlines.
Work-study	Need-based; encourages community service work or work related to your course of study. Pays by the hour, at least the federal minimum wage. Jobs may be on campus (usually for your school) or off (often with a nonprofit organization or a public agency).

financial situation. Search libraries and the Web, including your school's Web site, for information on everything that is possible.

Apply for government aid.　Fill out the Free Application for Federal Student Aid (FAFSA) form electronically. The form can be found through your college's financial aid office or Web site, or via the U.S. Department of Education's Web site at www.ed.gov/finaid.html. The U.S. Education Department has an online tool called FAFSA Forecaster, which you can use to estimate how much aid you qualify for. You will need to reapply every year for federal aid. This is a *free* form—if you hear about services that charge a fee for completing your FAFSA for you, avoid them.

Get help.　Consider asking a parent or relative to co-sign on a loan application or to loan you money directly. Web sites such as www.fynanz.com or www.GreenNote.com can help you create a legal document formalizing the agreement between you and the person offering the loan.

Consider a range of options.　Look at loans from all kinds of private lenders in addition to federal loans. Compare loans using Web sites like www.estudentloan.com. Consider transferring to a less expensive school. You may be able to get a comparable education while escaping post-graduation debt.

Applying for Aid

The number one rule is to apply—and apply by the deadline or, even better, early. The earlier you complete the process, the greater your chances of being

By the way . . .

according to a recent survey, although 78% of students indicate that the financial aid office is one of the most important resources on campus, only 17% report using it frequently.[11]

considered for aid, especially when you are vying for part of a limited pool of funds. Here are some additional tips from financial aid experts Arlina DeNardo and Carolyn Lindley of Northwestern University:[12]

- **Know what applications you need to fill out.** FAFSA is required at all colleges, but some also require a form called the CSS/Financial Aid Profile.

- **Note the difference between merit-based and need-based aid.** While some aid is awarded based on financial need, other aid is merit-based, meaning that it is linked to specifics such as academic performance, a particular major, or ethnic origin.

- **Be aware of the total cost of attending college.** When you consider how much money you need, add books, transportation, housing, food, and other fees to tuition.

- **If you receive aid, pay attention to the award letter.** Know whether the aid is a grant or a loan that needs to be repaid. Follow rules such as remaining in academic good standing. Note reapplication deadlines and meet them (many require reapplication *every year*).

Finally, don't take out more money than you need. If you max out on your total aid too early in your college career, you could run into trouble as you approach graduation. Look at your needs year by year, and make sure you are only taking out what is absolutely necessary.

Juggle Work and School

More than two-thirds of college students have some kind of job while in school. Key 3.6 shows the percentages of part-time and full-time college students who work.

If, like Sajid, you want to or need to work, try to do it in a way that allows you to focus on schoolwork.

Establish Your Needs

Think about what you need from a job before you begin your job hunt. Ask questions like these:

- How much money do I need to make—weekly, per term, for the year?
- What time of day is best for me? Should I consider night or weekend work?
- Can my schedule handle a full-time job, or should I look for part-time work?
- Do I want hands-on experience and/or connections in a particular field?
- What do I like and dislike doing?
- Does location matter? Where do I want to work, and how far am I willing to commute?

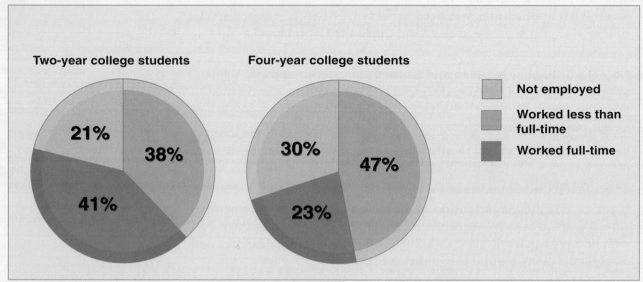

Two-year college students   **Four-year college students**

Not employed

Worked less than full-time

Worked full-time

21%   38%   41%

30%   47%   23%

Source: U.S. Department of Education, National Center for Educational Statistics, *Profile of Undergraduates in U.S. Postsecondary Educational Institutions: 2003-2004* (NCES 2006-184), June 2006, p.13.

- How flexible a job do I need?
- Can I, or should I, find work at my school or as part of a work-study program?

Analyze Effects of Working While in School

Working while in school can have both pros and cons. Here are some possibilities for each:

- **Pros:** general and career-specific experience; developing future contacts; enhanced school performance (working up to 15 hours a week may help you use your time more effectively)
- **Cons:** time commitment that reduces available study time; reduced opportunity for social and extracurricular activities; having to shift gears mentally from work to classroom; stretching yourself too thin and being tired all the time

Identify Options, Make a Choice, and Evaluate

Use what you learned about yourself when you apply for jobs. Continue to evaluate after you start a job. If the benefits you anticipated aren't there, or aren't enough, consider other possibilities at work or at school. Sajid might find, for example, that one job gives him enough money if he goes to school part time. He's okay with taking longer to get a degree because he realizes that he will almost certainly fail if he continues what he is doing.

Connect with your school's job placement office, career center and counselors, or Web site job board as you search for the right position. Keep in mind that work-study positions have many advantages for students: They are located on campus, and they don't involve weekend or holiday hours. Finally, if you do get a job off campus, make sure your employer knows that you are a student and that your schedule may change every term.

Manage Income and Expenses Through Budgeting

Creating a practical monthly **budget** that works means that you gather information about your resources (money flowing in) and expenditures (money flowing out) and analyze the difference. Next, you come up with ideas about how you can make changes. Finally, you adjust spending or earning so that you come out even or ahead.

Your biggest expense right now is probably the cost of your education. However, that expense may not hit you fully until after you graduate and begin to pay back your student loans. For now, include in your budget only the education costs you are paying while you are in school.

Budget
a plan to coordinate resources and expenditures; a set of goals regarding money.

Figure Out What You Earn

Add up all of the money you receive during the year—the actual after-tax money you have to pay your bills. Common sources of income include:

- Take-home pay from a regular full-time or part-time job during the school year
- Take-home pay from summer and holiday employment
- Money you earn as part of a work-study program
- Money you receive from your parents or other relatives for your college expenses
- Loans, scholarships, or grants

If you have saved money for college, decide how much you will withdraw every month for school-related expenses.

Figure Out What You Spend

Start by recording every check or electronic withdrawal going toward fixed expenses like rent, phone, and Internet service. Then, over the next month, record personal expenditures in a small notebook. Indicate any expenditure over $5, making sure to count smaller expenditures if they are frequent (for example, a bus pass for a month, coffee or lunch purchases per week).

Some expenses, like automobile and health insurance, may be billed only a few times a year. In these cases, divide the yearly cost by 12 to see how much you pay each month. Common expenses include:

- Rent or mortgage
- Tuition that you are paying right now (the portion remaining after all forms of financial aid)

- Books, lab fees, and other educational expenses
- Regular bills (electric, gas, oil, phone, water)
- Food, clothing, toiletries, and household supplies
- Child care
- Transportation and auto expenses (gas, maintenance, monthly bus or train pass)
- Credit cards and other payments on credit (car payments)
- Insurance (health, auto, homeowner's or renter's, life)
- Entertainment (cable TV, movies, restaurants, books and magazines, music downloads)
- Computer-related expenses, including the cost of your online service
- Miscellaneous unplanned expenses

Use the total of all your monthly expenses as a baseline for other months, realizing that your expenditures will vary depending on what is happening in your life and even the season (for example, the cost to heat your home may be much greater in the winter than in the summer).

Evaluate the Difference

Focusing again on your current situation, subtract your monthly expenses from your monthly income. Ideally, you have money left over—to save or to spend. However, if you are spending more than you take in, ask some focused questions.

© Shutterstock

- **Examine expenses.** Did you forget to budget for recurring expenses such as dental visits? Was your budget derailed by an emergency expense such as a major car repair?
- **Examine spending patterns and priorities.** Did you overspend on entertainment or clothes? Are you being hit by high interest payments or late fees on your credit card? Did you really need that new iPod, cell phone, car stereo, hair color, or movie club membership?
- **Examine income.** Do you bring in what you need? Do you need to look for another source of income—a job or financial aid?

Adjust Expenses or Earnings

If you need to make changes, brainstorm solutions that involve either increasing resources or decreasing spending. To increase resources, consider taking a part-time job, increasing hours at a current job, or finding aid. To decrease spending, look at what expenses you can trim or cut out. In addition, save money in day-to-day ways such as the following:

- Share living space
- Take advantage of free on-campus entertainment (movies and events)
- Rent movies or borrow them from friends or the library

- Eat at home more often
- Use grocery and clothing coupons
- Take advantage of sales, buy store brands, and buy in bulk
- Find discounted play and concert tickets for students
- Walk or use public transport
- Bring lunch from home
- Shop in secondhand stores or swap clothing with friends
- Bring coffee from home instead of buying it at expensive coffee shops
- Reduce credit hours
- Ask a relative to help with child care or create a babysitting co-op
- Cut back on air conditioning and use compact flourescent bulbs (CFLs)

Key 3.7 shows a sample budget of an unmarried student living with two other students in off-campus housing with no meal plan. Included are all

Key 3.7 How one student mapped out a monthly budget

- Wages: $12 an hour (after taxes) × 20 hours a week = $240 a week × 4⅓ weeks (one month) = $1,039
- Monthly withdrawals from savings (from summer earnings) = $200
- Total income per month = $1,239

MONTHLY EXPENDITURES	
School-related expenses (books, supplies, any expense not covered by financial aid)	$80
Public transportation	$90
Phone	$92
Food (groceries and takeout)	$285
Credit card payments	$100
Rent (including utilities)	$650
Entertainment (music, movies, tickets to events)	$90
Miscellaneous expenses, including clothing and personal items	$375
Total monthly spending:	$1,762
$1,239 (income) − $1,762 (expenses) = −$523	*$523 over budget*

Credit card offers pop up everywhere, as these women applying for Walmart cards know. Think carefully before applying for any type of card.

regular and out-of-pocket expenses with the exception of tuition, which the student will pay back after graduation in student loan payments. In this case, the student is $523 over budget, having spent more than $300 this month on miscellaneous expenses such as clothing, downloadable music, and a new cell phone. How would you make up the difference?

Consider your dominant multiple intelligences when planning your budget. For example, whereas logical–mathematical learners may take to a classic detail-oriented budgeting plan, visual learners may want to create a budget chart, or bodily–kinesthetic learners may want to make budgeting more tangible by dumping receipts into a big jar and tallying them at the end of the month. See the multiple intelligence strategies grid on the next page for MI-related ideas about how to manage your money.

Manage Credit Card Use

Credit card companies target college students with dozens of offers. Credit cards are a handy alternative to cash and can help build a strong credit history if used appropriately, but they also can plunge you into debt, affecting your credit rating and making it difficult to get loans or finance car or home purchases. Tough economic times often mean heavier reliance on credit to get by. Recent statistics show how college students use credit cards:[14]

- 84% of college students hold at least one credit card. The average number of cards is 4.6 and 50% have four or more.
- Students who hold credit cards carry an average outstanding balance of $3,173.
- 92% of students report charging school supplies or other education expenses. Nearly 30% report using cards to pay tuition.

Often cash-poor, college students charge books and tuition on cards (or "plastic") as well as expenses like car repair, food, and clothes. Before they know it, their debt becomes unmanageable. It's hard to notice trouble brewing when you don't see your wallet taking a hit.

How Credit Cards Work

Every time you charge a purchase, you create a debt that must be repaid. The credit card issuer earns money by charging interest on unpaid balances. Here's an example: Say you have a $3,000 unpaid balance on your card at an annual

Multiple Intelligence Strategies for Money Management

Briefly describe a money management problem you have.

_____

_____

Now, brainstorm potential solutions to your problem, linking each solution to an intelligence. Use the right-hand column to record your ideas.

INTELLIGENCE	SUGGESTED STRATEGIES	USE MI STRATEGIES TO COME UP WITH SOLUTIONS
Verbal-Linguistic	■ Talk over your financial situation with someone you trust. ■ Write out a detailed budget outline. If you can, store it on a computer file so you can update it regularly.	
Logical-Mathematical	■ Focus on the numbers; using a calculator and amounts as exact as possible, determine your income and spending. ■ Calculate how much money you'll have in 10 years if you start now to put $2,000 in a 5% interest-bearing IRA account each year.	
Bodily-Kinesthetic	■ Consider putting money, or a slip with a dollar amount, each month in envelopes for various budget items—rent, dining out, etc. When the envelope is empty or the number is reduced to zero, spending stops.	
Visual-Spatial	■ Set up a budgeting system that includes color-coded folders and colored charts. ■ Create color-coded folders for papers related to financial and retirement goals—investments, accounts, etc.	
Interpersonal	■ Whenever money problems come up, discuss them right away with a family member, partner, or roommate. ■ Brainstorm a five-year financial plan with one of your friends.	
Intrapersonal	■ Schedule quiet time to plan how to develop, follow, and update your budget. Consider financial-management software, such as Quicken. ■ Think through where your money should go to best achieve your long-term financial goals.	
Musical	■ Include a category of music-related purchases in your budget—going to concerts, buying CDs—but keep an eye on it to make sure you don't go overboard.	
Naturalistic	■ Analyze your spending by using a system of categories. Your system may be based on time (when payments are due), priority (must-pay bills vs. extras), or spending type (monthly bills, education, family expenses).	

TAKE ACTION
Map Out Your Budget

Use your logical–mathematical intelligence to see what you take in and spend and to decide what adjustments you need to make. Consider using an online calculator—such as www.calculatorweb.com—for this task.

Step 1: Estimate your current expenses in dollars per month, using the following table. This may require tracking expenses for a month, if you don't already have a record.

EXPENSE	AMOUNT SPENT
Rent/mortgage or room and board payment	$
Utilities (electric, heat, gas, water)	$
Food (shopping, eating out, meal plan)	$
Telephone (land line and mobile phone)	$
Books, lab fees, other educational expenses	$
Loan payments (educational or bank loans)	$
Car (repairs, insurance, payments, gas)	$
Public transportation	$
Clothing/personal items	$
Entertainment	$
Child care (caregivers, clothing/supplies, etc.)	$
Medical care/insurance	$
Other	$
TOTAL MONTHLY EXPENSES	$

Step 2: Calculate your average monthly income. If it's easiest to come up with a yearly figure, divide by 12 to derive the monthly figure. For example, if you have a $6,000 scholarship for the year, your monthly income would be $500 ($6,000 divided by 12).

INCOME SOURCE	AMOUNT RECEIVED
Regular work salary/wages (full-time or part-time)	$
Grants or work-study programs	$
Scholarships	$
Assistance from family members	$
Other	$
TOTAL	$

Step 3: Subtract the grand total of your monthly expenses from the grand total of your monthly income

INCOME PER MONTH	**$**
Expenses per month	– $
CASH FLOW	$

Step 4: If you have a negative cash flow, you can increase income, decrease spending, or both. List two workable ideas about how you can get your cash flow back in the black.

1. _____

2. _____

interest rate of 18%. If you make the $60 minimum payment every month, it will take you eight years to pay off your debt, *assuming that you make no other purchases*. The effect on your wallet is staggering:

- Original debt—$3,000
- Cost to repay credit card loan at an annual interest rate of 18% for 8 years—$5,760
- Cost of using credit—$5,760 – $3,000 = $2,760

As you can see, by the time you finish, you will repay nearly *twice* your original debt.

The first step in avoiding debt is to know as much as you can about credit cards, starting with the important concepts in Key 3.8 on the next page.

Managing Credit Card Debt

Think before you act in order to avoid debt. Ask questions before charging: Would I buy it if I had to pay cash? Can I pay off the balance in full at the end of the month? If I buy this, what else will I have to give up? The majority of American citizens have some level of debt, and many people go through periods when they have a hard time paying bills. If you use credit wisely while in school, however, you will build good habits that can improve your financial future.

A few basics will help you stay in control.

- **Choose your card wisely.** Students are often eligible for lower interest rate cards, cards with no annual fee, cards with useful rewards, or cards with a grace period (no penalty for late payments up to a certain number of days).

- **Pay bills on time, and make at least the minimum payment.** Remind yourself a week or so before the due date by creating an e-mail alert through your card account, making a note in your planner, or setting an alarm on your electronic planner.

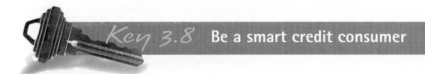

WHAT IS THIS?	WHAT DO YOU DO WITH IT?
Annual percentage rate (APR) is the amount of interest charged on the money you don't pay off in any given month. The higher your APR, the higher your finance charges.	Shop around for low rates (check www.studentcredit.com). Look for fixed rates. Watch out for low rates that skyrocket to more than 20% after a few months or a couple of late payments.
Cash advance is an immediate loan, in cash, from the credit card company.	Use a cash advance only in emergencies. Finance charges begin immediately, and you may also have to pay a transaction fee.
Credit limit is the top amount your card company allows you to charge, including all fees and cash advances.	Card companies generally set lower credit limits for students, but your limit may rise if you pay bills on time. Avoid charging up to the limit, so that you have credit available for emergencies.
Finance charges include interest and fees and are calculated each month.	The only way to avoid a finance charge is to pay your balance in full by the due date.
Minimum payment is set by the card company and refers to the smallest amount you can pay by the statement due date.	Make the minimum payment at the very least—not doing so may hurt your credit report. Remember that the more you can pay each month, the less you spend on fees.

Creditor
A person or company to whom a debt is owed, usually money.

- **Stay on top of problems.** If you get into trouble, call the **creditor** and see if you can set up a payment plan. Then, going forward, try to avoid what got you into trouble. Organizations such as the National Foundation for Credit Counseling (www.nfcc.org) can help you solve problems.
- **Reduce the load.** Cut up a credit card or two if you have too many.

Money is only a tool. It will take you wherever you wish, but it will not replace you as the driver.

Ayn Rand, writer and philosopher

Habit for Success

 think you before act

Below are examples of how you can put this habit into action in different situations. Use the three spaces to add your own ideas for actions you can accomplish now or in the future. Be specific, and be realistic.

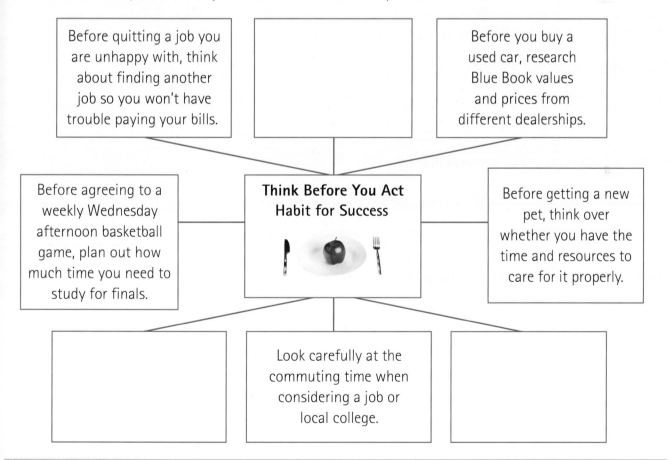

Before quitting a job you are unhappy with, think about finding another job so you won't have trouble paying your bills.

Before you buy a used car, research Blue Book values and prices from different dealerships.

Before agreeing to a weekly Wednesday afternoon basketball game, plan out how much time you need to study for finals.

Think Before You Act Habit for Success

Before getting a new pet, think over whether you have the time and resources to care for it properly.

Look carefully at the commuting time when considering a job or local college.

Building Skills
for successful learning

Note the Important Points

What do time and money have to do with college success?

Explain how your two key resources—money and time—are connected.

_____

_____

What kind of time and money manager are you?

Briefly describe yourself as a time manager.

_____

_____

Briefly describe yourself as a money manager.

_____

_____

How can you effectively manage your time?

Describe how to build a useful schedule.

_____

_____

Name three strategies that can help you put your schedule to work.

1. _____

2. _____

3. _____

How can you manage your money?

Describe two actions you can take to find financial aid.

1. _____

2. _____

Define what it means to "budget."

_____

Critical Thinking

applying learning to life

Discover How You Spend Your Time

Use the tables here to record data. Answer questions and write additional thoughts on separate paper or in a computer file.

Everyone has exactly 168 hours in a week. How do you spend yours? To warm up, make guesses, or estimates, about three particular activities. In a week, how much time do you spend . . .

1. Studying? _____ hours

2. Sleeping? _____ hours

3. Interacting with media and technology (computer, online services, cell phone, video games, television) for non-study purposes? _____ hours

Now, to find out the real story, record how you spend your time for seven days. The chart on pages 88–89 has blocks showing half-hour increments. As you go through the week, write in what you do each hour. Include sleep and leisure time. Record your *actual* activities instead of the activities you wished you did. There are no wrong answers.

TIME	Monday ACTIVITY	Tuesday ACTIVITY	Wednesday ACTIVITY	Thursday ACTIVITY
6:00 A.M.				
6:30 A.M.				
7:00 A.M.				
7:30 A.M.				
8:00 A.M.				
8:30 A.M.				
9:00 A.M.				
9:30 A.M.				
10:00 A.M.				
10:30 A.M.				
11:00 A.M.				
11:30 A.M.				
12:00 P.M.				
12:30 P.M.				
1:00 P.M.				
1:30 P.M.				
2:00 P.M.				
2:30 P.M.				
3:00 P.M.				
3:30 P.M.				
4:00 P.M.				
4:30 P.M.				
5:00 P.M.				
5:30 P.M.				
6:00 P.M.				
6:30 P.M.				
7:00 P.M.				
7:30 P.M.				
8:00 P.M.				
8:30 P.M.				
9:00 P.M.				
9:30 P.M.				
10:00 P.M.				
10:30 P.M.				
11:00 P.M.				
11:30 P.M.				
12:00 A.M.				
12:30 A.M.				
1:00 A.M.				
1:30 A.M.				
2:00 A.M.				

TIME	Friday ACTIVITY	Saturday ACTIVITY	Sunday ACTIVITY
6:00 A.M.			
6:30 A.M.			
7:00 A.M.			
7:30 A.M.			
8:00 A.M.			
8:30 A.M.			
9:00 A.M.			
9:30 A.M.			
10:00 A.M.			
10:30 A.M.			
11:00 A.M.			
11:30 A.M.			
12:00 P.M.			
12:30 P.M.			
1:00 P.M.			
1:30 P.M.			
2:00 P.M.			
2:30 P.M.			
3:00 P.M.			
3:30 P.M.			
4:00 P.M.			
4:30 P.M.			
5:00 P.M.			
5:30 P.M.			
6:00 P.M.			
6:30 P.M.			
7:00 P.M.			
7:30 P.M.			
8:00 P.M.			
8:30 P.M.			
9:00 P.M.			
9:30 P.M.			
10:00 P.M.			
10:30 P.M.			
11:00 P.M.			
11:30 P.M.			
12:00 A.M.			
12:30 A.M.			
1:00 A.M.			
1:30 A.M.			
2:00 A.M.			

After a week, add up how many hours you spent on each activity (round off to half-hours—that is, mark 40 minutes of activity as a half-hour, and 45 minutes as one hour). Log the hours in the boxes in the table below using tally marks, with a full mark representing one hour and a half-size mark representing one-half hour. In the third column, total the hours for each activity. Leave the "Ideal Time in Hours" column blank for now.

ACTIVITY	TIME TALLIED OVER ONE-WEEK PERIOD	TOTAL TIME IN HOURS	IDEAL TIME IN HOURS
Example: Class	⅄⅄⅄ l	16.5	
Class			
Work			
Studying			
Sleeping			
Eating			
Family time/child care			
Commuting/traveling			
Chores and personal business			
Friends and important relationships			
Telephone time			
Leisure/entertainment			
Spiritual life			
Other			

Add the totals in the third column to find your grand total. Use a separate sheet of paper to answer the following questions:

- What surprises you about how you spend your time?
- Where do you waste the most time? What do you think that is costing you?
- On what activities do you think you should spend more or less time?
- What are you willing to do to make a change?

Go back to the chart and fill in the "Ideal Time in Hours" column. Finally, write a short paragraph describing the time-management changes you plan to make to move closer to spending your time the way you want to.

Team Building

collaborative solutions

Brainstorm Day-to-Day Ways to Save Money

■ Gather in a group of three or four. Together, think about the ways you spend money in a typical month. Come up with three areas of spending that you have in common.

■ On your own, take five minutes to brainstorm ideas about how to reduce spending in those areas. What expense can you reduce or do without? Where can you look for savings? Can you exchange a product or service for one that a friend can provide?

■ Come together to share your ideas. Discuss which ones you would be most able and likely to put into action. Write your five most workable ideas here.

1. _____

2. _____

3. _____

4. _____

5. _____

On your own, give these a try and see how they can help you put some money toward your savings. To make the experiment tangible, put cash into a jar once a week in the amount you've saved by making these changes. See how much you have at the end of one month—and bank it.

Test Prep: Start It Now

Think Before You Act to Prepare for Midterm/Exam Week

It is never too early to get on top of what you will need to do to prepare for a big exam week (choose either midterm or finals week, depending on which is more challenging for you). Look at your schedule now, and note the date exactly three weeks before your first exam. Write that date here.

_____

Your goal is to find *three hours per day for each day of those three weeks* to study for your exams. First, subtract the hours allotted to Priority 1 activities—class, work, caring for children or others, and sleep. Then look at what is left. For each day in the three-week calendar here, write the date and indicate your planned study hours in whatever form you can manage them—for example, "2–5 p.m." or "10–11 a.m. and 9–11 p.m.," or even "1–2 p.m., 5–6 p.m., and 9–10 p.m."

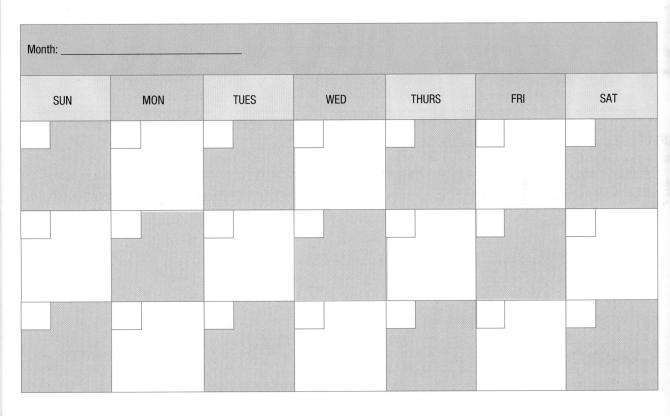

Enter this schedule into your planner, and do your best to stick to it. Life may get in the way of several of your study sessions, but commit to finding other times for them rather than giving them up entirely.

Time for a Change: take steps to improve a habit for success

For this exercise, refer back to the results of the assessment you took in Chapter 1 on page 19.

First: Write one of your three *strongest* Habits for Success here._____

_____

Why does it work for you? Name a result of this habit that helps you solve problems and move toward important goals. _____

_____

Now: Write one of your three *least developed* Habits for Success here. _____

_____

Why do you want to develop this habit—in other words, what positive effect do you think it will have on your ability to solve problems and achieve goals? _____

_____

Focus on this challenging habit more carefully. Answer the following questions on a separate piece of paper or computer file.

- Name two specific, short-term actions you can take to power up this habit. (Refer to the actions you listed in Chapter 1's Take Action exercise on page 14 if they connect to this habit).
- Name a support person and describe your plan for communicating your progress and getting encouragement (for example, have your person call, e-mail, or text you on a regular basis to check up on particular actions you've committed to taking).

Remember, the way to make a habit stick is to do it over and over again over a period of at least 21 days. *Right now*, commit to checking your progress on a regular basis over the next three weeks, using whatever method you prefer. Describe the method you will use to track your habit development.

- What will you use? (Example: date book, electronic planner, cell phone alarm, e-mail alert)
- When and how often will you use it? (Example: every day at bedtime, every other day when I get up, twice a week after a particular class)

It's time for a change—put your plan in motion *today*. You will revisit your progress at the ends of Chapters 6 and 9 (pages 186 and 277) as well as in Chapter 12.

setting and reaching goals

using values, stress management, and teamwork

lidia is experiencing overload. She is a full-time office assistant during the week and spends nights and weekends taking college accounting courses. With a toddler, a 10-year-old, and a husband who works nights, child care is a major problem. Her mother watches the kids on Mondays and Tuesdays, but she works too.

Lidia often has to drop everything in the middle of a study session to deal with her kids. She can't afford full-time child care, so she tries to find help day by day. She is trying to keep this up for another two years until her oldest can babysit his younger brother. In the meantime, she worries that she will be unable to stay on the path toward completing her courses and earning a degree.

In this chapter . . .

you explore answers to the following questions:

WHY are values the foundation of successful goal setting?   p. 96

HOW do you set and achieve goals?   p. 98

WHAT are ways to manage stress as you pursue your goals?   p. 104

HOW will learning to work with others help you reach your goals?   p. 113

© iStockphoto.com

Habit for Success

reach out to others

Goals are easier to reach with help from those around you. And when thinking through a problem, two (or more) heads are better than one.

- Powerful Questions about Reaching Out to Others   *p. 112*

- Real People Reach Out to Others   *p. 118*

- Habit Summary   *p. 119*

- Test Prep: Start It Now   *p. 125*

Why Are Values the Foundation of Successful Goal Setting?

To set the goals that are best for you—and, even more importantly, to move ahead toward achieving them—you need to identify the **core values** that motivate you. This chapter will show you how to set S.M.A.R.T. goals (specific, measurable, attainable, relevant, and linked to time frame) based on these values. It will also give you tools to manage the stress that can hinder your efforts to reach your target, and strengthen your ability to work with others so you can achieve goals faster and more efficiently than you could if you worked alone.

For the best chance at success, your core values should guide the goals you set and the choices you make. Lidia's choice to pursue a degree reflects her belief that a college education will help her get ahead, and focusing on child care shows that she prioritizes the needs of her family. Discovering what matters to *you* ensures that the changes you make in your life in the goal-setting process are meaningful and will keep you motivated.

Your values help you to:

- **Understand what you want out of life.** Your top goals reflect what you value most.

- **Define your educational path.** Values help you to explore what you want to learn, your major, and career goals.

- **Create "rules for life."** Values form the foundation for decisions and behavior. You will return repeatedly to them for guidance, especially when dealing with new problems.

Values are influenced by family, friends, culture, media, school, work, neighborhood, religion, world events, and more. Your strongest values are often linked to childhood experiences and family, but values may shift as you

Core Values
the principles and qualities that inform your beliefs and actions.

A goal without a plan is just a wish.

Larry Elder, radio talk show host

TAKE ACTION
Explore Your Core Values

Rate each of the following values on a scale from 1 to 5, 1 being least important to you and 5 being most important.

Knowing myself_____

Self-improvement_____

Political involvement_____

Leadership and teamwork skills_____

Getting a good job_____

Pursuing an education_____

Having a family_____

Helping others_____

Being liked by others_____

Taking risks_____

Being with friends_____

Political involvement_____

Being organized_____

Spiritual/religious life_____

Health and fitness_____

Participating in an online community_____

Having time to read_____

Time to myself_____

Lifelong learning_____

Competing and winning_____

Financial stability_____

Making a lot of money_____

Creative/artistic pursuits_____

Other (write below)_____

_____

Write your top three values here:

1. _____

2. _____

3. _____

Often, musical choices reflect values. Putting your musical intelligence to work, find a song that inspires you. Now imagine that you're creating a CD for a friend with that song on it. Write a quick note about why you included the song on the CD. Be sure to mention how it connects to one or more of your top values.

_____

_____

_____

_____

acquire knowledge and experiences and build new relationships. For example, a student whose family and friends were there for him after a serious accident may place greater value on relationships than he did before the accident.

Values form the bedrock of meaningful goals. The stronger the link between your values and your long-term goals, the happier, more motivated, and more successful you are likely to be in setting and achieving those goals.

How Do You Set and Achieve Goals?

Goal
an end toward which you direct your efforts.

When you set a **goal**, you focus on what you want to achieve and create a path that can get you there. Learning to set and achieve goals isn't just important for students. It is essential in your personal life and career.

Setting goals involves defining what you are aiming for in both long-term and short-term time frames. *Long-term* goals are broader objectives you want to achieve over a long period of time, perhaps a year or more. *Short-term* goals are smaller steps that move you toward a long-term goal, making it manageable and achievable, piece by piece (see Key 4.1).

Set Long-Term Goals

Take a moment to imagine: What do you want your life to look like in 5 years? In 10 years? In 20? What degree do you want to earn, what kind of job do you

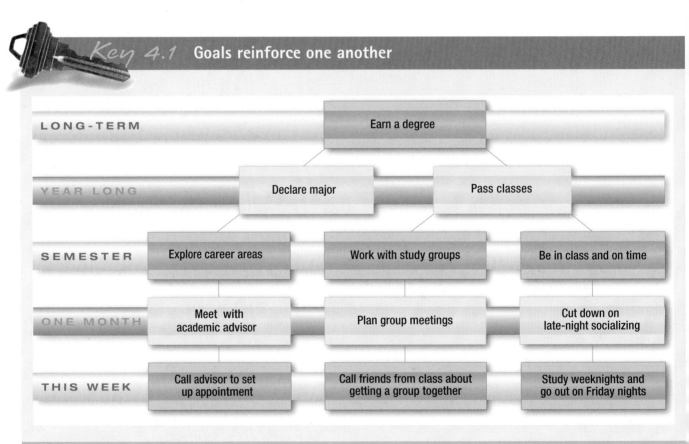

Key 4.1 **Goals reinforce one another**

LONG-TERM		Earn a degree		
YEAR LONG	Declare major		Pass classes	
SEMESTER	Explore career areas	Work with study groups		Be in class and on time
ONE MONTH	Meet with academic advisor	Plan group meetings		Cut down on late-night socializing
THIS WEEK	Call advisor to set up appointment	Call friends from class about getting a group together		Study weeknights and go out on Friday nights

want, where do you want to live? Your answers to questions like these help you identify your long-term goals.

Some long-term goals have an open-ended time frame. For example, if as a nursing student, your long-term goal is to stay on top of developments in medicine, you will pursue this goal throughout your professional life. Other goals, such as completing the required courses for your degree, have a more definite end and often fewer options for getting there.

One way to make long-term goals real is to put them in writing. For example:

My goal is to become a nurse practitioner, emphasizing preventative medicine, who works in a clinic in an underserved community.

To determine your long-term goals, think about what you want to accomplish while in school and after you graduate. For example, it is no surprise that Lidia, who values financial stability, is motivated to do well in her accounting courses.

By the way . . .

focusing on one goal at a time increases your chance of success. Studies show that switching back and forth too often, or trying to accomplish more than one goal at a time, reduces focus and can actually increase stress.[1]

Set Short-Term Goals

Lasting as short as an hour or as long as several months, *short-term* goals help you narrow your focus and encourage progress toward bigger dreams. The student aiming to be a nurse practitioner might set supporting short-term goals like these for her second year of college:

Choose courses that keep me on track to complete pre-med requirements. Locate a medical practice serving an underprivileged community and apply for a summer internship. Research graduate schools that offer a nurse-practitioner degree.

Getting more specific, this student may set these short-term goals for the next six months:

- I will learn the names and functions of every human bone and muscle.
- I will work with a study group to understand the muscular-skeletal system.

These goals can be broken down into even shorter time frames. Here are one-month goals:

- I will work with on-screen tutorials of the muscular-skeletal system.
- I will spend three hours a week with my study partners.

Your short-term goals may last a week, a day, or even a couple of hours. Here's how Lidia might use smaller short-term goals to support a month-long goal to set up weekend child care:

- **By the end of today:** Text and e-mail friends to see if they know of available sitters or are looking to pick up some extra cash themselves
- **One week from now:** Have at least two potential sitters to contact

- **Two weeks from now:** Have spoken to potential sitters and evaluated the possibilities
- **Four weeks from now:** Have plan in place for regular help for at least one weekend day

Your Syllabus: A Powerful Goal-Achievement Tool

Remember: For each course you take, your syllabus provides a clear layout of the goals you will target throughout the term and when you need to achieve them. Keep paper syllabi where you can refer to them frequently, and bookmark electronic syllabi if your instructors post them online. Key 4.2 shows a portion of an actual syllabus with important items noted.

Set Up a Goal-Achievement Plan

At any given time, you are working toward goals of varying importance. Prioritize goals so you can put the bulk of your energy and time toward those that matter most (see Chapter 3). Then draw up a plan, using the S.M.A.R.T. system to make your goals Specific, Measurable, Attainable, Relevant, and attached to a Time Frame (see Key 4.3).

Step 1: Define an attainable, relevant goal. *What do you want?* Is it attainable (within reach)? Is it relevant (connected to your needs)? To develop an attainable, relevant goal, consider your hopes, interests, abilities, and values. Then, reflect on whether your goal is possible, given your resources and circumstances. Write out a clear description of your goal.

Step 2: Define a specific path. *How will you get there?* Brainstorm different paths. Choose one; then map out its specific steps. Focus on behaviors and events that are under your control.

Step 3: Set a timetable. *When do you want to accomplish your goal?* Schedule steps within a realistic time frame. Create specific deadlines for each step you defined in Step 1. Charting your progress will help you stay on track.

Step 4: Measure your progress. *What safeguards will keep you on track?* Will you record progress in a weekly journal? Report to a friend? Use an alarm system on your smartphone to remind you to do something? Create a measurement system to evaluate your progress.

Step 5: Get unstuck. *What will you do if you hit a roadblock?* The path to a goal is often rocky and stressful. Anticipate problems and define **specific** ways to alter your plans if you run into trouble (stress management strategies are presented later in the chapter). Reach out to friends, family, and college personnel who can help you. Be ready to brainstorm other ideas if your plans don't work.

Step 6: Action time. Follow the steps in your plan until you achieve your goal.

ENG 122 Spring 2007

Instructor: Jennifer Gessner
Office Hours: Tue & Thur 12:30–1:30 (or by appointment) in DC 305
Phone: 303-555-2222
E-mail: jg@abc.xyz

How to connect with the instructor

Required Texts: *Good Reasons with Contemporary Arguments,* Faigley and Selzer
A Writer's Reference, 5th ed., Diana Hacker

Required Materials:
- a notebook with lots of paper
- a folder for keeping everything from this class
- an active imagination and critical thinking

Books and materials to get ASAP

Course Description: This course focuses on argumentative writing and the researched paper. Students will practice the rhetorical art of argumentation and will gain experience in finding and incorporating researched materials into an extended paper.

Writer's Notebook: All students will keep, and bring to class, a notebook with blank paper. Throughout the semester, you will be given writing assignments to complete in this book. You must bring to class and be prepared to share any notebook assignment. Notebook assignments will be collected frequently, though sometimes randomly, and graded only for their completeness, not for spelling, etc.

Course coverage, expectations, responsibilities

Grading:
- Major Writing Assignments worth 100 points each.
- Final Research Project worth 300 points.
- Additional exercises and assignments range from 10 to 50 points each.
- Class participation: Based on the degree to which you complete the homework and present this in a thoughtful, meaningful manner in class.
- Attendance: Attendance is taken daily and students may miss up to three days of class without penalty, but will lose 5 points for each day missed thereafter.
- Late work: All work will lose 10% of earned points per class day late. No work will be accepted after five class days or the last class meeting.

How grades are determined for this course

Final Grade: The average of the total points possible (points earned divided by the total possible points). 100–90% = A; 89–80% = B; 79–70% = C (any grade below 70% is not passing for this class).

Academic Integrity: Students must credit any material used in their papers that is not their own (including direct quotes, paraphrases, figures, etc.). Failure to do so constitutes plagiarism, which is illegal, unethical, <u>always recognizable</u>, and a guaranteed way to fail a paper. The definition of plagiarism is "to steal and use (the writings or ideas of another) as one's own."

Reflects schools academic integrity policy

Week 4
2/1   The Concise Opinion.
      HW: Complete paper #1 Rough Draft (5–7 pages double-spaced)

2/3   How Professionals Argue
      HW: Read Jenkins Essay (p 501 of *Good Reasons) and* Rafferty Essay (p 525); compare argumentative style, assess and explain efficacy of arguments.

Topics of that days class meeting

Notice of due date for paper draft

Notice of reading assignments to complete

Week 5
2/15   Developing an Argument
      Essay Quiz on Jenkins and Rafferty Essays
      HW: Chap 5 of *Good Reasons;* based on components of a definition of argument, write a brief explanation of how your argument might fit into this type.

2/17   Library Workday: Meet in Room 292
      PAPER #1 DUE

Notice of quiz

Notice of final due date for paper

Source: Jennifer Gessner, Community College of Denver.

Goal: To raise my algebra grade from a C to a B.

MY GOAL IS...	MEANING...	EXAMPLE
Specific	Name exactly how you will achieve your goal.	I will accomplish my goal by studying algebra at least an hour a day and working with a tutor once a week.
Measurable	Find ways to measure your progress over time.	I will look at my weekly quiz grades to see if I am making progress. I will also use the exercises in my text to take practice tests and use the answer key to grade my work.
Attainable	Set a goal that challenges you but isn't too far out of your reach.	Algebra is tough for me, but I know that I can manage to pull up my grade.
Relevant	Define a goal that is meaningful to you and your needs.	I need to pass this required course to move ahead in my major.
Time Frame	Set up a time frame for achieving your goal and the steps toward it.	I will do an extra problem set every Monday and Thursday night. I will get my grade point up by the end of the term.

Staying motivated on your way to a goal can be tough when you have years of work ahead of you. (As a student just beginning college and with your degree years away, you know what that feels like.) Your challenge is to find ways to "keep your eyes on the prize." You might visualize yourself accomplishing your goal or remind yourself of what you stand to gain when you complete your goal. Checking off short-term goals and seeing them as signs of progress will also help. Lidia, for example, might keep a photo of her kids in her notebook to remind herself of how getting a degree will help her support her family.

It will take work and persistence to pursue your goals. The changes—positive or negative—that happen along the way are likely to cause some stress. If managed well, however, it shouldn't stop you from reaching your goals. Next, we examine potential sources of stress and strategies for dealing with them.

Name a general area in which you want to change or improve this year.

Using the S.M.A.R.T. system and your visual intelligence, define a goal in this area by filling in this think link and the table underneath it.

6. Action time

Put your plan in motion.

5. Get unstuck

Think of a potential roadblock you might hit as you try reach your goal. Name two **specific** ways you can get back on track if this roadblock occurs.

_____

_____

4. Be accountable

Describe the system you will use to stay on track and **measure** your progress.

_____

_____

3. Set a timetable

What is a realistic **time frame** within which you can accomplish this goal?

_____

_____

2. Define a path

What are the **specific** steps? _____

_____

_____

1. Define your goal

Be **specific**. What exactly do you want to accomplish?

_____

Why is this goal **relevant**—how does it relate to what you need?

_____

What makes it **attainable**—enough of a challenge to motivate but not so tough that you give up?

_____

Define your path within the **time frame** from number 3. Use this grid to assign estimated dates to specific steps.

Step					
Date done					

Stress
physical or mental strain produced in reaction to pressure.

If you feel **stress** as you try to reach your goals, you are not alone. Stress levels among college students have increased (see Key 4.4). Handling stress involves identifying and defusing stress triggers, keeping your body and mind healthy so that you can handle increased pressures, and avoiding poor personal health choices that take you off your path.

For Lidia, and almost every other student, dealing with stress is an everyday challenge that can take a toll on your health and on your ability to achieve your goals. However, some amount of stress gives you energy to do well on tests, finish assignments on time, or prepare for a class presentation. Key 4.5 shows that stress can be helpful or harmful, depending on how much you experience. A manageable balance empowers you to forge ahead.

Key 4.4 How college students experience stress

- Students say that their top stressors are ... grades (71%), schoolwork (74%), and financial worries (62%).

- 62% of graduating seniors are worried about finding a full-time job after graduation.

- Stress had significant effects on many students. Some say that it interfered with their motivation (63%), made it tough to get work done (63%), and made them not want to participate in social activities (55%).

- 34% of students said they have felt depressed at some point in the last 3 months.

- 70% of students reported that they have never considered reaching out to a trained professional for help with stress or anxiety.

Source: mtvU and Associated Press College Stress and Mental Health Poll Executive Summary, Spring 2008. http://www.halfofus.com/_media/_pr/mtvU_AP_College_Stress_and_Mental_Health_Poll_Executive_Summary.pdf

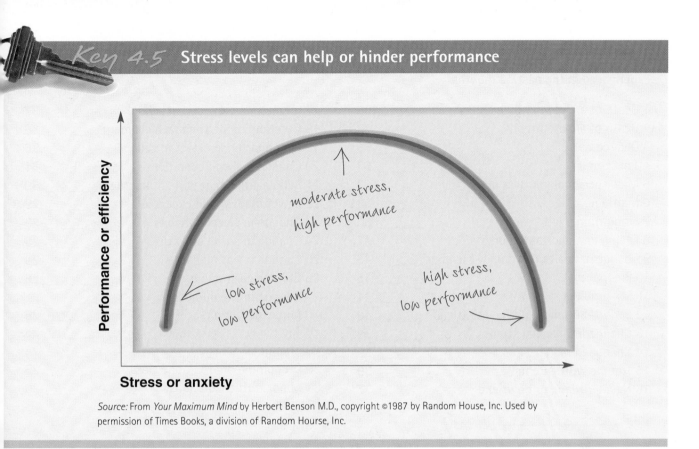

Source: From *Your Maximum Mind* by Herbert Benson M.D., copyright ©1987 by Random House, Inc. Used by permission of Times Books, a division of Random Hourse, Inc.

Identify and Address Stress Triggers

When psychologists T. H. Holmes and R. H. Rahe measured the intensity of people's reaction to specific changes, they found that stress is linked to both positive *and* negative events. On the next page is an adaptation, designed for college students, of the Holmes-Rahe scale. It delivers a "stress score," based on events in the past year, that indicates your likelihood of experiencing a stress-related health problem. Understanding your stress score can guide your actions in two ways:

- Seeing what you face on a regular basis can help you decide how to handle ongoing pressures.

- In a high-stress period of your life, understanding what's causing the pressure can help you re-evaluate and, if necessary, adjust your goals.

How can you cope with stress and prevent it from derailing your plans? First, remember:

- **The goal-setting strategies in this chapter are stress-management strategies.** When you set SMART goals and pursue them step by step with focus, reaching out to others along the way for help, you reduce stress.

- **The time-management strategies you learned in Chapter 3 are stress-management strategies.** When you create and follow a schedule, complete items on your to-do list, and avoid procrastinating, you reduce stress.

To determine your stress score, add up the number of points corresponding to the events you have experienced in the past 12 months.

1 Death of a close family member	_____ 100	17 Increase in workload at school	_____	37
2 Death of a close friend	_____ 73	18 Outstanding personal achievement	_____	36
3 Divorce	_____ 65	19 First quarter/semester in college	_____	36
4 Jail term	_____ 63	20 Change in living conditions	_____	31
5 Major personal injury or illness	_____ 63	21 Serious argument with an instructor	_____	30
6 Marriage	_____ 58	22 Lower grades than expected	_____	29
7 Firing from a job	_____ 50	23 Change in sleeping habits	_____	29
8 Failing an important course	_____ 47	24 Change in social activities	_____	29
9 Change in health of a family member	_____ 45	25 Change in eating habits	_____	28
10 Pregnancy	_____ 45	26 Chronic car trouble	_____	26
11 Sex problem	_____ 44	27 Change in the number of family gatherings	_____	26
12 Serious argument with close friend	_____ 40	28 Too many missed classes	_____	25
13 Change in financial status	_____ 39	29 Change of college	_____	24
14 Change in major	_____ 39	30 Dropping more than one class	_____	23
15 Trouble with parents	_____ 39	31 Minor traffic violations	_____	20
16 New girlfriend or boyfriend	_____ 37			

Total: _____

If your score is 300 or higher, you are at high risk for developing a health problem. If your score is between 150 and 300, you have a 50–50 chance of experiencing a serious health change within two years. If your score is below 150, you have a 30% chance of a serious health change.

Source: Paul Insel and Walton Roth, *Core Concepts in Health,* 4th ed., Palo Alto, CA: Mayfield Publishing Company, 1985, p. 29.

Here are some additional ways to keep stress under control:

Be realistic about commitments. Students who combine work and school may become overloaded and fall behind, increasing the risk of dropping out. If you need to work to pay tuition, set up a schedule you can realistically meet. You may need more than two years (for an associate's degree) or four years (for a bachelor's degree) to graduate, but taking extra time is much better than not graduating at all.

Work with your personality. If you are a night person, schedule your course work in the afternoon or evening—or, if there's no choice, use external (three alarm clocks) and internal strategies ("I'm determined to do well") to stick to the schedule. If you are fidgety, keep a squeezable object in your hands during class to help you stay focused. If you need to blow off steam with exercise, make time to go to the athletic center between classes.

Have some fun. Doing things you enjoy, such as meeting up with friends on a Thursday night for pizza, will take the edge off of stress. Put fun on your schedule so you are sure to have time.

Actively manage your schedule.　Get in the habit of checking your planner throughout the day. Also, try not to put off tasks. If you can take even one tiny step toward a goal, do it.

Try relaxation techniques.　Techniques that will help you relax and increase your awareness of your physical body can help calm you. These include various breathing techniques (some based in yoga), progressive relaxation (tensing and relaxing different muscles one by one), and visualization (focusing on a place that you find calming).

Check things off.　Use a physical action when you complete a task—check off the item, delete it from your task list, crumple up the Post-It note. A physical act can relieve stress and highlight the confidence that comes from getting something done. Consider listing the courses you need to complete your degree and checking off those you complete every term.

Manage family responsibilities.　Students with elderly parents, relatives with health-care issues, or young children often have to juggle family responsibilities as they try to study (see Key 4.6 for helpful suggestions on child-care issues).

Know when you need help—and ask for it.　Trying to do it all on your own may not be possible and can actually make things worse. Call on family and friends to take the pressure off. Switch shifts at work to free up study time, ask a friend to take your kids the day before a test, or have a family member take your car for servicing. Because her mother already babysits when she can, Lidia might talk to a neighbor about trading child care in a pinch.

Keep Your Body Healthy

Even the most driven goal achiever has trouble moving ahead when illness or injury hits. If you do your best to eat well, get exercise and sleep, and avoid substances that can throw you off your game, you will be in shape to stay in motion.

Eat Well

Eating well and getting exercise can be tough for students. The *food environment* in college is often filled with unhealthful choices,[2] and students tend to sit a lot, eat on the run, and get too busy to exercise. Healthy eating requires *balance*

Inside Tips from Sarah, Self-Management Coach

You can't get new results with the same old behaviors. To reach new goals, you may need to change some personal health habits, such as how much sleep you get per night. Start small, and go step by step: Target one specific problem and decide on a concrete change that you think will help (go to bed an hour earlier, send your last text at 11 p.m., go without refined sugar). Put this change in place for a week. If it makes a difference, keep it up—and maybe add another.

Keep Them Up to Date on Your Schedule

Let them know when you have a big test or project due and when you are under less pressure, and what they can expect of you in each case.

Explain What Your Education Means

Tell them how it will improve your life and theirs. This applies, of course, to older children who can understand the situation and compare it with their own schooling.

Find Help

Ask a relative or friend to watch your children or arrange for a child to visit a friend. Consider trading babysitting hours with another parent, hiring a sitter to come to your home, or using a day-care center.

Keep Them Active While You Study

Give them games, books, or toys. If there are special activities that you like to limit, such as watching videos or TV, save them for your study time.

Study on the Phone

You might be able to have a study session with a fellow student over the phone while your child is sleeping or playing quietly.

Offset Study Time with Family Time and Rewards

Children may let you get your work done if they have something to look forward to, such as a movie night or a trip for ice cream.

Special Notes for Infants

Study at night if your baby goes to sleep early, or in the morning if your baby sleeps late.

Study during nap times if you aren't too tired yourself.

Lay your notes out and recite information to the baby. The baby will appreciate the attention, and you will get work done.

Put the baby in a safe and fun place while you study, such as a playpen, motorized swing, or jumping seat.

(varying your diet) and *moderation* (eating reasonable amounts). Here are some ways to incorporate both into your life:

- **Vary what you eat and reduce portion size.** The government "food pyramid" recommends certain amounts of food in particular food groups. (Go to www.mypyramid.gov.)

- **Limit fat, cholesterol, sugar, white flour, and alcohol.** Try to eliminate *trans fats*, which increase the risk of heart disease. Minimize candy, desserts, sugar-filled drinks, and alcohol, which is calorie-heavy.

- **If you need to lose weight, reach out.** A campus counselor can help you find a support group, such as Weight Watchers or an on-campus organization, which can help you stay on target. Set reasonable weight-loss goals and work toward them gradually.

© Shutterstock

More than just transportation, bicycling provides great exercise. As this bike rack shows, many students at this college use bicycles to get around.

Exercise Regularly

Being physically fit increases your energy, helps you cope with stress, and keeps you goal-directed. Here are some ways to make exercise a regular part of your life:

- Walk to classes and meetings. When you reach your building, use the stairs.

- Use your school's fitness facilities in between classes.

- Play team recreational sports at school or in your community.

- Find activities you can do on your own time, such as running or pick-up basketball.

- Work out with friends or family to combine socializing and exercise.

During solo exercise sessions, although your body is occupied, your mind is often free. Whether you are walking, using an elliptical trainer, or doing laps, you can brainstorm new goal-achievement strategies. Be open to the ideas that pop into your head.

Get Enough Sleep

Research indicates that eight to nine hours of sleep a night is ideal for students. But the average student sleeps only six to seven hours a night—and often gets much less.[3] Overwhelmed students often prioritize schoolwork over sleep, staying up regularly until the wee hours of the morning to study or pulling "all-nighters" to get through a tough project or paper.

Being sleep deprived hinders your ability to concentrate, raises stress levels, and makes you more susceptible to illness. For the sake of your health, your goals, and your GPA, find a way to get the sleep you need. Sleep expert Gregg D. Jacobs, Ph.D., has the following practical suggestions for improving sleep habits:[6]

- **Reduce consumption of alcohol and caffeine.** Caffeine may keep you awake, especially if you drink it late in the day. Alcohol can prevent you from sleeping deeply.

By the way . . .

a survey of nearly 10,000 students at the University of Minnesota showed that students who reported getting adequate sleep had a higher average GPA than those who reported sleep difficulties.[4] Lack of sleep is also linked to greater risk of illness.[5]

- **Nap.** Taking short afternoon naps can reduce the effects of sleep deprivation.
- **Be consistent.** Try to establish a regular sleep time and wake-up schedule.
- **Complete tasks an hour or so before sleep.** Give yourself a chance to wind down.

Avoid Alcohol and Drug Abuse

Some students choose to use alcohol and other potentially addictive substances to alleviate stress temporarily or for other reasons. Actually, using these substances can affect your life in ways that *increase* stress. The abuse of these substances can have potentially serious consequences, including sending you way off the track that leads to your goals.

Alcohol is a depressant and the most frequently abused drug on campus. Of all alcohol consumption, **binge drinking** is associated with the greatest problems. Students who binge drink are more likely to miss classes or work, perform poorly, experience physical problems (memory loss, headache, stomach issues), become depressed, and engage in unplanned or unsafe sexual activity.[7] Even a few drinks affect muscle coordination and, more importantly, the ability to reason and make sensible decisions. All of these effects can send your stress level skyrocketing.

College students may use drugs to relieve stress, be accepted by peers, or just to try something new. In most cases, the negative consequences of drug use outweigh any temporary high. Drug use violates federal, state, and local laws, and you may be arrested, tried, and imprisoned for possessing even a small amount of drugs. You can jeopardize your reputation and your student status if you are caught using drugs or if drug use impairs your performance. Finally, long-term drug use can damage your body and mind. Every consequence of drug use has the potential to derail you from the goals that mean the most to you.

If you drink or take drugs, think carefully about the effects on your health, safety, and academic performance. Consider the positive and negative effects of your choice. If you believe you have a problem, reach out for help. Your college and community resources can help you generate options and develop practical plans for recovery.

Keep Your Mind Healthy

Although feeling anxious is normal at times, especially when you have a lot to do, some people react to high levels of stress in more serious ways. Mental health disorders interfere with your ability to reach your goals, and they can be caused or worsened by problematic health decisions. If you recognize yourself in any of the following descriptions, contact your student health center or campus counseling center for help or a referral to a specialist. These disorders include:

- **Panic disorder.** Specific situations bring on "panic attacks" that may include heart palpitations, rapid breathing, dizziness, and fear.

Binge Drinking
having five or more drinks (for men) or four or more (for women) at one occasion.

Multiple Intelligence Strategies for Stress Management

Briefly describe a stress-related problem you have.

_____

_____

Now, brainstorm potential solutions to your problem, linking each solution to an intelligence. Use the right-hand column to record your ideas.

INTELLIGENCE	SUGGESTED STRATEGIES	USE MI STRATEGIES TO COME UP WITH SOLUTIONS
Verbal–Linguistic	■ Keep a journal of what situations, people, or events cause stress. ■ Write letters or e-mail friends about your problems.	
Logical–Mathematical	■ Think through problems using a problem-solving process, and devise a detailed plan. ■ Analyze the negative and positive effects that may result from a stressful situation.	
Bodily–Kinesthetic	■ Choose a physical activity that releases tension—running, yoga, team sports—and do it regularly. ■ Plan physical activities during free time—go for a hike, take a bike ride, go dancing with friends.	
Visual–Spatial	■ Enjoy things that appeal to you visually—visit an exhibit, see an art film, shoot photos with your camera. ■ Use a visual organizer to plan out a solution to a stressful problem.	
Interpersonal	■ Reach out for help to people who care about you and are supportive. ■ Shift your focus by listening to others who need to talk about their stresses.	
Intrapersonal	■ Schedule time when you can think through what is causing stress. ■ Allow yourself five minutes a day to meditate: Visualize positive resolutions to your stressful situation.	
Musical	■ Listen to music that relaxes, inspires, and/or energizes you. ■ Write a song about what is bothering you.	
Naturalistic	■ Try to categorize what's bothering you to identify solvable patterns. ■ If nature calms you, spend time outdoors, watch nature-focused TV, or read about nature or science.	

reach
out to
others

- **Post-traumatic stress disorder.** Past trauma (rape, war experiences, assault) triggers flashbacks, irritability, emotional distance, and sometimes violence.

- **Eating disorders.** *Anorexia nervosa* (severe restriction of eating), *bulimia* (eating excessive amounts of foods followed by purging), or *binge-eating disorder* (bingeing on foods without purging) cause serious health problems.

- **Clinical depression (depressive disorder).** At varying levels of severity, sometimes leading to threats of suicide.

Of these disorders, depression in particular has become fairly common on college campuses, due in part to the wide range of stressors that students experience. Recent research reports that nearly half of surveyed students reported feelings of depression at some point, with more than 30% saying that the level of depression made it difficult to function at times.[8] Key 4.7 shows possible causes of depression as well as some typical symptoms and offers helpful coping strategies.

At its worst, depression can lead to suicidal thoughts and attempts. A recent survey conducted by the American Psychological Association of students at 70 colleges and universities found that 15% of students had thought seriously about committing suicide, and 5% had made actual attempts. Many of these students reported that they did not seek help when in crisis.[9]

These disorders have the power to derail goals and dreams, so get medical care. The right help can change—or even save—your life.

Nearly all goals seem more reachable and less stressful when you work with others. As you will see next, getting the most out of your personal relationships requires both knowledge and skill.

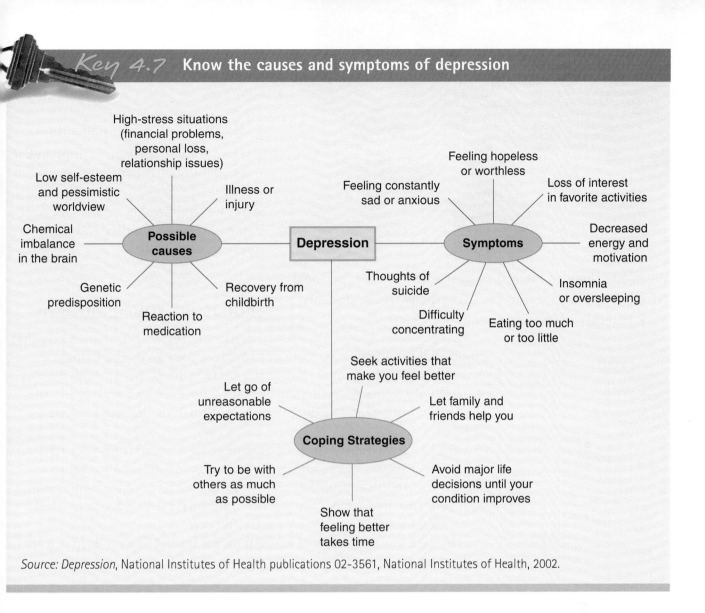

High-stress situations
(financial problems,
personal loss,
relationship issues)

Low self-esteem
and pessimistic
worldview

Illness or
injury

Chemical
imbalance
in the brain

**Possible
causes**

Genetic
predisposition

Recovery from
childbirth

Reaction to
medication

Depression

Feeling hopeless
or worthless

Feeling constantly
sad or anxious

Loss of interest
in favorite activities

Symptoms

Decreased
energy and
motivation

Thoughts of
suicide

Insomnia
or oversleeping

Difficulty
concentrating

Eating too much
or too little

Seek activities that
make you feel better

Let go of
unreasonable
expectations

Let family and
friends help you

Coping Strategies

Try to be with
others as much
as possible

Avoid major life
decisions until your
condition improves

Show that
feeling better
takes time

Source: *Depression*, National Institutes of Health publications 02-3561, National Institutes of Health, 2002.

How Will Learning to Work with Others Help You Reach Your Goals?

In school, as at work and in your personal life, being able to achieve your goals depends on your ability to relate effectively to others. Students taking the same course may work on projects together, create and perform a presentation (see Chapter 11), or form a study group that aims to prepare for an exam. Math and science instructors sometimes initiate student study groups, known as *peer-assisted study sessions* or *supplemental instruction,* to help students improve performance in those courses. Students in online courses may meet in chat rooms for virtual study group sessions or project work. No student is an island!

© Patrick White/Merrill Education

When you share an interest or goal with someone, personal differences may fade into the background. These students work together on an assignment.

To work well with others on the way to your most important goals, you need to know:

- How emotions affect relationships
- How to value and benefit from diverse people and their perspectives

Start by examining how to manage your own emotions and understand the emotions of others.

Focus on Your Emotions

Psychologist Daniel Goleman says that **emotional intelligence** is essential to achieve your goals and helps you make the most of personal relationships. He believes that you can develop the ability to know yourself, manage your emotions, and understand the emotions of others.[10] The qualities of emotional intelligence are found in Key 4.8.

The key is staying aware of what your goals demand from your relationships. For example, succeeding in the classroom might require that you present yourself in appropriate ways both in the classroom and in meetings with your instructor. Lidia can use her emotional intelligence to get help from others with both academics and child care.

Here are some examples of how emotional intelligence can help you set and pursue goals:

- "Because I get bored quickly, I need to emphasize short-term goals."
- "Because I enjoy hands-on experiences, I will explore majors in the sciences that require lab courses."
- "My project partner is not himself today, so I'll reschedule our study session and see if he wants to go for coffee after class and talk instead."

You are building your emotional intelligence throughout your work in this text. Some of the Habits for Success—thinking before you act, for example, and being flexible—involve looking at your emotions and needs before deciding how to move ahead. Also, the self-assessments in each chapter help you learn more about who you are and how you react to a variety of situations.

Often the people you work with have different values and cultural backgrounds. In an increasingly global world, learning to appreciate that diversity and to understand and accept those who differ from you will help you work with others more successfully.

Emotional Intelligence
the ability to perceive, assess, and manage one's own emotions as well as understand the emotions of others.

Each quality is written as an affirmative statement. Make a commitment to live by them and to get in touch with how emotions affect you and others. Reaffirm each statement before joining a study group. If a problem arises and you have trouble controlling your feelings, go back to these qualities for direction.

PERSONAL COMPETENCE	SOCIAL COMPETENCE
Self-Awareness	**Social Awareness**
I know my emotions and how they affect me.	I sense the feelings and perspectives of others.
I understand my strengths and limits.	I help others reach their goals.
I am confident in my abilities.	I know how to relate to people from different
I am open to improvement.	cultures.
	I can sense how to serve the needs of others.
Self-Management	**Social Skills**
I can control my emotions and impulses.	I know how to work in a team.
I can delay gratification when there is something	I can inspire people to act.
more important to be gained.	I understand how to lead a group.
I am trustworthy.	I know how to persuade people.
I can adapt to change and new ideas.	I can make positive change happen.
I persist toward my goals despite obstacles.	

Source: Based on Daniel Goleman, *Working with Emotional Intelligence*, New York: Bantam Books, 1998, pp. 26–27.

Become Culturally Competent

Most academic goals that you set will require you to work with other students, teachers, and administrators. Work goals will require you to work with clients, colleagues, and employers. Chances are that you will work with others who differ from you in ways both visible (race, ethnicity) and invisible (communication styles, values). The goal of **cultural competence** is to develop the ability to understand and appreciate diversity and adjust your behavior to improve how you get along with the people around you.

Building cultural competence means taking the following actions:[11]

1. Learn more about why and how people differ from you, and what tends to happen when differences in culture occur.

2. Become self-aware about your own perceptions and attitudes, including whether you have any **prejudices** or judge based on **stereotypes**. Challenge yourself to set them aside as you get to know and work with others.

3. Find ways to adjust to the differences of others that will create opportunities. Look past external characteristics, put yourself in other people's shoes, and recognize what you have in common with people everywhere.

Cultural Competence
the ability to understand and appreciate differences and to respond to people of all cultures in a way that values their worth, respects their beliefs and practices, and builds communication and relationships.

Prejudice

a preconceived judgment or opinion formed without just grounds or sufficient knowledge.

Stereotype

a standardized mental picture that represents an oversimplified opinion or uncritical judgment.

For instance, if Lidia couldn't attend her study group as often because of family commitments, cultural competence could help both her and her study group to solve the problem. Realizing that she has responsibilities as a parent, a study group member could ask her to come up with a way to help the group when she's not there. She could then offer to work at home to combine notes from the text and class for a week. This contribution will help her and the group reach their goals of learning the course material.

Maximize Your Team Work

Whether you aim to complete a project or study for an exam, what can you gain from working with others?

Increased knowledge. When group members share knowledge, each member spends less time and energy learning the material. Another benefit: Talking about concepts or teaching them to others helps solidify what you know.

More motivation. Knowing that you are accountable to others and that they will see how prepared you are—or aren't—may encourage you to work hard.

Better teamwork skills. Nothing teaches you how to work effectively in groups better than experience. What you learn will be invaluable throughout college and in the workplace.

Strength from diversity. Working with students from a variety of backgrounds creates team strength. The more diverse the team, the more varied the approach to problem solving.

Strategies for Group Success

The way a group operates may depend on members' personalities, motivation, and knowledge; what you are studying; group size; and where you are meeting. These general strategies will help all groups succeed:

- **Set long-term and short-term goals.** At your first meeting, decide what the group wants to accomplish. You may want to have an *agenda* (a meeting plan) for each meeting.

- **Set a regular schedule.** Determine how many meetings are needed and what members' schedules can handle. If you are studying for a final, you might start a month before the test with a weekly meeting. As test day nears, you may decide to meet more frequently.

- **Choose a leader for each meeting.** Rotating the leadership among members willing to lead helps everyone take ownership of the group.

- **Share the workload.** Your willingness to pitch in and work is more important than how much you know.

For groups with a study focus, here are further tips:

- **Create materials for one another.** Give each group member one topic to compile, photocopy, and review for the others.

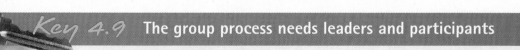

For Participant	For Leader
• Do your share of the work. • Stay organized and focused. • Be open and willing to discuss. • Perform your responsibilities on schedule.	• Define projects, and focus everyone's efforts. • Assign work tasks, and set a schedule and deadlines. • Set meeting and project goals. • Keep everyone on target and moving ahead. • Set a fair, respectful, and encouraging tone. • Evaluate progress, and make changes if needed.

- **Help each other learn.** Have group members teach each other information, work on problems, give feedback on responses to essay questions, or go through flash cards together.

- **Pool your note-taking resources.** Compare notes and fill in any information you don't have (see Chapter 9 for more on note taking).

Study groups and other teams need both leaders *and* participants to accomplish their goals.[12] Lidia, who rarely has time or energy to take a leadership role, needs to understand that she is a crucial part of a group no matter which role she plays (see Key 4.9).

Defuse Potential Problems

As beneficial as it is to work in a team, issues can arise. Be prepared to address them if they happen to you:

- **People not pulling their weight.** At some point in almost every group, one or more people will not fulfill their responsibilities. If it's a one-time incident due to an illness or a personal problem, it's best to let it go. However, if it happens regularly, take action. Try reassigning tasks or having a group problem-solving session.

- **Trouble scheduling.** Finding a time and location that works for a group of people can be challenging. Coordinate everything on a group e-mail first. Once you find a time a day that works, schedule meetings consistently. You may want to rotate locations if there isn't one that is convenient for all group members.

- **Too much talking.** Although it may not be realistic to keep friends out of your study group, you can set boundaries. Set up some talking time at the end as a "reward" for accomplishing a goal.

Identifying your core values, setting goals that reflect them, learning techniques to manage the stress that can keep you from reaching your goals, and tapping the wisdom of the group will help you stay on target toward what you most want to achieve in college and beyond.

Louise Gaile Edrozo

Gaile Edrozo was on track to earn a biology degree in a year's time and then begin medical school in her native Philippines. However, financial difficulties got in the way of her plans.

Graduate of the Registered Nursing Program at Highline Community College, Des Moines, Washington

Aiming for more opportunity to work and earn a living, she and her family came to the United States in 2004. Because of her immigration status, she knew that she would be considered an international student when she started college.

Stop and Think

Have you experienced a sudden change, like Gaile's, that forced you to rethink your plans? What happened, and where did it take you?

As she and her family adjusted to living in Washington state, Gaile decided to explore nursing and enrolled as a nursing student at Highline Community College in the fall of 2004.

Gaile was on course to a meaningful, productive goal, but the cost of her education was too high for her family to manage. Even more frightening was the possibility that Gaile would lose her status in the U.S. if she were unable to stay in school and would have to return to the Philippines alone.

"My fears were so many I was drowning in them," says Gaile. "I wanted nothing more than to become a nurse, have a career I love, and help

my family at the same time. I wanted it so much it hurt to think it could all be taken away—again."

Stop and Think

Gaile thought that academic success would be a key to many doors—and found that this was not true because of her immigration status. When have you thought that a skill or accomplishment was a sure thing only to find out that it wasn't enough? How did you react?

It was time to reach out for help. Gaile had heard about a course at Highline that helped students explore scholarship opportunities, prepare portfolio and résumé materials, and look at four-year institutions. She registered for Honors 100. In this course she met Dr. Barbara Clinton, her instructor and the head of the honors program at Highline.

With Dr. Clinton's help, Gaile was able to see the positive in her challenges, focus on what made her unique, and express those qualities in her portfolio and résumé so that they made a statement. When she shared her financial concerns, Dr. Clinton helped her find—and win—scholarships for which she was eligible. "The most

beautiful thing is that Dr. Clinton did not stop helping me after the class was over. She became my greatest resource."

With the confidence she gained from her mentor, Gaile has forged ahead to success. After getting employment authorization from the Immigration and Naturalization Service, she worked as a critical care nurse technician while finishing her nursing studies. She graduated in 2007 and started working as a registered nurse. She has also completed a baccalaureate degree in nursing from the University of Washington at Tacoma and will soon change her immigration status to permanent resident. She considers Dr. Clinton a resource for life and understands firsthand the value of reaching out to others.

Think about Gaile and Think about Yourself

- As the old saying goes, "No person is an island." What have you accomplished with a partner or team that you could not have done alone?
- How could reaching out to someone help you at school? Whom can you call? What help would you ask for?

Source: Highline College Honors Scholar Program Success Stories (adapted with permission from original story, online at http://flightline.highline.edu/honors/success/gaile.h

You can reach out to others for help, or you can reach out to others to help *them*. **Salma Hayek** has done both. After coming to the U.S. from her native Mexico to pursue an acting career, Hayek got her first big break from director Roberto Rodriguez. Now an international star, Salma produces Latin-themed films and supports UNICEF in its drive to provide vaccinations to poor children.

© Peter Kramer/AP Images

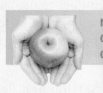

Sticks in a bundle are unbreakable.

Kenyan proverb

Habit for Success

reach out to others

Below are examples of how you can put this habit into action in different situations. Use the three spaces to add your own ideas for actions you can accomplish now or in the future. Be specific, and be realistic.

Get advice from close friends or family about how not to overdo the alcohol when you need to relax on weekends.

Find writing and math help at your school's writing center or tutoring center.

When thinking about different majors, talk to students majoring in areas that interest you.

**Reach Out to Others
Habit for Success**

When you can't get to a chore or need support with family responsibilities, ask for help—or trade something you do for something you need done.

Post notes and questions to online communities that can provide advice as you work to lose weight.

Building Skills

Note the Important Points

Why are values the foundation of successful goal setting?

Describe three ways that identifying your values can help you achieve college and life goals.

_____

_____

_____

How do you set and achieve goals?

Explain what short-term and long-term goals are and how they relate.

_____

_____

List the steps to take toward achieving a goal.

1. _____

2. _____

3. _____

4. _____

5. _____

6. _____

What are ways to manage stress as you pursue your goals?

In your own words, define the word "stress" in the context of your life as a student.

_____

_____

Name the three general categories of what to do to get stress under control, and include one strategy for each category.

1. _____

2. _____

3. _____

How will learning to work with others help you reach your goals?

Describe what emotional intelligence is.

_____

_____

Give some ways to participate effectively in a group setting.

_____

_____

Critical Thinking

Use Short-Term Goals to Explore Majors

Declaring a major is a long-term goal made up of short-term goal steps. Although many entering students don't yet know what they want to study, it's smart to explore possibilities now so that you can match your talents, skills, and dreams with an academic path. Use the following short-term goals to get moving.

Short-term goal #1: Identify interests and talents. If you can choose a major that focuses on what interests you and what you do well, you are more likely to have a positive attitude and perform effectively. To pinpoint areas that may work for you, consider questions like the following:

■ What are my favorite courses, topics to read about, activities?

■ Am I a "natural" in any academic or skill area?

■ How do I learn and work with others most effectively? (See Chapter 2.)

Based on your exploration, write down two majors that you think are worth considering.

■ _____

■ _____

Short-term goal #2: Explore general academic options.

Use the course catalog, the school Web site, or other resources to explore the following:

■ When do you have to declare a major? _____

■ What majors are offered at your school? (No need to write here; just read through the list.)

■ What are the options in majoring? (double majors, minors, "interdisciplinary" majors that combine more than one academic area) _____

_____

■ What is the process for changing a major once you have declared?

_____

_____

Short-term goal #3: Explore details of selected majors. Use the table to nail down specifics for each of the three majors that interest you. Check your course catalog and school Web site, talk to people currently majoring in this subject, and consult your academic advisor.

MAJORS	#1: _____	#2: _____
Minimum GPA for being accepted		
Minimum GPA required in coursework for the major		
Number of courses required		
Career areas that relate to this major		
Department head name		
Department secretary name and contact information		
How many students declare this major each year		
Where the department is located		
Courses you would have to take in the next year		

Finally, name the exact calendar date here when you will need to have declared your major:

_____ Put it in your planner and stick to it!

Team Building

Actively Dealing with Stress

Working alone, look back at the college stress scale on page 106. Note the stressors you included in your "stress score" for the past year. As a class, identify four stressors most commonly experienced by students. Divide into four groups, and assign a stressor to each. With your group:

- Discuss your stressor and the effects it has on people

- Brainstorm solutions and strategies, making sure to include ones that relate to health and teamwork (eating, sleeping, exercise, substances, getting help)

- List best coping strategies

- Choose a group member to present strategies

Finally, each group makes a presentation to the rest of the class about ways to handle this stressor. Groups may want to make extra copies of their lists for every member of the class.

Test Prep: Start It Now

reach
out to
others

Work with Others to Prep for Tests

Remember all of the advantages to studying in a group (see page 116)? Make them yours by setting up a study group now for your next big test. Check your syllabi and note here the topic, date, and course for your closest upcoming test:

Test topic _____

Test date and time _____

Course _____

Set up a study group with between one and four classmates. Write their names and contact information here:

_____   _____

_____   _____

_____   _____

_____   _____

How much time do you have from now until the test?_____

Plan at least two sessions during that time—one two days before the test and one a week or so earlier. For each, name the date, time, and location (put this information in your planner).

Session 1: _____

_____

Session 2: _____

_____

Finally, read over the strategies for group work success, and communicate with your group before you meet in order to set goals and decide who will serve as leader for both sessions.

critical and creative thinking
solving problems and making decisions

terrell generally doesn't agonize over problems. He makes a decision quickly and moves on to the next. Rapid-fire thinking serves him well in his part-time job as a short-order cook, where everything runs at breakneck speed. But it is creating problems at school.

In his work as an applied science major headed for a career as a paramedic–EMT, Terrell feels overloaded. In sociology, talking in groups about health-care delivery problems wears him out, and he loses patience with his instructor's teaching style. In anatomy and physiology, he just wants to memorize the parts of the body, not answer questions about how they work. He is so uncomfortable with it all that he is rethinking his career choice.

In this chapter . . .

you explore answers to the following questions:

WHY is it important to ask and answer questions? p. 128

HOW can you improve your critical thinking skills? p. 129

HOW can you improve your creative thinking skills? p. 138

HOW can you solve problems and make decisions effectively? p. 144

© PhotosToGo

create
and
imagine

Every person has the power to create. Use your creative power to imagine and activate new ideas or to solve problems.

Why Is It Important to Ask and Answer Questions?

As a college student, you ask questions and seek answers every day. You go through a process of questioning when you:

- Choose a term paper topic by looking at the topic list, thinking about available library and Internet sources, and considering personal interest and the instructor's approval

- Decide between two courses by reading course descriptions and talking to your advisor

- Offer an opposing opinion after listening to one point of view in a class discussion

You may not consider asking questions to be a big deal, and you may even feel that people who know what they are doing don't *have* to ask questions. Consider this: *Only through questioning are you engaged in the act of thinking.* According to Richard Paul of the Center for Critical Thinking and Moral Critique, thinking is what happens when you ask questions and move toward the answers.[1] "To think through or rethink anything," says Paul, "one must ask questions that stimulate . . . thought. Questions define tasks, express problems and delineate issues. . . . Only students who have questions are really thinking and learning."[2]

As you *answer* questions, you transform pieces of information into knowledge you can use. A computer programming student may ask how a certain code can make software perform a task. A pharmacy technology student may question which drug works best for a particular illness. An accounting student may ask how to set up a spreadsheet. All of these questioners seek information that they will use to achieve goals.

The best way to have a good idea is to have lots of ideas.

Linus Pauling, American scientist and peace activist

The questioning process may not be straightforward or quick, as Terrell is finding out. Sometimes the answer doesn't come right away. Often the answer leads to further, and more specific, questions. Having a clear purpose will help you pose targeted questions. Defining your purpose starts with a question: "What am I trying to accomplish, and why?"

As a college student, you are required to think in ways that go beyond the ability to memorize and retain what you learn. You are thinking *critically* and *creatively*, and you accomplish both through asking questions.

Critical thinking. This can be defined as the process of gathering, analyzing, and evaluating information for the purposes of gaining understanding, solving a problem, or making a decision.

Creative thinking. This term has a few definitions. Some researchers define creativity as combining existing elements in an innovative way to create a new purpose or result. (Using a weak adhesive to mark pages in a book, a 3M scientist created Post-it Notes.) Others see creativity as the ability to generate new ideas from looking at how things are related. (Noting what ladybugs eat inspired organic farmers to bring them in to consume crop-destroying aphids.)[4] Psychologist Robert Sternberg notes that creative people tend to have ideas that go against the norm—ideas that are often rejected at first but later are widely accepted.[5]

The rest of this chapter will describe critical and creative thinking in detail and will explain how to use both in problem solving and decision making. Remember that, as you improve your thinking skills, you will also improve your performance at school and at work. Critical and creative thinkers are in demand because of their ability to apply what they know, think through situations, create new ideas, solve problems, and make decisions effectively.

By the way . . .
you can improve your ability to think. Studies have shown that the brain develops throughout life if you continue to ask questions and learn new information and processes.[3]

How Can You Improve Your Critical Thinking Skills?

The first step in critical thinking is to define your purpose by asking what you want to examine and why. Then you gather the necessary information, analyze and clarify the ideas, and evaluate what you've found. Throughout the process, you will come up with new questions that may take you in new directions or even change your purpose.

The library is a great place to read information critically. Resources there can help you verify accuracy, locate support for ideas, and explore other perspectives.

To illustrate the actions of critical thinking, this section will use the example of writing a research paper. When working through a problem or decision, use the same actions to analyze and evaluate potential solutions and choices.

Gather Information

Information is the raw material for thinking. Choosing what to gather requires a careful exploration of how much information you need, how much time to spend gathering it, and whether the information is relevant. Say, for instance, that you have to write a paper on one aspect of the media (TV, radio, Internet) and its influence on a particular group. If you gathered every available resource on the topic, the course would be over long before you began writing.

Here's how asking questions will help you target your assignment:

- Reviewing the assignment, you ask how long it has to be (10 pages) and what it has to accomplish (describe at least three significant points of media influence).

- At the library and online, you find thousands of articles on the topic. After an hour, you ask what information threads you are uncovering. You decide to focus your paper on how the Internet influences young teens (ages 13–15).

- As you read six comprehensive articles, you ask which ones are most complete. You choose three in-depth sources.

Through questioning, you achieve a short-term goal—you select your writing sources—and set yourself up to achieve your long-term goal of writing a well-crafted paper.

Analyze and Clarify Information

Your next step is to analyze the information to determine whether it is *reliable* (accurate and trustworthy) and useful in helping you answer your questions.

Break Information into Parts

When analyzing information, you break information into parts and examine the parts so that you can see how they relate to each other and to what you already know. Use the following strategies to accomplish this goal.

Separate the ideas.   If you are reading about how teens aged 13–15 use the Internet, you might discuss methods of access, popular Web sites, and how people interact via social networking sites and blogs.

Compare and contrast.   Examine similarities and differences. You might explore how teen subgroups (boys versus girls, for example) use social networking sites like Facebook and MySpace.

Examine cause and effect.   Look at the possible reasons why something happened (true causes) and its consequences (effects, both positive and negative). You might examine the effect that Internet use has on how young teens spend their time outside of school.

An important caution: Avoid jumping to conclusions about cause-and-effect relationships and getting distracted by "false causes" (things that seem to cause a problem but are not the actual causes). In other words, while A may be related to B, A may not be the cause of B. For example, while it is tempting to say that young teens are spending less time with friends as a result of the Internet, their behavior may also be influenced by other factors, including parental and school pressures.

Look for themes, patterns, and categories.   Note connections that form as you examine how bits of information relate to one another. For example, you might notice patterns that link boys and girls with different types of Internet use.

Once ideas are broken down, you can examine whether evidence supports a general idea, whether information is fact or opinion, whether it has a biased perspective, and whether there are hidden assumptions.

Examine the Evidence

How useful an idea is to your work may depend on whether, or how well, it is backed up by solid evidence. *Evidence* includes clear logic, facts, expert opinion, research findings, personal experience, and so on. Concrete, specific examples are a form of evidence.

Many reading materials present a particular **argument** for you to consider. Use questioning to judge the quality of the evidence used in the argument and whether it supports the central idea. For example, a blog written by a 13-year-old may make statements about what kids do on the Internet; however, the word of one person who may or may not be telling the truth is not adequate support. On the other hand, a study of kids' technology use by the Department of Commerce under the provisions of the Children's Internet Proctection Act is more likely to be trustworthy. With this examination, you can decide whether to explore the materials further or set them aside.

Evidence examination is especially important when you research on the Internet, because its resources vary widely in reliability. In fact, your Internet research is only as strong as your critical thinking. Robert Harris, professor and Web expert, has developed an easy-to-remember system for evaluating Internet information called the CARS test for information quality (Credibility, Accuracy, Reasonableness, Support). Use the information in Key 5.1 to question any

Argument
a set of connected ideas, supported by examples, that prove or disprove a point.

CREDIBILITY	ACCURACY	REASONABLENESS	SUPPORT
Examine whether a source is believable and trustworthy.	Examine whether information is correct—i.e., factual, comprehensive, detailed, and up to date (if necessary).	Examine whether material is fair, objective, moderate, and consistent.	Examine whether a source is adequately supported with citations.
What are the author's credentials?	*Is it up to date, and is that important?*	*Does the source seem fair?*	*Where does the information come from?*
Look for education and experience, title or position of employment, membership in any known and respected organization, reliable contact information, biographical information, and reputation.	If you are searching for a work of literature, such as Shakespeare's play *Macbeth*, there is no "updated" version. However, you may want reviews of its latest productions. For most scientific research, you will need to rely on the most updated information you can find.	Look for a balanced argument, accurate claims, and a reasoned tone that does not appeal primarily to your emotions.	Look at the site, the sources used by the person or group who compiled the information, and the contact information. Make sure that the cited sources seem reliable and that statistics are documented.
Is there quality control?	*Is it comprehensive?*	*Does the source seem objective?*	*Is the information corroborated?*
Look for ways in which the source may have been screened. For example, materials on an organization's Web site have most likely been approved by several members; information coming from an academic journal has to be screened by several people before it is published.	Does the material leave out any important facts or information? Does it neglect to consider alternative views or crucial consequences? Although no one source can contain all of the available information on a topic, it should still be as comprehensive as is possible within its scope.	While there is a range of objectivity in writing, you want to favor authors and organizations who can control their bias. An author with a strong political or religious agenda or an intent to sell a product may not be a source of the most truthful material.	Test information by looking for other sources that confirm the facts in this information—or, if the information is opinion, sources that share that opinion and back it up with their own citations. One good strategy is to find at least three sources that corroborate each other.

(continued)

CREDIBILITY	ACCURACY	REASONABLENESS	SUPPORT
Is there any posted summary or evaluation of the source?	*For whom is the source written, and for what purpose?*	*Does the source seem moderate?*	*Is the source externally consistent?*
You may find abstracts of sources (summary) or a recommendation, rating, or review from a person or organization (evaluation). Either of these—or, ideally, both—can give you an idea of credibility before you decide to examine a source in depth.	Looking at what the author wants to accomplish will help you assess whether it has a bias. Sometimes biased information will not be useful for your purpose; sometimes your research will require that you note and evaluate bias (such as if you were to compare Civil War diaries from Union soldiers with those from Confederate soldiers).	Do claims seem possible, or does the information seem hard to believe? Does what you read make sense when compared to what you already know? While wild claims may turn out to be truthful, you are safest to check everything out.	Most material is a mix of both current and old information. External consistency refers to whether the old information agrees with what you already know. If a source contradicts something you know to be true, chances are higher that the information new to you may be inconsistent as well.
Signals of a potential lack of credibility:	*Signals of a potential lack of accuracy:*	*Signals of a potential lack of reasonableness:*	*Signals of a potential lack of support:*
Anonymous materials, negative evaluations, little or no evidence of quality control, bad grammar or misspelled words	Lack of date or old date, generalizations, one-sided views that do not acknowledge opposing arguments	Extreme or emotional language, sweeping statements, conflict of interest, inconsistencies or contradictions	Statistics without sources, lack of documentation, lack of corroboration using other reliable sources

Source: Robert Harris, "Evaluating Internet Research Sources," November 17, 1997, VirtualSalt (www.virtualsalt.com/evalu8it.htm).

source you find as you conduct research. You can also use it to test the reliability of non-Internet sources.

Focus on Logical Connections

As you read, be on the lookout for mistakes in logic, or *logical fallacies* (see Key 5.2). They are prevalent and have the power to convince you that an argument is well reasoned when, in fact, it is flawed. Writing expert and author Dr. Lynn Quitman Troyka explains: "Most logical fallacies masquerade as reasonable statements, but they are in fact attempts to manipulate readers by reaching their emotions instead of their intellects, their hearts rather than their heads."[6]

Critical and Creative Thinking

Statement: "We cannot trust the company's CEO, and he should resign."

FALLACY	EXAMPLE
Appeal to authority: *Statement is true because someone important says it is.*	"A powerful financial analyst has a low opinion of him."
False cause: *It's true because an unrelated point is true.*	"The company's stock dropped by 20% when a competitor introduced a new product that consumers are buying."
Hasty generalization: *Because this is true of one person or situation, it is true of all.*	"Corporate executives bend the rules for their own benefit and are dishonest. I know of one CEO who stole millions of dollars."
Personal attack: *It's true because of personal characteristics that have nothing to do with the situation.*	"He is impatient and doesn't seem to be a nice person."

Perspective
a characteristic way of thinking about people, situations, events, and ideas.

Finding credible, reliable information with which to answer questions and come up with ideas enables you to separate fact from opinion.

Distinguish Fact from Opinion

A *statement of fact* is verifiable—that is, you can prove that it is true ("The Internet is a research tool"). In contrast, a *statement of opinion* is a belief, conclusion, or judgment that is difficult, and sometimes impossible, to verify ("The Internet is always the best and most reliable research tool"). Key 5.3 defines important characteristics of fact and opinion.

Looking carefully at whether an argument is based on fact or opinion will help you determine how reliable it is. You can use opinions if you determine that they are backed up by facts. However, it is important first to recognize that you are dealing with an opinion and then to look for underlying perspectives and assumptions.

Examine Perspectives and Assumptions

A **perspective** can be broad, such as a generally optimistic or pessimistic view of life. Or it can be more focused, such as an attitude about whether students should commute or live on campus.

Perspectives are associated with **assumptions**. For example, the perspective that there are many ways to handle the problem of children spending too much time on an unregulated and sometimes dangerous Internet leads to assumptions such as "Parents can control children's Internet use" and "Children can access the Internet without being exposed to inappropriate content."

Assumption
a judgment, generalization, or bias influenced by experience and values.

FACTS INCLUDE STATEMENTS THAT . . .	OPINIONS INCLUDE STATEMENTS THAT . . .
. . . *deal with actual people, places, objects, or events.* Example: In the 2008 presidential election, Barack Obama won 365 electoral votes compared with John McCain's 173 votes.	. . . *show evaluation.* Words such as *bad, good, pointless,* and *beneficial* indicate opinion-based value judgments. Example: "Barack Obama's candidacy benefited from the downturn in the economy as voters looked for change."
. . . *use concrete words or measurable data.* Example: "The charity event raised $50,862."	. . . *use abstract words.* Vague, imprecise words like *misery* or *success* usually indicate a personal opinion. Example: "The charity event was a smashing success."
. . . *describe current events in exact terms.* Example: "Mr. Barrett's 9:00 A.M. course has 378 students."	. . . *predict future events.* Statements about future occurrences are often opinions. Example: "Mr. Barrett's course is going to set a new enrollment record this term."
. . . *avoid emotional words and focus on the verifiable.* Example: "Citing dissatisfaction with the instruction, 7 out of the 25 students in that class withdrew in September."	. . . *use emotional words.* Emotions are unverifiable. Words like *delightful* or *miserable* express an opinion. Example: "That class is a miserable experience."
. . . *avoid absolutes.* Example: "Some students need to have a job while in school."	. . . *use absolutes.* Absolute **qualifiers,** such as *all, none, never,* and *always,* often express an opinion. Example: "All students need to have a job while in school."

Source: Adapted from Ben E. Johnson, *Stirring Up Thinking*, New York: Houghton Mifflin, 1998, pp. 268–270.

How do you perceive yourself as a critical thinker? For each statement, circle the number that feels right to you, from 1 for "not at all true for me" to 5 for "very true for me."

1. I recognize and define problems effectively.   1 2 3 4 5
2. I see myself as "a thinker," "analytical," "studious."   1 2 3 4 5
3. I need to see convincing evidence before accepting information as fact.   1 2 3 4 5
4. In a group setting, I like to break down a problem into parts and evaluate them.   1 2 3 4 5
5. I notice when ideas are not backed up by solid evidence.   1 2 3 4 5
6. I focus on whether ideas are logically connected.   1 2 3 4 5
7. I read everything carefully—even e-mails—to make sure that I understand what the writer intends to say.   1 2 3 4 5

Total your answers here: _____

If your total ranges from 5 to 14, you consider your critical-thinking skills to be *weak.*

If your total ranges from 15 to 24, you consider your critical-thinking skills to be *average.*

If your total ranges from 25 to 35, you consider your critical-thinking skills to be *strong.*

Bias
a preference or inclination, especially one that prevents even-handed judgment.

Perspectives and assumptions color nearly everything you read, and being able to examine them carefully enables you to judge whether material is free of **bias.** Biased material strongly reflects the author's perspective and intent. For example, if the author of an article urging no Internet controls is a well-known proponent of free speech in all forms, the article is likely to reflect his bias.

Your personal perspective and assumptions can affect your ability to fairly evaluate information that differs from your point of view. A student who thinks that the death penalty is wrong, for example, may have a hard time analyzing arguments that defend it. Try to set aside your personal perspectives and assumptions when you analyze information. Come to the classroom or your reading materials ready to think about the merits of new ideas.

Key 5.4   Ask questions at every stage of the critical-thinking process

To gather information, ask:	■ What kinds of information do I need to meet my goal? ■ What information is available? Where and when can I get to it? ■ Of the sources I found, which ones will best help me achieve my goal?
To analyze, ask:	■ What are the parts of this information? ■ What is similar to this information? What is different? ■ What are the reasons for this? Why did this happen? ■ What ideas, themes, or conclusions emerge from this material? ■ How would you categorize this information?
To see if evidence or examples support an idea, ask:	■ Does the evidence make sense? ■ How do the examples support the idea/claim? ■ Are there examples that might disprove the idea/claim?
To distinguish fact from opinion, ask:	■ Do the words in this information signal fact or opinion? ■ What is the source of this information? Is the source reliable? ■ If this is an opinion, is it supported by facts?
To examine perspectives and assumptions, ask:	■ What perspectives might the author have, and what may be emphasized or deemphasized as a result? ■ What assumptions might lie behind this statement or material? ■ How could I prove, or disprove, an assumption? ■ How might my perspective affect the way I see this material?
To evaluate, ask:	■ What information will support what I'm trying to prove or accomplish? ■ Is this information true or false, and why? ■ How important is this information?

Source: Adapted from "Questions That Probe Reasons and Evidence" (www-ed.fnal.gov/trc/tutorial/taxonomy.html), based on Richard Paul, *Critical Thinking: How to Prepare Students for a Rapidly Changing World,* Santa Rosa, CA: Center for Critical Thinking, 1993; and from Barbara Fowler, "Bloom's Taxonomy and Critical Thinking," 1996, Longview Community College (http://mcckc.edu/longview/ctac/blooms.htm).

Consider the statement below. Use your critical-thinking skills and logical-mathematical intelligence to answer the questions that follow:

"The Internet is the best place to find information about any topic."

Is this statement fact or opinion? Why?

_____

What assumption(s) underlie the statement, and how might these assumptions affect how you complete research assignments?

_____

What examples can you think of that support or disprove this statement?

_____

_____

As a result of your critical thinking, what is your evaluation of this statement?

_____

_____

_____

Evaluate Information

You've gathered and analyzed your information. You have examined its components, its evidence, its reliance on fact or opinion, and its underlying assumptions. With what you've learned, you now *evaluate* whether an idea or piece of information is important or unimportant, applicable or unrelated, strong or weak, and why. You set aside what is not useful and use the rest to create your argument.

Evaluation, like every stage of critical thinking, requires that you return to your foundational approach: careful, thorough questioning. See Key 5.4 for some questions that engage critical-thinking skills.

In preparing your paper on young teens and the Internet, for example, you've gathered pertinent information, came up with an idea you wanted to write about, researched information and materials, and analyzed how your research applied to your position. You then drafted your paper, presenting what you learned in an organized, persuasive way.

Meeting expectations at school may require more than critical thinking. It may also involve thinking creatively about how to use what your thinking has uncovered.

How Can You Improve Your Creative Thinking Skills?

Even though some people seem to be more creative than others, creative thinking is a skill that can be developed if you keep a flexible mind. Creativity expert Roger von Oech explains: "Like race-car drivers who shift in and out of different gears depending on where they are on the course," you can enhance creativity by learning to "shift in and out of different types of thinking depending on the needs of the situation at hand."[7]

The following actions will help you make those shifts. Because creative ideas often pop up randomly, get in the habit of writing them down as they occur to you. Keep a pen and paper by your bed, your electronic planner in your pocket, or a digital recorder in your backpack.

Brainstorm

Brainstorming — letting your mind free-associate to come up with different ideas.

Brainstorming is also referred to as *divergent thinking:* You start with a question and then let your mind diverge—go in many different directions—in search of solutions. Brainstorming is *deliberate* creative thinking. When you brainstorm, generate ideas without thinking about how useful they are; evaluate their quality later. Brainstorming works well in groups because group members can become inspired by, and make creative use of, one another's ideas.[8]

One way to inspire ideas when brainstorming is to think of similar situations—in other words, to make *analogies* (comparisons based on a resemblance of things otherwise unlike). For example, Velcro is a product of analogy: When imagining how two pieces of fabric could stick to each other, the inventor thought of a burr sticking to clothing.

When you brainstorm, don't get hooked on finding the one right answer. Questions may have many "right answers"—or many answers that have degrees of usefulness. The more possibilities you generate, the better your chance of finding the best one. Also, don't stop when you think you have the best answer—keep going until you are out of steam. You never know what may come up in those last gasps of creative energy.[9]

real people

create and imagine

At Kenyon College in Ohio, Charlie Reinhardt was president of his fraternity, a bass player in a rock band, and a mediocre student.

Graduate student in hotel management, Temple University, Philadelphia, Pennsylvania

He knew that academics were supposed to be important, yet he only did enough to get by. Without a sense of what he wanted from school, he couldn't imagine what he wanted out of life.

Stop and Think

Do you have times when, like Charlie, you have trouble imagining what is possible for you beyond your responsibilities of the next 24 hours? What effect does that have on your motivation?

After graduation, Charlie took a job in Chicago as a currency trader, but he soon realized that the work wasn't for him. He began to question why he was a college graduate without direction, and realized that he was still working through all the issues related to his amputated right leg. Born with a rare condition called pseudoarthrosis, he had a below-the-knee amputation when he was 5 years old and wore a prosthesis. As a result, in college, nothing mattered more than being a "regular guy." Being studious was not part of his regular-guy profile.

Unhappy and ready to do something about it, he gave himself permission to think creatively, imagining

what he might want to do with his life. He decided to become a chef, a dream that had been in the back of his mind for a long time. Both of his parents were gourmet cooks, and Charlie had always felt happy in the kitchen.

A year after he graduated college, Charlie began attending the Cooking and Hospitality Institute of Chicago at night while working during the day. He loved every exhausting minute.

Stop and Think

Charlie's leg amputation affected his sense of self. Do you have any personal factors that influence your ability to achieve your full potential?

With culinary degree in hand, Charlie worked in prestigious Manhattan restaurants for five years.

His next career move literally took him halfway around the world when he got a job managing a large kitchen staff at a Kempinski resort in Djibouti, Africa. Charlie thrived on the work, but he faced recurring leg problems. Not wanting to lose him, Charlie's managers thought creatively about what he could do. They offered him a position that combined his cooking

experience with his background in finance. The position would allow him to sit and put him on a track to become a general manager.

After two years with Kempinski, Charlie is now working as a chef in Philadelphia while working toward his master's degree in hotel management.

When he thinks about it all, he knows that he is where he is because he imagined what he loved doing, seized an outlandish opportunity that changed his life, and had the creativity to adjust to a wide variety of job situations. Despite a slow start and mid-course corrections, he doesn't regret a minute of it.

Think about Charlie and Think about Yourself

- A wise person once said: "*Start with something you love and then figure out how to make money doing it.*" Why are you more likely to persist when you enjoy your work?

- If you allow your creative mind to imagine what might be possible for you, as Charlie did, what would you want to do in your working life?

© Ben Margot/AP Images

Larry Page and **Sergey Brin,** two computer science students at Stanford University in the 1990s, imagined that there must be a more effective way to search for materials online. Working together, they created a search engine that would list the most popular Web pages first when listing search "hits." Although it was first called BackRub, you now know it as Google.

create
and
imagine

Take a New and Different Look

If no one ever questioned established opinion, people would still think the sun revolved around the earth. Here are some ways to change how you look at a situation or problem:

Challenge assumptions. Don't assume something has to be done a certain way because it *always* has been done that way. Break the mold. In the late 1960s, conventional wisdom said that school provided education and television provided entertainment. Jim Henson, a pioneer in children's television, asked, "Why can't we use TV to educate young children?" From that question, the characters of *Sesame Street,* and eventually a host of other educational programs, were born.

Shift your perspective. Try on new perspectives by asking others for their views, reading about new ways to approach situations, or deliberately going against your first instinct.[10] Then use those perspectives to inspire creativity. For a fun example of how looking at something in a new way can unearth a totally different idea, look at the perception puzzles in Key 5.5.

Ask "what if" questions. Set up hypothetical environments in which new ideas can grow: "What if I had unlimited money or time?" For example, the founders of Seeds of Peace, faced with generations of conflict in the

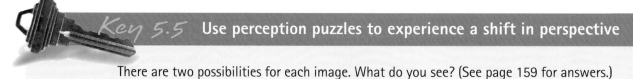

Key 5.5 **Use perception puzzles to experience a shift in perspective**

There are two possibilities for each image. What do you see? (See page 159 for answers.)

Source of middle puzzle: "Sara Nadar" illustration from *Mind Sights* by Roger Shepard. Copyright © 1990 by Roger Shepard. Reprinted by permission of Henry Holt and Company, LLC.

Middle East, asked: What if Israeli and Palestinian teens met at a summer camp in Maine so that the next generation has greater understanding and respect? And what if follow-up programs and reunions are set up to cement friendships so that relationships change the politics of the Middle East? Based on the ideas that came up, they created an organization that helps teenagers from the Middle East develop leadership and communication skills.

Set the Stage for Creativity

Use these strategies to give yourself the best possible chance at generating creative ideas.

Choose, or create, environments that free your mind.   Find places that energize you. Play music that moves you. Seek out people who inspire you.[11]

Be curious.   Try something new and different: Take a course outside of your major, listen to a new genre of music, or read a book on an unfamiliar topic. Try something you don't think you would like in order to see if you had misjudged your reaction. Seeking out new experiences will give you more raw materials with which to build creative ideas.[12]

Give yourself time to "sit" with a question.   American society values speed, so much so that being "quick" means being smart.[13] However, creative ideas often come when you give your brain permission to "leave the job" for a while.[14] Take breaks when figuring out a problem—get some exercise, take a

POWERFUL
QUESTIONS

Grace Murray Hopper, a Navy admiral as well as an accomplished mathematician, once said, "A ship in port is safe, but that's not what ships are built for."

What does this say to you about

your creativity and imagination? Consider what goals you think your "ship"—your mind—is built to pursue. Choose one to think about carefully. What kinds of risks are you willing to take to accomplish that goal?

create
and
imagine

Critical and Creative Thinking

nap, talk with a friend, work on something else, take a shower, or do something fun.

Take Risks

Creative breakthroughs can come from sensible risk taking.

Fly in the face of convention.   Wanting to make the Internet more efficient through human connection, entrepreneurs and computer specialists came up with the idea of MySpace. The possibility of failure did not stop them from risking money, time, energy, and reputation to achieve a truly unique and creative goal.

Let mistakes be okay.   Open yourself to the learning that comes from mistakes. When a pharmaceutical company failed to develop a new treatment for multiple sclerosis, the CEO said, "You have to celebrate the failures. If you send the message that the only road to career success is experiments that work, people won't ask risky questions, or get any dramatically new answers."[15]

As with critical thinking, asking questions powers creative thinking. See Key 5.6 for examples of the kinds of questions you can ask to get your creative juices flowing.

When you combine critical thinking, creativity, and emotional and social intelligence, you have a powerful set of skills. Put them into action together to solve problems and make decisions.

How do you perceive yourself as a creative thinker? For each statement, circle the number that feels right to you, from 1 for "least like me" to 5 for "most like me."

1. I tend to question rules and regulations.   1 2 3 4 5
2. I see myself as "unique," "full of ideas," "innovative."   1 2 3 4 5
3. Too much routine in my work or schedule drains my energy.   1 2 3 4 5
4. When working with a group, I generate a lot of ideas.   1 2 3 4 5
5. If you say something is too risky, I'm ready to give it a shot.   1 2 3 4 5
6. I feel comfortable allowing myself to make mistakes as I test out ideas.   1 2 3 4 5
7. I often wonder if there is a different way to get something done.   1 2 3 4 5

Total your answers here: _____

If your total ranges from 5 to 14, you consider your creative-thinking skills to be *weak*.

If your total ranges from 15 to 24, you consider your creative-thinking skills to be *average*.

If your total ranges from 25 to 35, you consider your creative-thinking skills to be *strong*.

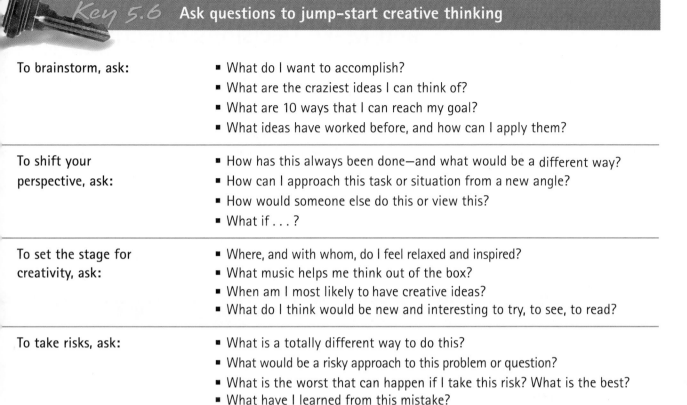

To brainstorm, ask:	■ What do I want to accomplish? ■ What are the craziest ideas I can think of? ■ What are 10 ways that I can reach my goal? ■ What ideas have worked before, and how can I apply them?
To shift your perspective, ask:	■ How has this always been done—and what would be a different way? ■ How can I approach this task or situation from a new angle? ■ How would someone else do this or view this? ■ What if . . . ?
To set the stage for creativity, ask:	■ Where, and with whom, do I feel relaxed and inspired? ■ What music helps me think out of the box? ■ When am I most likely to have creative ideas? ■ What do I think would be new and interesting to try, to see, to read?
To take risks, ask:	■ What is a totally different way to do this? ■ What would be a risky approach to this problem or question? ■ What is the worst that can happen if I take this risk? What is the best? ■ What have I learned from this mistake?

TAKE ACTION
Gather Evidence of Your Creativity

First, think about the past month; then, list three creative acts you performed.

1. While I studied, I _____

2. In my personal life, I _____

3. In the classroom, I _____

Now, engaging your intrapersonal intelligence, think of a problem or situation that is on your mind. Brainstorm one new creative idea for how to deal with it.

_____

_____

Now, let the question sit for *at least* 24 hours. Come back to this page, and write one more idea.

_____

_____

How Can You Solve Problems and Make Decisions Effectively?

Problem solving and decision making follow similar paths. Both require you to identify and analyze a situation, generate possible solutions, choose one, follow through, and evaluate its success. Key 5.7 gives an overview of the paths, indicating how you think at each step. Keys 5.9 and 5.10 on pages 147 and 149 will show you how to use this path, through a visual organizer, to map out problems and decisions.

Even though problem solving and decision making follow the same plan of action, they differ in important ways:

- Problem solving generally requires that you focus on coming up with possible solutions. In contrast, in decision making, your choices are often determined.

Key 5.7   Solve problems and make decisions using a plan of action

PROBLEM SOLVING	THINKING SKILL	DECISION MAKING
Define the problem—recognize that something needs to change, identify what's happening, look for true causes.	Step 1 Define	Define the decision—identify your goal (your need) and then think though a decision that will help you get it.
Analyze the problem—gather information, break it into pieces, verify facts, check the support, look at perspectives and assumptions, evaluate information.	Step 2 Analyze	Examine needs and motives—carefully consider layers of needs; try to focus on what is most important.
Generate possible solutions—use creative strategies to think of ways you could address the causes of this problem.	Step 3 Create	Name and/or generate different options—use creative questions to come up with choices that would fulfill your needs.
Evaluate solutions—look carefully at potential pros and cons of each, and choose what seems best.	Step 4 Evaluate	Evaluate options—look carefully at potential pros and cons of each, and choose what seems best.
Put the solution to work—persevere, focus on results, and believe in yourself as you go for your goal.	Step 5 Choose and act	Act on your decision—go down the path and stay on target.
Evaluate how well the solution worked—look at the effects of what you did.	Step 6 Re-evaluate	Evaluate the success of your decision—look at whether it accomplished what you had hoped.
In the future, apply what you learned. Use this solution, or a better one, when a similar situation arises.	Step 7 Apply results	In the future, apply what you learned. Make this choice, or a better one, when a similar decision arises.

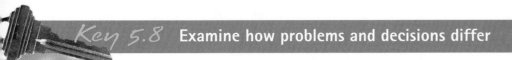

SITUATION	YOU HAVE A PROBLEM IF . . .	YOU NEED TO MAKE A DECISION IF . . .
Planning summer activities	Your low GPA means you need to attend summer school—and you've already accepted a summer job.	You've been accepted into two summer abroad internship programs.
Declaring a major	It's time to declare, but you don't have all the prerequisites for the major you want.	There are three majors that appeal to you and you qualify for them all.
Handling communications with instructors	You are having trouble following the lecture style of a particular instructor.	Your psychology survey course has seven sections taught by different instructors; you have to choose one.

- A problem exists when a situation has negative effects, and problem solving aims to remove or counteract those effects. In contrast, decision making aims to fulfill a need.

See Key 5.8 for some examples. Remember, too, that whereas all problem solving involves some decision making, only some decision making requires you to solve a problem.

Solving a Problem

Use these strategies as you move through the problem-solving process outlined in Key 5.9.

Use probing questions to define problems.   Focus on causes. Engage your social and emotional intelligence. If you are not happy in a class, for example, you could ask questions like these:

- What do I think about when I feel unhappy?
- Do my feelings stem from how I interact with my instructor or classmates?
- Is the subject matter difficult? Uninteresting? The volume of work too much?

Chances are that how you answer one or more of these questions may lead to a clear definition—and ultimately to the right solution.

Analyze carefully.   Gather information for a comprehensive examination. Consider how the problem is similar to, or different from, other problems. Clarify facts. Note your own perspective, and ask others for theirs. Make sure your assumptions don't cloud your analysis.

Generate possible solutions based on causes, not effects. Addressing a cause provides a lasting solution, whereas "fixing" an effect cannot. Say, for example, that your shoulder hurts when you use your computer. Getting a friend to massage it is a helpful but temporary solution, because the pain returns whenever you go back to work. Changing the height of your keyboard and mouse is a better idea, because it eliminates the cause of your pain.

Consider how possible solutions affect you and others. What would suit you best? What takes other people's needs into consideration?

Evaluate your solution and let it lead to future action. Once you choose a solution and put it into action, ask yourself: What worked that you would do again? What didn't work that you would avoid or change in the future?

What happens if you don't work through a problem comprehensively? Take, for example, Terrell's problems with his instructor. He may get into an argument with the instructor, stop showing up to class, or take a quick-and-dirty approach to assignments. All of these choices have negative consequences. Now look at how he might use his critical- and creative-thinking skills to work through the problem. Key 5.9 shows how his effort can pay off.

Making a Decision

As you use the steps in Key 5.7 to make a decision, remember these strategies.

Look at the given options—then try to think of more. Some decisions have a given set of options. For example, your school may allow you to major, double major, or major and minor. However, you may be able to work with your advisor to come up with another option—an interdisciplinary major. As with problem solving, consider similar situations you've been in or heard about, what decisions were made, and what resulted from those decisions.

Look at the long-term effects. As with problem solving, a final evaluation is crucial. For important decisions, do a short-term evaluation

DEFINE PROBLEM HERE:	ANALYZE THE PROBLEM
I don't like my Sociology instructor	We have different styles and personality types—I am not comfortable working in groups and being vocal. I'm not interested in being there, and my grades are suffering from my lack of motivation.

Use boxes below to list possible solutions:

POTENTIAL POSITIVE EFFECTS	SOLUTION #1	POTENTIAL NEGATIVE EFFECTS
List for each solution: Don't have to deal with that instructor Less stress	Drop the course	*List for each solution:* Grade gets entered on my transcript I'll have to take the course eventually; it's required for my major
Getting credit for the course Feeling like I've honored a commitment	**SOLUTION #2** Put up with it until the end of the semester	Stress every time I'm there Lowered motivation Probably not such a good final grade
A chance to express myself Could get good advice An opportunity to ask direct questions of the instructor	**SOLUTION #3** Schedule meetings with advisor and instructor	Have to face instructor one-on-one Might just make things worse

Now choose the solution you think is best—circle it and make it happen.

ACTUAL POSITIVE EFFECTS	PRACTICAL ACTION	ACTUAL NEGATIVE EFFECTS
List for chosen solution: Got some helpful advice from advisor Talking in person with the instructor actually promoted a fairly honest discussion I won't have to take the course again	I scheduled and attended meetings with both advisor and instructor and opted to stick with the course.	*List for chosen solution:* Still have to put up with some group work I still don't know how much learning I'll retain from this course

FINAL EVALUATION: Was it a good or bad solution?

The solution has improved things. I'll finish the course, and I got the chance to fulfill some class responsibilities on my own or with one partner. I feel more understood and more willing to put my time into the course.

Source: Based on heuristic created by Frank T. Lyman Jr. and George Eley, 1985.

and another evaluation after a period of time. Examine whether your decision sent you down a positive path or whether you should rethink your choice.

Consider all factors.   Psychologists who study decision making realize that a variety of factors influence choices. For example, you may choose a major, not because you love the subject, but because you think your parents will approve of it. The goal is to make decisions that are right for you.

What happens when you make important decisions too quickly or base them on factors that are actually pretty low on the priority list? You may regret them. Consider a student trying to decide whether to transfer schools. If she makes her decision because a close friend goes to the other school, but then finds that the school doesn't suit her, she may wish she had made a different choice.

Now look at how this student might make an effective decision. Key 5.10 shows how she used her critical and creative thinking in the process.

Stay in Touch with Yourself and Others

Remember that emotional intelligence and cultural competence are key tools for problem solving and decision making. Terrell's success in his sociology course, for example, may depend as much if not more on finding a way to get along with his instructor than on answering multiple-choice questions on a test. Your emotional intelligence can help you to:

- Define a problem effectively by understanding the negative effects a situation has on you
- Brainstorm potential solutions that take your abilities and level of motivation into account
- Persist through a problem-solving or decision-making process
- Consider how potential solutions and choices may affect others
- Behave in social situations in a way that motivates people to work with you

Your cultural competence can help you to:

- Value the diverse perspectives people bring to the discussion
- Gather different ideas from others who may have been in similar situations
- Be aware of, and try to avoid, problematic stereotypes and assumptions
- Focus on the needs of others involved in the problem or decision

Groups often solve problems effectively because different people generate different ideas to consider. This group works together on a math problem.

© Mark Richards/PhotoEdit

DEFINE THE DECISION	EXAMINE NEEDS AND MOTIVES
Whether or not to transfer schools	My father has changed jobs and can no longer afford my tuition. My goal is to become a physical therapist, so I need a school with a full physical therapy program. My family needs to cut costs. I need to transfer credits.

Use boxes below to list possible choices:

POTENTIAL POSITIVE EFFECTS	CHOICE #1	POTENTIAL NEGATIVE EFFECTS
List for each solution:	Continue at the current college	*List for each solution:*
No need to adjust to a new place or new people		Need to finance most of my tuition and costs on my own
Ability to continue course work as planned		Difficult to find time for a job
		Might not qualify for aid

POTENTIAL POSITIVE EFFECTS	CHOICE #2	POTENTIAL NEGATIVE EFFECTS
Many physical therapy courses available	Transfer to the community college	No personal contacts there that I know of
School is close so I could live at home and save room costs		Less independence if I live at home
Reasonable tuition; credits will transfer		No bachelor's degree available

POTENTIAL POSITIVE EFFECTS	CHOICE #3	POTENTIAL NEGATIVE EFFECTS
Opportunity to earn tuition money	Stop out for a year	Could forget so much that it's hard to go back
Could live at home		Could lose motivation
Status should be intact		A year might turn into more

Now choose the one you think is best—circle it and make it happen.

ACTUAL POSITIVE EFFECTS	PRACTICAL ACTION	ACTUAL NEGATIVE EFFECTS
List for chosen solution:	Go to community college for two years; then transfer to a four-year school to get a B.A. and complete physical therapy course work.	*List for chosen solution:*
Money saved		Loss of some independence
Opportunity to spend time on studies rather than on working to earn tuition money		Less contact with friends
Availability of classes I need		

FINAL EVALUATION: Was it a good or bad choice?
I'm satisfied with the decision. It can be hard being at home at times, but my parents are adjusting to my independence and I'm trying to respect their concerns. With fewer social distractions, I'm really getting my work done. Plus the financial aspect of the decision is ideal.

Source: Based on heuristic created by Frank T. Lyman Jr. and George Eley, 1985.

Multiple Intelligence Strategies for Team Problem Solving

Briefly describe a situation where you find it challenging to work through a problem with one or more people.

_____

_____

Now, brainstorm potential solutions to your problem, linking each solution to an intelligence. Use the right-hand column to record your ideas.

INTELLIGENCE	SUGGESTED STRATEGIES	USE MI STRATEGIES TO COME UP WITH SOLUTIONS
Verbal-Linguistic	■ Find opportunities to express your thoughts and feelings to others—either in writing or in person. ■ Listen actively to understand the other person's point of view.	
Logical-Mathematical	■ Think through a problem before discussing it. Clarify your thoughts by writing them out. ■ When communicating with others who are not as logic-focused, ask specific questions to learn the facts you need.	
Bodily-Kinesthetic	■ Pay attention to your own body language. Make sure it supports what you want to communicate. ■ Hone in on the signals from other people's body language.	
Visual-Spatial	■ Make a drawing or diagram of points you want to communicate during an important discussion. ■ If you are in a formal classroom or work setting, use visual aids to explain your main points.	
Interpersonal	■ Consider how you tend to operate in a group. If you tend to dominate, focus on listening; if you prioritize others' opinions, try to express your opinion more assertively. ■ Stay aware of what others need to hear from you, and respond accordingly.	
Intrapersonal	■ Spend time thinking about what you want to say so that it comes out exactly right. ■ Use your understanding of yourself to tune into what others feel and think.	
Musical	■ Before communicating difficult thoughts or feelings, listen to music that relates to what you are thinking. ■ Be sensitive to the rhythms of a conversation. Sense when to voice your opinion and when to hang back.	
Naturalistic	■ Use your ability to recognize patterns to evaluate communication situations. Employ patterns that work well and avoid those that do not. ■ When appropriate, make an analogy from the natural world to clarify a point in a conversation.	

Keep Your Balance

No one has equal strengths in critical and creative thinking. Effective problem solvers and decision makers are able to assess their abilities, develop creative ideas that maximize their strengths and support their weaknesses, and take action. Staying as balanced as possible requires that you:

- Use what you've learned in this chapter and the rest of the text to maximize your critical- and creative-thinking skills
- Reflect on what you do well and focus on strengthening weaker skills
- Engage your emotional and social intelligence as you solve problems and make decisions
- Believe in your skills as a thinker and a doer

In school, in your personal life, and at work, you will face obstacles of all kinds. Use what you learned here about questioning and thinking to face those obstacles, work through them, and move toward a better place.

Creativity comes from trust. Trust your instincts. And never hope more than you work.

Rita Mae Brown, writer and poet

Habit for Success

create and imagine

Below are examples of how you can put this habit into action in different situations. Use the three spaces to add your own ideas for actions you can accomplish now or in the future. Be specific, and be realistic.

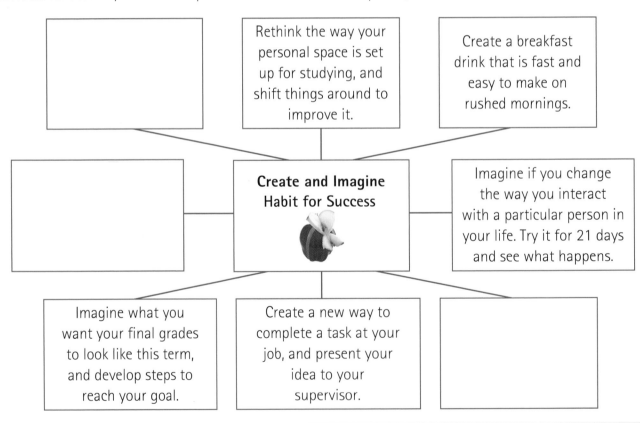

Rethink the way your personal space is set up for studying, and shift things around to improve it.

Create a breakfast drink that is fast and easy to make on rushed mornings.

Create and Imagine Habit for Success

Imagine if you change the way you interact with a particular person in your life. Try it for 21 days and see what happens.

Imagine what you want your final grades to look like this term, and develop steps to reach your goal.

Create a new way to complete a task at your job, and present your idea to your supervisor.

Note the Important Points

Why is it important to ask and answer questions?

How can you ask useful questions?

_____

_____

How can you improve your critical-thinking skills?

Name four ways that you can analyze information.

1. _____   2. _____

3. _____   4. _____

What is the difference between a fact and an opinion?

_____

_____

How can you improve your creative-thinking skills?

Give two examples of creativity that do not involve music, visual arts, or performing.

1. _____

2. _____

Name two strategies you can use to build your ability to think creatively.

1. _____

2. _____

Critical and Creative Thinking

How can you solve problems and make decisions effectively?

Name the steps of the problem-solving and decision-making path.

_____

_____

_____

Critical Thinking
applying learning to life

Make an Important Decision

Put the decision-making process to work on something that matters to you. Use a separate sheet of paper if you need more space.

Step 1: Define the decision.   First, describe an important decision that you need to make soon. (Example: Should you take a part-time job?)

_____

_____

What goal are you working toward? (Example: You are trying to pay your tuition bill.)

_____

_____

Step 2: Examine needs.   Who and what will be affected by your decision? How will they be affected? (Example: How might your work schedule and your increased income have a positive or negative effect on your family and friends?)

_____

_____

_____

_____

Step 3: Name possible options. Look at any options you can imagine. Consider options even if they seem impossible or unlikely; you can evaluate them later. Some decisions only have two options (such as to look for a new apartment mate or not); others have more. List two possible options for your decision. (Examples: Take fewer courses to make room in my schedule to work or step out for a year and work full time to save money.)

Option 1: _____

Option 2: _____

Step 4: Evaluate potential effects. What might result from choosing each option?

Option 1: _____

Positive effects: _____

Negative effects: _____

Option 2: _____

Positive effects: _____

Negative effects: _____

Consider whether you or someone else you know ever made a similar decision. If so, what can you learn from that decision?

_____

_____

Step 5: Decide on a plan and take action. Taking your entire analysis into account, decide what to do. Write your decision here.

_____

_____

Next is perhaps the most important part of the process: <u>Act on your decision</u>.

Step 6: Evaluate the result. After you take action, evaluate how things turn out. What were the effects on you? On others? On the situation? To what extent were they positive, negative, or mixed? List two effects here, circle whether each was positive or negative, and explain your evaluation.

Effect: _____

Positive/Negative _____

Why? _____

_____

Effect: _____

Positive/Negative _____

Why? _____

_____

Final evaluation: Think about the entire process and indicate whether you think you made the right decision and why. List any adjustments you could have made to improve the outcome.

_____

_____

_____

_____

_____

_____

Team Building

collaborative solutions

Solve a Problem

On a 3-by-5 card or a plain sheet of paper, each student in the class writes an academic problem; this could be specific to one class or general to all classes. Problems might involve a fear, a challenge, or a roadblock. Students hand these in without names. The instructor writes the list on the board.

Divide into groups of two to four. Each group chooses a different problem to work on. Use the empty problem-solving flowchart (Key 5.11 on the next page) to fill in your work.

1. **Define the problem.** Start by stating your specific problem. Together, explore what is causing the problem and what negative effects come from it.

2. **Examine the problem.** Pick it apart to see what's happening. Gather information from all group members, verify facts, and go beyond assumptions.

3. **Generate possible solutions.** From the most likely causes, derive possible solutions. Record all the ideas that group members offer. After 10 minutes or so, each group member should choose one possible solution to evaluate.

4. **Evaluate each solution.** Independently, each group member should take a couple of minutes to weigh potential positive and negative effects of this solution and think about how the solution addresses the causes of the problem. Is it a good one? Will it work?

5. **Choose a solution.** Group members then come together, share observations and recommendations, and take a vote: Which solution is the best? Try to find the solution that most people agree on, or consider combining elements of different solutions to create a new one. Then, together, come up with a plan for putting your solution to work.

6. **Evaluate your solution.** As a group, discuss whether you think the chosen solution can be successful. List the positive and negative effects you think it may have.

DEFINE PROBLEM HERE: ANALYZE THE PROBLEM

Use boxes below to list possible solutions:

POTENTIAL POSITIVE EFFECTS	SOLUTION #1	POTENTIAL NEGATIVE EFFECTS
List for each solution:		*List for each solution:*

SOLUTION #2

SOLUTION #3

Now choose the solution you think is best—circle it and make it happen.

ACTUAL POSITIVE EFFECTS	ACTION TAKEN	ACTUAL NEGATIVE EFFECTS
List for chosen solution:		List for chosen solution:

FINAL EVALUATION: Was it a good or bad solution?

Source: Based on heuristic created by Frank T. Lyman Jr. and George Eley, 1985.

Test Prep: Start It Now

create
and
imagine

Use Your Analytical Thinking Skills to Broaden Your Knowledge

Many essay tests require you to take your thinking beyond recall and into the realm of critical thinking. Name a course you are currently taking that will have at least one essay test:

_____

Now, name an important topic in the course that you need to know inside out.

_____

On a separate sheet of paper or on a computer file, use what you learned on pages 130–136 to prepare yourself for the test. Create notes on:

- Themes and patterns that define the topic

- Facts and opinions about this topic and evidence that supports them

- How parts of this topic are similar to or different from one another as well as other topics

- Causes and effects that are part of this topic

- Arguments you might make to support your point of view

- Assumptions that people tend to make about this topic

When you are done, you should be ready to handle an essay question on your chosen topic.

Answers to perception puzzles on p. 140
First puzzle: A duck or a rabbit
Second puzzle: A face or a musician
Third puzzle: Lines or the letter E

memory

maximizing recall for test success

tammy is studying hard—in six-hour stretches if she can keep her eyes open—for mid-terms coming at the end of the month. She reads her textbook and class notes over and over again and, to be sure the material is fresh in her mind, she studies until four in the morning before each test. When she gets back her grades, she is shocked: a C+ in two courses, a C in a third, and a C– in a fourth. "How could this have happened?" she groans to a friend. "I studied so hard. I really thought this stuff was in my brain."

In this chapter. . .

you explore answers to the following questions:

© Kristin Piljay/Pearson Science/Pearson Education

put your senses to work

Note—and then look beyond—what you see and hear. Open your sensory pathways up to all kinds of information. Using all five senses as you learn can help you lock information into long-term memory in a meaningful way.

- Real People Put Their Senses to Work   *p. 166*

- Powerful Questions about Putting Your Senses to Work   *p. 180*

- Habit Summary   *p. 181*

- Test Prep: Start It Now   *p. 185*

How Does Memory Work?

Memory forms the foundation for both learning and test success. Doing well on exams requires that you understand and memorize key information. Memorization puts concepts, facts, processes, formulas, and so on at your fingertips so you can answer knowledge-based questions.

Memorization also gives you the tools to tackle higher level thinking questions. Moving from lower thinking levels (knowledge and understanding) to higher ones (application, analysis, synthesis, and evaluation) requires that you have good recall of information. You will study this concept, known as Bloom's Taxonomy, in Chapter 7.

To avoid Tammy's struggle, you need to retain what you learn. This chapter provides a host of memory-improvement techniques that you can make your own with a positive attitude and active involvement. Your first step is to explore how memory works.

Repetition can reinforce memory. This student is comparing classroom notes to her text, strengthening her memory of the information by reading it again in the chapter.

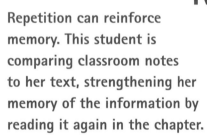

© Patrick White/Merrill Education

The Information Processing Model of Memory

Memory refers to the way the brain stores and recalls information or experiences that are acquired through the five senses. While you take in thousands of pieces of information every second—everything from the shape and color of your chair to how your history text describes Abraham Lincoln's presidency—you remember few. Unconsciously, your brain sorts through stimuli and stores only what it considers important.

The more mental gymnastics you do, the more agile and the quicker your brain becomes.

Nathan Tublitz, University of Oregon neurobiologist[1]

Sensory registers
brain filters through which sensory information enters the brain and is sent to short-term memory.

Look at Key 6.1 as you read how the brain forms lasting memories:

1. Raw information, gathered through the five senses, reaches the brain.

2. This information enters **sensory registers**, where it stays for only seconds.

3. You then choose to pay attention to some information in the sensory register. When you selectively look, listen, smell, taste, or feel the information, you move it into **short-term memory**, also known as working memory, which contains what you are thinking at any moment and makes information available for further processing. Short-term memory lasts no more than about 30 seconds and has limited storage.

Key 6.1 Information processing model of memory

LONG-TERM MEMORY
(PERMANENT MEMORY STORAGE) ⑤

④ REHEARSAL   ⑥ RETRIEVAL

SHORT-TERM MEMORY
OR WORKING MEMORY ③

SENSORY REGISTERS
(SENSORY MEMORY) ②

①

Short-term Memory
the brain's temporary information storehouse in which information remains for a few seconds.

Long-term Memory
the brain's permanent information storehouse from which information can be retrieved.

By the way . . .

research shows that even short-term stress can interfere with cell communication in the learning and memory regions of the brain. When stress eases, memory returns to normal.[2]

4. Through *rote rehearsal*—the process of repeating information to yourself or even out loud—you keep information in short-term memory. (You use rote rehearsal when dialing a phone number you just learned.) This is only temporary learning unless you move the information into long-term memory.

5. You keep information in **long-term memory** through diligent, active rehearsal over time. Long-term memory is the storage house for everything you know from Civil War battle dates to the lyrics of a favorite song. There are no limits to how much information long-term memory can hold or how long it can hold it.
Long-term memory has three separate storage houses:

- **Storage of procedural memory.** This area stores information about *procedures*, or, in other words, how to do things—ride a bike, drive a car, blow into the mouthpiece of a trombone. It takes awhile to develop these memories, but they are difficult to lose.
- **Storage of declarative memory.** Memories of facts, concepts, formulas, etc. are stored here. These are relatively easy to learn but are easy to forget without continual review.
- **Storage of episodic memory.** Memories of events linked to personal experiences are stored here.

6. When you need a piece of information from long-term memory, the brain retrieves it and places it in short-term memory. On test day, this enables you to choose the right answer on a multiple-choice question or lay out a reasoned, fact-based argument for an essay question.

The movement of information into the sensory register, then into short-term and long-term memory, then back again into short-term memory strengthens the connections among brain cells, called *neurons*. Memories are built at the *synapses*—the junctions through which brain cells communicate. When you learn an algebra formula, for example, your brain forms new connections. Every time you review the formula, the connections get stronger.

Why You Forget

Problems like head injuries and poor nutrition can cause memory problems, but the most common reason that information fails to stay in long-term memory is ineffective studying—not doing what is needed to retain what you learn. As Key 6.2 shows, retaining information over time requires continual review. You are still learning information 10 minutes after you hear it the first time. If you review the material over time—after 24 hours, after a week, a month, six months, and more—you will hold onto the knowledge. If you do not review, the neural connections will weaken, and eventually you will forget.

In a classic study conducted in 1885, researcher Herman Ebbinghaus memorized a list of meaningless three-letter words such as CEF and LAZ. He then examined how quickly he forgot them. Within one hour, he had forgotten more than 50% of what he had learned; after two days, he knew less than 30% of the memorized words. Although Ebbinghaus's recall of the nonsense syllables remained fairly stable after that, his experiment shows how fragile

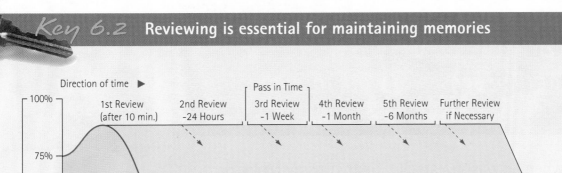

Direction of time ▶

Pass in Time

| 1st Review (after 10 min.) | 2nd Review –24 Hours | 3rd Review –1 Week | 4th Review –1 Month | 5th Review –6 Months | Further Review if Necessary |

Amount Recalled

100%

75%

50%

25%

0%

Area of maintained knowledge for person who does review

Area of maintained knowledge for person who does not review

1 day

2 days

To Long-Term Memory

Source: From *Use Both Sides of Your Brain* by Tony Buzan, © 1974, 1983 by Tony Buzan. Used by permission of Dutton, a division of Penguin Group (USA) Inc.

memory can be—even when you take the time and expend the energy to memorize information.[3]

If forgetting is so common, why do some people have better memories than others? Some may have an inborn talent. More often, though, they succeed because they actively and consistently use techniques for improving recall.

How Can You Improve Your Memory?

As you learn new material, your goal is to anchor information in long-term memory. Memory strategies will help you succeed.

Have Purpose, Intention, and Emotional Connection

Why can you remember the lyrics to dozens of popular songs but not the functions of the pancreas? Why can you remember where you were on September 11, 2001, the day the World Trade Center towers were attacked, but not how to record business transactions for your accounting course? Perhaps this is because you have an emotional tie to the lyrics and what happened on 9-11. When you care about something, your brain responds differently, and you learn and remember more easily.

Henry Gustav Molaison

A man without a memory[4]

In 1935, when he was 9 years old, Henry Gustav Molaison was run down by a bicycle. He fell and hit his head hard on the pavement. Soon after, he began suffering severe seizures, which worsened over the years.

By the time Henry was 27, he endured as many as 10 seizures a day. Blacking out, convulsing, and unable to work, he was desperate for help and agreed to undergo experimental surgery.

His surgeon inserted a metal tube into his brain and removed two finger-sized pieces of tissue from a portion of the brain called the hippocampus. The operation reduced Henry's seizures but robbed him of the ability to form *current* memories. His only lasting memories were of his early life.

Brain researcher David Amaral explained how this changed Henry's life. When Henry was in his 70s, "I asked him to describe what he looked like. He said without hesitation that he had dark curly hair. He was recalling what he looked like before the surgery. He didn't have the ability to remember that he had aged. Think about it. Every time Henry looked in the mirror, he saw a stranger."

Stop and Think

Imagine living without the ability to form memories. Would you be the same person? Would you be able to fulfill your goals and dreams?

From the time of his surgery in 1953 to his death in 2008, Henry was the most studied individual in medical science. "Before Henry, scientists had no idea how memory was organized," said brain researcher Larry Squire. From their work with Henry, they learned that two separate brain systems controlled memory formation. The first, known as declarative memory and located in the hippocampus, is responsible for the ability to remember names, faces, and new experiences; store them in long-term memory; and retrieve them when needed. The second memory system, located in another brain region, controls procedural memory (how to perform physical actions like walking). This part of Henry's brain was unaffected.

Stop and Think

Thinking about the separate declarative and procedural memory systems, consider your own ability to form memories. Do you have an easier time with one form of memory than the other?

Remarkably, Henry's short-term memory was strong—he could hold onto thoughts for about 20 seconds—but without a hippocampus, he couldn't move them into long-term memory. So each time he met one of his long-time researchers, it was like he was meeting him for the first time.

For many years after his surgery, Henry lived with his parents. He was able to do the ordinary tasks of life—making lunch, watching television, mowing the lawn—by relying on what he remembered from his pre-surgery years. He seemed to sense that he was part of a major breakthrough, although he was not sure what it was. One thing that he never forgot was his own name.

Think about Henry and Think about Yourself

What does Henry's story tell you about the connection between who you are and what you know and remember? Respond to this statement: *Knowing how memories are formed convinces me that my brain has enormous power to gather and remember sensory information and that I can use that power to succeed.*

© Kaylin Bowers/AP Images

Knowing that he was dying of pancreatic cancer, Professor **Randy Pausch** gave a "last lecture" about what mattered most to him and about the preciousness of every experience and sensation. His book, titled *The Last Lecture,* is read on college campuses all over the country, and videos of his lecture are available on YouTube.

put
sens
worl

To achieve the same results in school, try to create a purpose and will to remember by becoming emotionally involved with what you are studying. For example, an accounting student might think of a friend who is running a small business and needs to keep his records in order—to pay bills on time, to record income, to meet tax payments. Without proper accounting, the business cannot operate. Putting himself in the position of his friend's accountant, the student connects learning accounting principles with making a difference in a friend's life.

Understand What You Memorize

Something that has meaning is easier to recall than something that makes little sense. This basic principle applies to everything you study. Figure out logical connections, and use these connections to help you learn. For example, in a plant biology course, memorize plant families; in a history course, memorize events by linking them in a cause-and-effect chain.

When you are having trouble remembering something new, think about how the new idea fits into what you already know. A simple example: If you can't remember what a word means, look at the word's root, prefix, or suffix. Knowing that the root *bellum* means "war" and the prefix *ante* means "before" will help you recognize that *antebellum* means "before the war."

Use Critical Thinking

Critical thinking encourages you to associate new information with what you already know. Imagine you have to remember information about the signing of the Treaty of Versailles, which ended World War I. How can critical thinking help?

- Recall everything that you know about the topic.
- Think about how this event is similar to other events in history.
- Consider what is different and unique about this treaty in comparison with other treaties.
- Explore the causes that led up to this event, and look at the event's effects.
- Evaluate how successful you think the treaty was.

This critical exploration makes it easier to remember the material you are studying.

Limit and Organize the Items You Are Processing

This involves three activities:

Separate main points from unimportant details. Ask yourself, "What is the most important information?" Highlight only the key points in your texts, and write notes in the margins about central ideas (see Key 7.6).

Identify the course that interests you the most this term. Engaging your intrapersonal intelligence, think about the roles that memorization and critical thinking are likely to play in your studying. Then complete the following:

Describe some material you have to memorize:

_____

_____

_____

Describe specific ways in which you will use critical thinking to learn and retain the material:

_____

_____

_____

Evaluate how the material you have to remember will be important to your working and/or personal life after college. Describe the connection:

_____

_____

_____

_____

Chunking
placing disconnected information into smaller units that are easier to remember.

Divide material into manageable sections. Generally, when material is short and easy to understand, studying it from start to finish improves recall. With longer material, however, you may benefit from dividing it into logical sections, mastering each section, putting all the sections together, and then testing your memory of all the material. **Chunking** increases the capacity of short-term and long-term memory. For example, while it is hard to remember these 10 digits—4808371557—it is easier to remember them in three chunks—480 837 1557. In general, try to limit groups to 10 items or fewer.

Day 8 (in eight days, you'll be taking a test)

Planning Day

- List everything that may be on the exam. (Check your syllabus and class notes; talk with your instructor.)
- Divide the material into four learning chunks.
- Decide on a study schedule for the next seven days—when you will study, with whom you will study, the materials you need, etc.

Day 7 (Countdown: seven days to go)

Study Chunk A

- Use the techniques described in Chapters 7–9 to study Chunk A.
- Memorize key concepts, facts, formulas, etc. that may be on the test.
- Take an active approach to learning: take practice tests, summarize what you read in your own words, use critical thinking to connect ideas, etc.

Day 6 (Countdown: six days to go)

- *Use the same techniques to study chunk B.*

Day 5 (Countdown: five days to go)

- *Use the same techniques to study chunk C.*

Day 4 (Countdown: four days to go)

- *Use the same techniques to study chunk D.*

Day 3 (Countdown: three days to go)

- *Combine and review chunks A and B.*

Day 2 (Countdown: two days to go)

- *Combine and review chunks C and D.*

Day 1 (Countdown: one day to go)

Put it all together: Review chunks A, B, C, and D.

- Take an active approach to review all four chunks.
- Make sure you have committed every concept, fact, formula, process, etc. to memory.
- Take a timed practice test. Write out complete answers so that concepts and words stick in your memory.
- Create a sheet with important information to memorize (again) on test day.

Test Day—Do Your Best Work

- Look at your last-minute study sheet right before you enter the test room so that difficult information sticks.
- As soon as you get your test, write down critical facts on the back of the paper.

The eight-day study plan in Key 6.3 relies on chunking as it links test success to memorization.[5] The plan starts eight days before a big exam and ends on test day.

Use organizational tools. Rely on an outline, a think link, or another organizational tool to record material and the logical connections among the elements (see Chapter 9 for more on note taking). These tools expose gaps in your understanding as they help you study and learn.

Recite, Rehearse, and Write

When you *recite* material, you repeat key concepts aloud, in your own words, to aid memorization. You also summarize these concepts. *Rehearsing* is similar to reciting but is done silently. *Writing* is reciting on paper. All three processes actively involve you in learning and remembering material. Use these steps to get the greatest benefit:

- Focus as you read on *main ideas*, which are usually found in the topic sentences of paragraphs (see Chapter 7). Then recite, rehearse, or write the ideas down.

- Convert each main idea into a key word, phrase, or visual image—something that is easy to recall and that will set off a chain of memories that will bring you back to the original material. Write each key word or phrase on an index card.

- One by one, look at the key words on your cards and recite, rehearse, or write all the associated information you can recall. Check your recall against the original material.

These steps are part of the process of consolidating and summarizing lecture and text notes as you study (see Chapter 9).

Reciting, rehearsing, and writing involve more than rereading material and then parroting words out loud, in your head, or on paper. Because rereading does not necessarily require involvement, you can reread without learning, which Tammy may have done in her marathon study sessions. However, you cannot help but think and learn when you convert text concepts into key points, rewrite main ideas as key words and phrases, and assess what you know and what you still need to learn.

Study During Short, Frequent Sessions

You can improve your chances of remembering material if you learn it more than once. A pattern of short sessions, say three 20-minute study sessions, followed by brief periods of rest is more effective than continual studying with little or no rest. (Tammy would probably have retained more had she followed this advice.)

Try studying on your own or with a classmate during breaks in your schedule. Although studying between classes isn't for everyone, you may find that it can help you remember more. If you study in bed—even for short periods—try to sit up straight to avoid dozing.

When you finish studying for an exam the next day, try to go to sleep. Sleep improves memory as it reduces interference from new information. When you can't go to sleep right away, put off studying other subjects until your exam is over. When studying for several tests at once, avoid studying two similar subjects back to back. Your memory may be more accurate when you study history after biology rather than chemistry after biology.

By the way . . .

shortchanging your sleep during the week impairs your ability to remember and learn, even if you try to make up for it by sleeping all weekend.[6]

Practice the Middle

When you are trying to learn something, you usually study some material first, attack other material in the middle of the session, and approach still other topics at the end. The weak link is likely to be what you study midway. Knowing this, try to give this material special attention.

Use Flash Cards

Flash cards give you short, repeated review sessions that provide immediate feedback. Use the front of a 3-by-5-inch index card to write a word, idea, or phrase you want to remember. Use the back for a definition, explanation, and other key facts. Key 6.4 shows two flash cards used to study for a psychology exam.

Here are some suggestions for making the most of your flash cards:

- **Use the cards as a self-test.** As you go through them, divide them into two piles—the material you know and the material you are learning.
- **Carry the cards with you and review them frequently.** You'll learn the most if you start using cards early in the course, well ahead of exam time.
- **Shuffle the cards and learn the information in various orders.** This will help you avoid putting too much focus on some items and not enough on others.
- **Test yourself in both directions.** First, look at the terms and provide the definitions or explanations. Then turn the cards over and reverse the process.

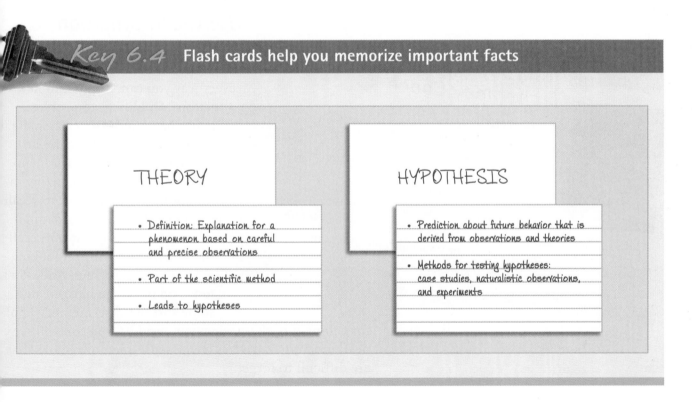

Key 6.4 Flash cards help you memorize important facts

THEORY

- Definition: Explanation for a phenomenon based on careful and precise observations
- Part of the scientific method
- Leads to hypotheses

HYPOTHESIS

- Prediction about future behavior that is derived from observations and theories
- Methods for testing hypotheses: case studies, naturalistic observations, and experiments

- **Reduce the stack as you learn.** Eliminate cards when you are sure of your knowledge. As you watch the pile shrink, your motivation will grow. As test time approaches, put all the cards together again for a final review.

Use Audio Strategies

Although all students can benefit from these strategies, they are especially useful if you learn best through hearing.

Create audio flash cards. Record short-answer study questions and leave 10 to 15 seconds between questions, so you can answer out loud. Record the correct answer after the pause for immediate feedback. For example, part of a recording for a writing class might say, "Three elements that require analysis before writing are . . . (*10- to 15- second pause*) . . . topic, audience, and purpose."

Use podcasts. Audio segments that are downloadable to your computer or MP3 player, podcasts are especially helpful to students who learn best through listening. Ask your instructors if they intend to make any of their lectures available in podcast format. Podcasts with coaching tips are available on MyStudentSuccessLab.

Technology has made many audio learning and study strategies possible. These students are using MP3 players and other electronic devices to study in the library.

Inside Tips from Joyce, Technology Coach

Several technology tools exist to support your memory. Electronic flash cards enable to you copy and paste articles from the Web and organize them as you would a stack of 3-by-5 cards (example: www.flashcardexchange.com). Another useful tool is mind-mapping software, which enables you to outline your information in a visual way and then turn the visual diagram into a formal outline at the click of a button (example: www.gliffy.com).

Use the Information

In the days after you learn something new, try to use the information in every way you can. Apply it to new situations, and link it to problems. Explain the material to a classmate. Test your knowledge to make sure the material is in long-term memory. "Don't confuse recognizing information with being able to recall it," says learning expert Adam Robinson. "Be sure you can recall the information without looking at your notes for clues. And don't move on until you have created some sort of sense-memory hook for calling it back up when you need it."[7] As you will see next, mnemonic devices create sense-memory hooks that are difficult to forget.

On a scale of 1 to 10, with 1 being the lowest and 10 being the highest, rate yourself on your memory skills. Then indicate where you want to be at the end of this course.

MEMORY SKILL	RATING NOW	RATING GOAL
Making emotional connections with material		
Understanding what you memorize		
Using critical thinking		
Using rehearsal techniques		
Chunking and organizing material		
Getting enough sleep		
Making a smart study schedule		
Practicing material in the middle		
Using flash cards		
Using digital recordings and podcasts		
Using what you just learned		
Using different mnemonic devices		

How Can Mnemonics Boost Recall?

Certain performers entertain audiences by remembering the names of 100 strangers or flawlessly repeating 30 ten-digit numbers. Although these performers probably have superior memories, they also rely on memory techniques, known as **mnemonic devices** (pronounced neh-MAHN-ick), for assistance. Mnemonics include visual images, associations, and acronyms.

Mnemonics depend on vivid associations (relating new information to other information) that engage your emotions. Instead of learning new facts by *rote* (repetitive practice), associations give you a "hook" on which to hang these facts and retrieve them later. Mnemonics make information unforgettable through unusual mental associations and visual pictures.

Mnemonics take time and effort to create, and you'll have to be motivated to remember them. Because of this, use them only when necessary—for instance, to

Mnemonic Devices
memory techniques that use vivid associations and acronyms to link new information to what you already know.

distinguish confusing concepts that consistently trip you up. Also know that no matter how clever they are and how easy they are to remember, *mnemonics have nothing to do with understanding.* Their sole objective is to help you memorize.

Create Visual Images and Associations

Turning information into mental pictures helps improve memory, especially for visual learners. To remember that the Spanish artist Picasso painted *The Three Women,* you might imagine the women in a circle dancing to a Spanish song with a pig and a donkey (pig-asso). The best images involve bright colors, three dimensions, action scenes, inanimate objects with human traits, and humor.

Here is another example: Say you are trying to learn some Spanish vocabulary, including the words *carta, río,* and *dinero.* Instead of relying on rote learning, you might come up with mental images such as those in Key 6.5.

Use Visual Images to Remember Items in a List

Using the *mental walk* strategy, you imagine storing new ideas in familiar locations. Say, for example, that on your next biology test you have to remember the body's major endocrine glands. To do this, think of your route to the library. You pass the college theater, the science center, the bookstore, the cafeteria, the athletic center, and the social science building before reaching the library. At each spot along the way, you "place" a concept you want to learn. You then link the concept with a similar-sounding word that brings to mind a vivid image (see Key 6.6):

- At the campus theater, you imagine bumping into the actor Brad **Pitt** (pituitary gland).
- At the science center, you visualize a body builder with bulging **thighs** (thyroid gland).

Key 6.5 Visual images aid recall

SPANISH WORD	DEFINITION	MENTAL IMAGE
carta	letter	A person pushing a shopping cart filled with letters into a post office.
río	river	A school of sharks rioting in the river. One of the sharks is pulling a banner inscribed with the word *riot*. A killer shark bites off the *t* in riot as he takes charge of the group. "I'm the king of this river," he says.
dinero	money	A man eating lasagna at a dinner. The lasagna is made of layers of money.

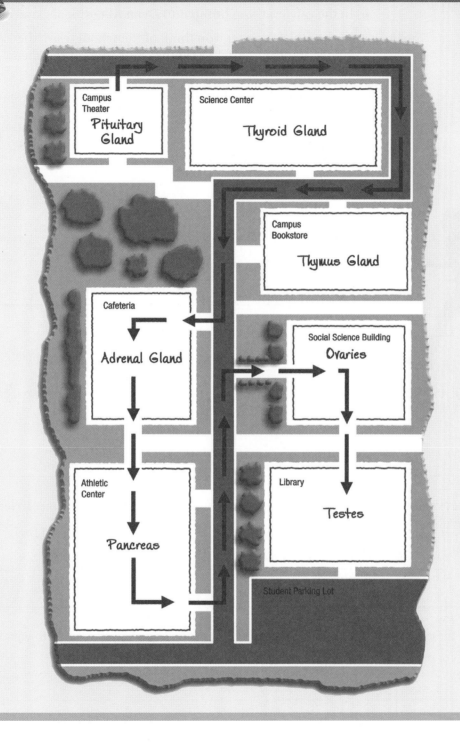

- At the campus bookstore, you envision a second body builder with his **thighs** covered in **mus**tard (thymus gland).
- In the cafeteria, you bump into **Dean Al** (adrenal gland).
- At the athletic center, you think of the school team, the Panthers—nicknamed the Pans—and remember the sound of the cheer "**Pans-R-Us**" (pancreas).
- At the social science building, you imagine receiving a standing **ova**tion (ovaries).
- And at the library, you visualize sitting at a table taking a **test** that is **easy** (testes).

TAKE ACTION
Create Your Own Mnemonic

Identify material you have to memorize for a course. Then complete the following:

Create a mnemonic to help you memorize the details. (If you need more space, use separate paper.)

_____

_____

Describe the images you used in the mnemonic. Were they visual images? Were they sounds? Were they humorous, ridiculous, or colorful?

_____

_____

Why do you think these types of images help you retain information? How did they tap into your visual or your musical intelligence?

_____

_____

_____

_____

Create a Vocabulary Cartoon

Visual cartoons use the *DAP method*—definition, association, and picture—to harness the power of humor to remember challenging vocabulary. Use the following steps to create your own vocabulary cartoons:

Step 1. Write down the new vocabulary word followed by its pronunciation and definition. For example:

> **word: histrionic**
> **pronunciation: (his tree AHN ik)**
> **definition: overly dramatic, theatrical**

Step 2. Think of a link word—an *association*—that rhymes with your word or sounds like it:

> **association: history**

Step 3. Create a *picture* or simple cartoon with the main word and the link word, to serve as a visual mnemonic. Then write a caption that connects the word you are trying to learn with the link word and visually illustrates its meaning:

> **"Professor Bradley liked his history on the histrionic side—with a lot of theatrics."**

Step 4. Use the word in sentences of your own:

> **The histrionic child threw herself on her bed when she didn't get her way.**
> **The histrionic actor's portrayal of the calm professor did not ring true.**

HISTRIONIC
(his tree AHN ik)
overly dramatic, theatrical
Link: HISTORY

Source: Sam Burchers, *Vocabulary Cartoons: Building an Educated Vocabulary with Visual Mnemonics,* Punta Gorda, FL: New Monic Books, 1997, p.40. Reprinted with permission.

Create Acronyms

Another helpful association method involves **acronyms**. In history class, you can remember the Allies during World War II—Britain, America, and Russia—with the acronym BAR. This is an example of a *word acronym*, because the first letters of the items you want to remember spell a word. The word (or words) spelled don't necessarily have to be real words. See Key 6.7 for an acronym—the name Roy G. Biv—that will help you remember the colors of the spectrum.

Other acronyms take the form of an entire sentence, in which the first letter of each word in each sentence stands for the first letter of the memorized term. This is called a *list order acronym*. When astronomy students want to

Acronym
a word formed from the first letters of a series of words created to help you remember the series.

red
orange
yellow
green
blue
indigo
violet

R O Y G B I V

remember the list of planets in order of their distance from the sun (Mercury, Venus, Earth, Mars, Jupiter, Saturn, Uranus, and Neptune), they might learn this sentence: *My very elegant mother just served us nectarines.*

Suppose you want to remember the names of the first six U.S. presidents. You notice that the first letters of their last names—Washington, Adams, Jefferson, Madison, Monroe, and Adams—together read W A J M M A. To remember them, first you might insert an e after the J and create a short nonsense word—*wajemma*. Then, to make sure you don't forget the nonsense word, you might picture the six presidents sitting in a row and wearing pajamas.

Use Songs or Rhymes

Some of the classic mnemonics involve rhymes. This one helps you remember a spelling rule:

> **I before E, except after C, or when sounded like A as in "neighbor" and "weigh." Four exceptions if you please: either, neither, seizure, seize.**

Make up your own poems or songs, linking familiar tunes or rhymes with information you want to remember. Thinking back to the "wajemma" example, imagine that you want to remember the presidents' first names as well. You might set those first names—George, John, Thomas, James, James, and John—to the tune of "Happy Birthday." Or, to extend the history theme, you might use the first musical phrase of the national anthem.

Multiple Intelligence Strategies to Boost Your Memory

Briefly describe a memory problem that you're having in one of your courses.

_____

_____

Now brainstorm potential solutions to your problem, linking each solution to an intelligence. Use the right-hand column to record your ideas.

INTELLIGENCE	SUGGESTED STRATEGIES	USE MI STRATEGIES TO COME UP WITH SOLUTIONS
Verbal–Linguistic	■ Develop a story line for a mnemonic first, then work on the visual images. ■ Write out answers to practice essay questions.	
Logical–Mathematical	■ Create logical groupings that help you memorize knowledge chunks. ■ When you study material in the middle, link it to what comes before and after.	
Bodily–Kinesthetic	■ Create a mnemonic story board on a poster board. Tape the board to a wall and walk back and forth as you memorize. ■ Record information onto a digital recorder and listen as you walk between classes.	
Visual–Spatial	■ Focus on visual mnemonics such as mental walks or vocabulary cartoons. ■ Use markers to add color to the images.	
Interpersonal	■ Do flash-card drills with a study partner. ■ Recite critical material to a study partner.	
Intrapersonal	■ Listen to an audio podcast that reviews test material. ■ Create vocabulary cartoons and test yourself on the material.	
Musical	■ Play music while you brainstorm ideas. ■ Create a mnemonic in the form of a musical rhyme.	
Naturalistic	■ Organize what you have to learn so that you know how everything fits together. ■ Sit outside and go through your flash cards.	

Why Do You Need a Good Memory When You Have the Internet?

With computers, smartphones, and wireless connections bringing the Internet to you whenever you need it, it is reasonable to ask why memorization skills are important when you can look almost everything up. The best answer is because the reservoir of facts in your long-term memory powers your intellectual potential. With a well-stocked reservoir that is constantly being replenished, you can put new ideas together and think of unique approaches to problems. With one that is nearly empty, you are a blank slate.

A final thought: The facts that you store in your memory help define who you are as a person and can lead to fulfilling academic, career, and life choices. If you love baseball and memorize World Series statistics, for example, your passion will make an impression on everyone you meet and will communicate something meaningful about you to friends, teachers, and prospective employers.

POWERFUL QUESTIONS

put your senses to work

Dr. Linus Pauling used his memory of an obscure scientific fact to make a major discovery about the chemical bond and how proteins are structured—one that would win him the Nobel Prize for Chemistry. He made this breakthrough while doodling during a long train ride, which created the environment for an "aha" moment that would change modern medicine.[8]

Have you ever put important ideas together during unexpected times—during a morning shower or an afternoon run, while cooking dinner or looking through a digital photo album? Why do you think unrelated sensory experiences lead to new ideas?

As an airline pilot, "good memorization skills helped me to quickly become familiar with thousands of pages of flight manuals, aircraft limitations, procedures, terminology, etc. I'm sure 'good memorizers' in other professions feel the same way."

Jim Erdos, from a letter in response to a newspaper article on why memorizing sports trivia is good for the brain[9]

Habit for Success

put your senses to work

Below are examples of how you can put this habit into action in different situations. Use the three spaces to add your own ideas for actions you can accomplish now or in the future. Be specific, and be realistic.

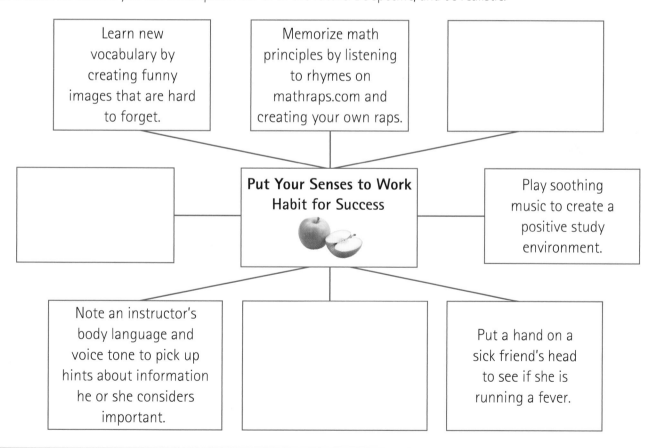

Learn new vocabulary by creating funny images that are hard to forget.	Memorize math principles by listening to rhymes on mathraps.com and creating your own raps.	

Put Your Senses to Work Habit for Success

		Play soothing music to create a positive study environment.
Note an instructor's body language and voice tone to pick up hints about information he or she considers important.		Put a hand on a sick friend's head to see if she is running a fever.

Building Skills
for successful learning

Note the Important Points

How does memory work?

Describe two reasons why memory is the basis for learning.

_____

_____

Describe what each of the following does in the information processing model of memory:

sensory registers _____

short-term memory _____

long-term memory _____

How can you improve your memory?

Describe three memory strategies you learned in this chapter that you are likely to start using.

1. _____

2. _____

3. _____

How can mnemonics boost recall?

Explain how mnemonic devices help you remember material._____

_____

Describe two different types of mnemonics you learned about in the chapter that you are likely to use.

1. _____

2. _____

Why do you need a good memory when you have the Internet?

Explain why it is important to "know something" even when you can easily look it up.

_____

_____

Critical Thinking
applying learning to life

Evaluate Your Memory in Three Different Areas

Next to these classifications of information in long-term memory, write down two examples from your personal experience:

Episodic memory (events)

Sample: I remember the first time I conducted an experiment in chemistry class.

Example #1: _____

Example #2: _____

Declarative memory (facts)

Sample: I know that the electoral college must vote before a new U.S. president is officially elected.

Example #1: _____

Example #2: _____

Procedural memory (motion)

Sample: I know how to type without looking at the keyboard.

Example #1: _____

Example #2: _____

Which type of memory is easiest for you to remember over a long period of time?

_____

Which type of memory is hardest for you to remember over a long period of time?

_____

Most exams test declarative memory. List three actions you can take when you study for your next exam to improve your declarative memory.

1. _____

2. _____

3. _____

Team Building

collaborative solutions

Assess Your Memory and Then Boost Its Power

Gather as a class if there are fewer than 20 people, or divide into two groups if it is larger. Then do the following. (You'll need a timer or a stopwatch.)

- Each person in your group should place at least one item on a table (try to avoid repeats). When all the items are laid out, allow one minute to look at them.
- Then cover the items and have each person list as many items as possible.
- Compare the lists to the actual items to see how you did.
- Talk as a group about the results, what you didn't remember and why, and what helped you remember. List your observations here and on a separate sheet, if necessary.

_____

_____

_____

Now repeat the exercise using a mnemonic device. For example, create a new group of items, and then allow five minutes to look at them and to develop a mnemonic in that time. Then cover the items and make lists again. Finally, talk about whether this helped you remember more items. Write your findings here.

_____

_____

_____

Test Prep: Start It Now

put your
senses to
work

Improve Your Memory for Test Success

Nearly every student has memory challenges that affect test grades. But nearly every student also has the ability to improve. Start here:

Describe your biggest memory challenge that limits your ability to remember test material.

_____

_____

Describe two strategies you learned in this chapter that you will use to get better test results. Focus on engaging your senses.

1. _____

_____

2. _____

_____

Now use these techniques to improve your grade on an upcoming test:

Course and date of test: _____

Date when you will use each technique. (Place a checkmark in the box after you use it.)

Technique #1: _____

Technique #2: _____

Evaluate the results: How do you think these techniques improved your test performance?

_____

_____

_____

_____

Time for a Change: take steps to improve a habit for success

For this exercise, refer back to the results of the assessment you took in Chapter 1 on page 19.

First: Write the second of your three *strongest* Habits for Success here (a different strong habit than the one you explored on page 93). _____

_____

Why does it work for you? Name a result of this habit that helps you solve problems and move toward important goals. _____

_____

Now: Write the second of your three *least developed* Habits for Success here (a different habit than the one you explored on page 93). _____

_____

Why do you want to develop this habit—in other words, what positive effect do you think it will have on your ability to solve problems and achieve goals? _____

_____

_____

Focus on this challenging habit more carefully. Name two specific, short-term actions you can take to power up this habit. (Refer to the actions you listed in Chapter 1's Take Action exercise on page 14 if they connect to this habit).

1. _____

2. _____

Name a support person, and briefly describe your plan for communicating your progress and getting encouragement (for example, have your person call, e-mail, or text you on a regular basis).

_____

_____

Remember, the way to make a habit stick is to do it over and over again over a period of at least 21 days. *Right now,* commit to checking your progress on a regular basis over the next three weeks, using whatever method you prefer.

Describe the method you will use to track your habit development.

What will you use? (example: date book, electronic planner, cell phone alarm, e-mail alert)

_____

When and how often will you use it? (example: every day at bedtime, every other day when I get up, twice a week after a particular class)

_____

It's time for a change—put your plan in motion *today*. You will revisit your progress at the end of Chapter 9 (page 277) as well as in Chapter 12.

Revisit Your Progress

Look back at the Time for a Change exercise at the end of Chapter 3 on page 93. Take a moment to describe how you have developed this habit, including how consistently you perform your chosen actions, how well you document your progress, the helpfulness of your support system, and whether you are satisfied with your progress. If you are not satisfied, describe how you will adjust your actions in order to move ahead.

_____

_____

_____

_____

_____

_____

_____

_____

reading and studying

focusing on print and online materials

hanh never had trouble keeping up with her high school reading assignments, but after four weeks of college she is already snowed under. With midterms coming in two weeks, she stays awake at night thinking about how much she has to learn. It seems as if all the reading she has done this term—particularly what she has read on the computer—has gone in one side of her brain and out the other, so she feels she has to start at the beginning. She has the sense that *the way* she is reading may be a problem, but it worked for her in the past, so why change now?

In this chapter . . .

you explore answers to the following questions:

HOW can SQ3R help you own what you read? p. 190

WHAT improves reading comprehension? p. 200

HOW do you customize a text with highlighting and notes? p. 205

HOW can you read online materials effectively? p. 208

Habit for Success

ask questions

Questions are the backbone of learning. They help you see what you do—and don't— understand. Asking questions as you read print and online materials will broaden and anchor your knowledge.

How Can SQ3R Help You Own What You Read?

Like Hanh, you may be surprised at how much reading there is in college. On any given day, you may be faced with assignments like these:

- A textbook chapter on the history of South African apartheid (world history)
- A research study linking sleep deprivation and memory problems (psychology)
- A journal article on police in society (criminal justice)
- A technical manual on the design of antivirus programs (computer software design)

Your succcess in every course depends on handling this load with a can-do attitude and an action plan. This chapter will help you improve your **reading comprehension** so that you don't fall into the trap that snared Hanh—turning pages without learning. When you learn concepts that you thought were impossible on first reading, you'll be proud of your ability to persist.

The place to begin is with the SQ3R study system, which was developed decades ago by Francis Robinson.[1] SQ3R is an acronym for *survey, question, read, recite,* and *review.* As you move through the stages of SQ3R, you will skim and scan your text. **Skimming** involves the rapid reading of such chapter elements as section introductions and conclusions, boldfaced or italicized terms, pictures, tables, charts, and chapter summaries. The goal of

Reading Comprehension
understanding concepts and being able to show your knowledge on exams and use it to solve problems.

Skimming
rapid reading of key chapter elements to get an overview and find main ideas.

Reading is to the mind what exercise is to the body.

Sir Richard Steele, 18th century Irish journalist and playwright

skimming is a quick construction of the main ideas. **Scanning** involves the careful search for particular information.

SQ3R works best if you adapt it to your needs. For example, you and another classmate may focus on elements in a different order when you survey, write different questions, or favor different review strategies. Explore strategies, evaluate what works, and then make the system your own. (Note that SQ3R is not appropriate for literature.)

Scanning
rapid reading in search of specific information.

Survey

Surveying, the first stage in SQ3R, involves previewing, or pre-reading, your assignment. Most textbooks include elements that provide a big-picture overview of the main ideas and themes. You need the big picture to make sense of the information nuggets contained in the text and to learn the order of topics and how extensively each is covered.

Front matter.   Skim the *table of contents* for the chapter titles, the main topics in each chapter, and the order in which they will be covered, as well as special features. Then skim the *preface* in which the author tells you what the book will cover and her point of view. For example, the preface for the American history text *Out of Many* states that it highlights "the experiences of diverse communities of Americans in the unfolding story of our country."[2] In other words, cultural diversity is a central theme.

Chapter elements.   Generally, text chapters use different devices to structure the material and highlight content, including:

- Chapter title, which establishes the topic and often the author's perspective
- Chapter introduction, outline, list of objectives, or list of key topics
- First-, second-, and third-level headings, including those in question form
- Information in the margins including definitions, quotes, questions, and exercises
- Tables, charts, photographs, and captions that express important concepts
- Sidebar boxed features that are connected to text themes

When you have a textbook reading assignment, find an environment that works for you—this student prefers the library—and survey the key elements of your chapter first.

© iStockphoto.com

- Different styles or arrangements of type (**boldface**, *italics*, <u>underlining</u>, larger fonts, bullet points, boxed text) that call attention to vocabulary or important ideas
- End-of-chapter summary that reviews chapter content
- Review questions and exercises that help you understand and apply content

In Key 7.1, which shows a typical page from the college textbook *Psychology: An Introduction,* by Charles G. Morris and Albert A. Maisto, how many elements do you recognize? How do these elements help you grasp the subject even before you read it?[3]

Back matter.   Some texts include a *glossary,* which defines text terms. You may also find an *index* to help you locate topics and a *bibliography* that lists additional readings.

Question

Your next step is to *ask questions* to discover knowledge on your own. As you pose questions and find answers, you teach yourself the material.

Step 1: Ask yourself what you know about the topic.   Before you start, take a few minutes to summarize in writing what you already know about the topic, if anything. In all cases, but especially in your major, concepts you learn in introductory courses prepare you for higher level courses. For example, while you may learn the term *market research* in an introductory business text, an upper level text may link market research to consumer behavior.

Step 2: Write questions linked to chapter headings.   Next, examine chapter headings and, on a separate page or in the text margins, write questions linked to them. When you encounter a reading without headings, divide the material into logical sections, and then develop questions based on what you think is the main idea of each section.

Key 7.2 shows how this works. The column on the left contains primary- and secondary-level headings from a section of *Out of Many.*[4] The

Key 7.1   Create questions from headings

Freedom and Resistance	What did freedom mean for slaves, and how did they resist their oppression?
African American Religion	What role did religion play in sustaining the enslaved?
Other Kinds of Resistance	What did slaves do to escape?
Slave Revolts	What were slave revolts, and how often did they occur?
Free African Americans	How many slave owners freed their slaves, and how did their actions affect the mood of the South?

Classical (or Pavlovian) conditioning The type of learning in which a response naturally elicited by one stimulus comes to be elicited by a different, formerly neutral stimulus.

Unconditioned stimulus (US) A stimulus that invariably causes an organism to respond in a specific way.

Unconditioned response (UR) A response that takes place in an organism whenever an unconditioned stimulus occurs.

Conditioned stimulus (CS) An originally neutral stimulus that is paired with an unconditioned stimulus and eventually produces the desired response in an organism when presented alone.

Conditioned response (CR) After conditioning, the response an organism produces when only a conditioned stimulus is presented.

you are experiencing insight. When you imitate the steps of professional dancers you saw last night on television, you are demonstrating observational learning. Like conditioning, cognitive learning is one of our survival strategies. Through cognitive processes, we learn which events are safe and which are dangerous without having to experience those events directly. Cognitive learning also gives us access to the wisdom of people who lived hundreds of years ago, and it will give people living hundreds of years from now some insight into our experiences and way of life.

Our discussion begins with *classical conditioning*. This simple kind of learning serves as a convenient starting point for examining what learning is and how it can be observed.

Classical Conditioning

How did Pavlov's discovery of classical conditioning help to shed light on learning?

Ivan Pavlov (1849–1936), a Russian physiologist who was studying digestive processes, discovered classical conditioning almost by accident. Because animals salivate when food is placed in their mouths, Pavlov inserted tubes into the salivary glands of dogs to measure how much saliva they produced when they were given food. He noticed, however, that the dogs salivated before the food was in their mouths: The mere sight of food made them drool. In fact, they even drooled at the sound of the experimenter's footsteps. This aroused Pavlov's curiosity. What was making the dogs salivate even before they had the food in their mouths? How had they learned to salivate in response to the sound of the experimenter's approach?

To answer these questions, Pavlov set out to teach the dogs to salivate when food was not present. He devised an experiment in which he sounded a bell just before the food was brought into the room. A ringing bell does not usually make a dog's mouth water but, after hearing the bell many times just before getting fed, Pavlov's dogs began to salivate as soon as the bell rang. It was as if they had learned that the bell signaled the appearance of food, and their mouths watered on cue even if no food followed. The dogs had been conditioned to salivate in response to a new stimulus—the bell—that would not normally have prompted that response (Pavlov, 1927). Figure 5–1, shows one of Pavlov's procedures in which the bell has been replaced by a touch to the dog's leg just before food is given.

Elements of Classical Conditioning

Generally speaking, **classical (or Pavlovian) conditioning** involves pairing an *involuntary* response (for example, salivation) that is usually evoked by one stimulus with a different, formerly neutral stimulus (such as a bell or a touch on the leg). Pavlov's experiment illustrates the four basic elements of classical conditioning. The first is an **unconditioned stimulus (US)**, such as food, which invariably prompts a certain reaction—salivation, in this case. That reaction—the **unconditioned response (UR)**—is the second element and always results from the unconditioned stimulus: Whenever the dog is given food (US), its mouth waters (UR). The third element is the neutral stimulus—the ringing bell—which is called the **conditioned stimulus (CS)**. At first, the conditioned stimulus is said to be "neutral" with respect to the desired response (salivation), because dogs do not salivate at the sound of a bell unless they have been conditioned to react in this way by repeatedly presenting the CS and US together. Frequent pairing of the CS and US produces the fourth element in the classical conditioning process: the **conditioned response (CR)**. The conditioned response is the behavior that the animal has learned in response to the conditioned stimulus. Usually, the unconditioned response and the conditioned

TAKE ACTION
Survey a Text

Surveying improves with practice, so use this or another text to fine-tune your skills.

Skim the front matter, including the table of contents and preface. What does this material tell you about the theme? About the book's approach and point of view?

_____

_____

Now look at a typical chapter. List devices that structure and organize the content. (Pay special attention to tables and charts if you are a visual-spatial learner.)

_____

_____

After skimming the chapter, what do you know about the material? What elements helped you skim quickly?

_____

_____

Finally, skim the back matter. What back matter elements can you identify?

_____

_____

How do you plan to use each of these elements when you begin studying?

_____

_____

column on the right rephrases these headings in question form. There is no "correct" set of questions. Given the same headings, you could create different questions. Your goal is to engage the material as you begin to think critically about it.

Use Bloom's Taxonomy to Formulate Questions

Educational psychologist Benjamin Bloom developed *Bloom's taxonomy* because he believed that not all questions are created equal.[5] While some questions ask for a simple recall, said Bloom, others ask for higher level thinking. Key 7.3 shows Bloom's six levels of questions: knowledge, understanding, application, analysis, synthesis, and evaluation. It also identifies verbs that are associated with each level. As you read, use these verbs to formulate questions. As you answer essay questions on a test, use your knowledge of these verbs to respond at the right level.

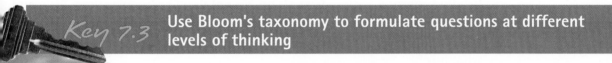

Key 7.3 Use Bloom's taxonomy to formulate questions at different levels of thinking

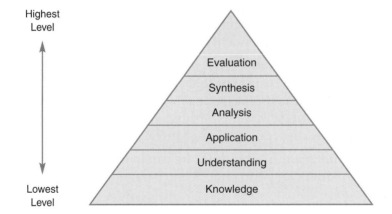

Verbs That Indicate Each Level

1. *Knowledge:* arrange, define, duplicate, label, list, memorize, name, order, recognize, relate, recall, repeat, reproduce, state.
2. *Understanding:* classify, describe, discuss, explain, express, identify, indicate, locate, recognize, report, restate, review, select, translate.
3. *Application:* apply, choose, demonstrate, dramatize, employ, illustrate, interpret, operate, practice, schedule, sketch, solve, use, write.
4. *Analysis:* analyze, appraise, calculate, categorize, compare, contrast, criticize, differentiate, discriminate, distinguish, examine, experiment, question, test.
5. *Synthesis:* arrange, assemble, collect, compose, construct, create, design, develop, formulate, manage, organize, plan, prepare, propose, set up, write.
6. *Evaluation:* appraise, argue, assess, attach, choose, compare, defend, estimate, judge, predict, rate, score, select, support, value, evaluate.

Read

Surveying and questioning give you a starting point for *reading,* the first R in SQ3R. Retaining what you read requires an active approach:

- **Focus on the key points of your survey.** Pay special attention to points raised in headings, boldface type, chapter objectives, and the summary.

- **Focus on your Q-stage questions.** Read with the purpose of answering each question. Write down or highlight ideas and examples that relate to your questions.

- **Mark up your text, and take text notes.** Write notes in the margins or on separate paper, circle ideas, or highlight key points that you want to study for exams. Text-marking and note-taking techniques will be examined later in the chapter.

- **Create text tabs.** Place plastic index tabs or adhesive notes at the start of different chapters so you can flip back and forth with ease.

Find the Main Idea

Reading comprehension depends on your ability to recognize *main ideas* and link other ideas to them. Most main ideas are in the first sentence or two of a paragraph. When the main idea is unclear, use this three-step approach to find what it is:[6]

1. **Search for the topic of the paragraph.** The topic of the paragraph is not the same as the main idea. Rather, it is the broad subject being discussed— for example, President Barack Obama, hate crimes on campus, or the Internet.

2. **Identify the aspect of the topic that is the paragraph's focus.** If the general topic is President Obama, the author may focus on different aspects of that topic, such as his health-care policies, his place as the first African-American president, or his public-speaking talent.

3. **Find what the author wants you to know about that aspect; this is the main idea.** The main idea of a paragraph on President Obama as a public speaker may be:

   > **President Obama is a charismatic speaker who uses his oratorical skills to encourage the American people in times of crisis.**

Prioritize Reading Assignments

Ask yourself what is important to remember and what is not, says Adam Robinson, co-founder of *The Princeton Review*: "Trying to digest and understand all the information in a textbook is... an excellent way to become quickly and hopelessly confused."[7] The following questions will help you target material for in-depth study:

- Is the information stressed in headings, charts, tables, captions, key terms, and definitions? In mid-chapter and end-of-chapter exercises? In the chapter introduction and summary? (Surveying before reading will enable you to answer these questions.)

- Is the information a definition, a crucial concept, an example, an explanation of a variety or type, or a critical relationship or comparison?

- Did your instructor stress the information in class? In your syllabus? Does your assignment ask you to focus on something specific?

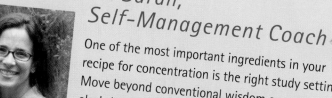

Inside Tips from Sarah, Self-Management Coach

One of the most important ingredients in your recipe for concentration is the right study setting. Move beyond conventional wisdom or anyone else's habit as you define what works best for you. Try different locations, times, atmospheres, and noise levels. A quiet corner of the library first thing in the morning can be as effective for one student as a busy outdoor cafe in the afternoon can be for another. Remember, too, that you might prefer different settings for different academic materials or tasks.

When trying to figure out what to study and what to skim, ask yourself whether your instructor would expect you to know the material. If you are unsure, and if the topic is not on your syllabus, ask your instructor.

Recite

Once you finish reading a topic, stop and answer the questions you raised in the Q-stage of SQ3R. *Even if you have already done this during the reading phase, do it again now— with the purpose of learning and committing the material to memory.*

You may decide to *recite* each answer aloud, silently speak the answers to yourself, "teach" the answers to another person, or write them down. Whatever your method, make sure you know how ideas connect to one another and to the general concept.

Writing is the most effective way to learn new material because it gives you immediate feedback: When you can use your own words to explain concepts, you know the material. When you can't, you still need work. When you write comprehensive responses to your Q-stage questions, you can compare what you write with the text and make adjustments, a process that will help you learn. Your responses then become a tool for review.

Keep your learning styles in mind when you explore different strategies. For example, an intrapersonal learner may prefer writing, while an interpersonal learner may choose to recite answers aloud to a classmate. A logical-mathematical learner may want to organize material into charts, while a musical learner might chant information aloud to a rhythm.

When do you stop to recite? Waiting for the end of a chapter is too late; stopping at the end of a paragraph is too soon. The best plan is to recite at the end of each text section, right before a new heading. Repeat the question-read-recite cycle until you complete the chapter. If you fumble for thoughts, reread the section until you feel you've got it.

Review

Review soon after you finish a chapter. Reviewing both immediately and periodically in the days and weeks after you read will help you learn and memorize material and prepare for exams. If you close the book after reading it once, you will probably forget almost everything. This is why students who read material for the first time before a test often have trouble. *Reviewing is your key to learning.*

Reviewing the same material over time will also help you identify knowledge gaps. It's natural to forget material between study sessions, especially if it's complex. When you come back after a break, you can focus on the areas where you need the most help.

Here are some reviewing techniques. Try them all, and use what works best:

- Reread your notes. Then summarize them from memory.
- Review and summarize in writing the text sections you highlighted or bracketed. Try to condense the material so that you can focus on key ideas.
- Answer the end-of-chapter review, discussion, and application questions.
- Recite concepts to yourself, or record and play them back on a digital recorder.
- Make flash cards with a word or concept on one side and a definition, examples, or other related information on the other. Test yourself.
- Quiz yourself, using the questions you raised in the Q-stage. If you can't answer a question, scan the text for the answer.
- Discuss the concepts with a classmate or in a study group. Use Q-stage questions to help one another learn.
- Ask your instructor about difficult material. Define exactly what you want to discuss, and then schedule a meeting during office hours or e-mail your questions.

On a scale of 1 to 10, with 1 being the lowest and 10 being the highest, rate yourself on your ability to complete each SQ3R stage *right now*. Then indicate where you want to be at the end of this course.

Stage	Description	Rating Now	Rating Goal
Survey	Pre-reading a book before studying it—skimming and scanning front matter, chapter elements, and back matter for clues about content and organization	———	———
Question	Developing questions linked to chapter headings and to what you already know	———	———
Read	Reading to answer Q-stage questions and find main ideas; taking notes as you read or highlighting your text	———	———
Recite	Answering, perhaps for a second time, your Q-stage questions; reciting the answers aloud or silently to yourself, teaching them to a study partner, or recording them in writing	———	———
Review	Learning the material through summarizing notes; answering study questions; writing outlines or think links; reciting concepts, using flash cards, thinking critically, and so on	———	———

real people
ask questions

Candace Payne

George Washington University Pre-Med Student[8]

For some people, a decade is a long time between attempts at being a full-time college student. But not for Candace Payne, a native of Trinidad who grew up in Miami and who was determined to become a medical doctor.

Candace first tried college at Florida's Trinity International University, where she got five A's her first semester. But the tuition put her $4,000 in debt, and she wanted to pay it off before taking more classes. So she stepped back from school and began working as a nanny in nearby Boca Raton. Although she promised herself that her detour would be temporary, she got into a work rut that lasted for years.

During that time, she took one course a semester at Palm Beach Community College, including English, chemistry, biology, and math, and she questioned her life. Is being a nanny what she really wanted? Was she smart enough to take a full load of pre-med courses and be accepted to medical school? How would she pay for it all? An aunt, who was a doctor, helped Candace get over her fear of failure. Hard work, she told her, was as important in medical school as IQ points.

Stop and Think

How did the questions Candace asked herself help clarify what she really wanted to do? How would asking yourself tough questions help you?

With newfound confidence, Candace decided to go for her dream and began taking even more rigorous science and math courses at PBCC. Chemistry professor Richard R. Shreve said she stood out from her peers because of her ability to manage her time, set priorities, and learn. "The key to the success of Candace," he said, "is that she questioned until she learned. When the time came for me to name the number 1 student in chemistry for the year, the honor went to Candace."

Stop and Think

Do you think that a person who questions personal goals is more likely to take a questioning approach to learning? Explain how you see yourself as a questioner.

Pursuing a pre-med program would mean transferring to a four-year school, so Candace began applying for scholarships, including one for transfer students offered by the Jack Kent Cooke Foundation. Getting the scholarship changed her life. Not only was her tuition paid, she could also apply to colleges in different parts of the country. George Washington University in Washington, D.C., was her pick.

Being older than the average student at GW, Candace's maturity gave her focus. She was also prepared because the courses she took at PBCC were textbook-driven, which meant that she had covered the same material as other students and could hit the ground running.

There are adjustments to make, but Candace is on the right track. She has to adapt to taking more than one course at a time, to finding tutoring and other services to help her succeed, and to living in an apartment with roommates. In some of her classes, she did not perform as well as she has in the past. But she is settling in, reaching out for support, and consistently improving. She is determined—and happy. "Every week I'm like, 'I can't believe I'm going to this school. I can't believe I'm here.'"

Think about Candace and Think about Yourself

Adjusting to college is challenging. List three questions you can ask yourself to cope better with the academic and social problems you face during the first weeks of class. Brainstorm solutions, and pursue those that are likely to help.

In 1977, Coloradan **Ken Salazar** was the first Hispanic-American to be elected to the U.S. Senate, and, in 2009, he was the first to join President Barack Obama's cabinet. As the Secretary of the Interior during difficult economic times, Secretary Salazar must ask tough questions about how to protect the environment while encouraging economic growth.

ask questions

Refreshing your knowledge is easier and faster than learning it the first time. Make a review schedule—for example, once a week—and stick to it until you're sure you know everything. Use different reviewing techniques to get a solid grasp of the material.

What Improves Reading Comprehension?

SQ3R is the key to building reading comprehension. As you will see next, having the right attitude and adopting some practical measures also help.

Take an Active Approach to Difficult Texts

First of all, start reading with an open mind. Don't prejudge reading assignments as impossible or a waste of time. Here are more active reading strategies:

Don't expect to master material on the first pass. Create a multi-step plan: Start with an overview of key concepts and interrelationships. On subsequent readings, learn new ideas and link them to what you know. By your last reading, you should know the material well enough to apply it to problems. (Time pressures may limit the number of times you read material, but real learning requires more than one pass.)

Know that some texts require extra work and concentration. If the material doesn't click, look back at last term's text or other background material to refresh your memory about key concepts. Be determined to make your way through the material.

Make sure concepts are clear. Ask instructors and study group partners for help. Check print and online references. Bookmark valuable Web sites.

Concentration
focusing on one topic at a time and avoiding distractions so that you can learn material.

You have different purposes for different reading materials. This student shopping at the bookstore may need textbooks, literary works, instructional packets, or even software.

© Bill Aron/PhotoEdit

Learn to Concentrate

When you pay attention to one thing and one thing only, you are **concentrating**, Without **concentration**, your mind tends to wander, and you are unlikely to remember the material. The strongest motivation to concentrate comes from within—not from the fear of failing a test—and is the result of connecting what you study to your short- and long-term goals. Following are some ways to focus on your work:

- **Make studying Job #1.** Place a purpose statement on your desk. For example: "I'm concentrating on the Bill of Rights, which will be on Friday's exam."

- **Know what you will study and for how long before you begin.** No one can concentrate for hours, so set realistic goals and have a plan for dividing your time.
- **Put aside unrelated thoughts.** Write them down so you can deal with them later. If something is really bothering you, take a break and deal with it. If you're feeling stressed for no particular reason, try exercising. You may be more efficient when you return.
- **Keep your social life separate.** Separate study time from fun time.
- **Plan a reward.** Have something to look forward to when you finish.
- **Evaluate.** If you studied for two hours, how much of that time did you actually concentrate? If not enough, figure out what disrupted your work. Then make changes before you study again.

Become Emotionally Involved

You are more likely to remember ideas that make you angry, happy, or curious than ideas you don't care about. Try these suggestions to inject emotions into "dry" materials:

- Think about your reaction to ideas, to the author's point of view and writing style, to chapter features and text design, and even to the chapter order.
- Discuss specific points with classmates and have spirited discussion when you disagree.
- Ask yourself how a concept applies to the real world.

Define Your Reading Purpose

To define your purpose, complete this sentence: "In reading this material, I intend to define/learn/answer/achieve … " *Write down your goal before you begin, and look at it whenever you lose focus or get bogged down in details.*

Purpose Determines Reading Strategy and Pace

You may have one or more of the following purposes for any "reading event":

- **Purpose 1: Read for understanding.** Take in concepts and details. Details explain or support concepts, and concepts provide a framework for details.
- **Purpose 2: Read to evaluate critically.** Examine causes and effects, examine similarities and differences, and question arguments. Critical reading goes beyond basic information recall.

By the way . . . .

eating less may actually improve your memory. In a recent study, people who cut their calories by 30% improved their memory performance by 20%. Researchers suspect that cutting calories reduces brain insulin levels and inflammation, which, in turn, helps brain function. [9]

- **Purpose 3: Read for practical application:** When you read a textbook preface or a software instruction booklet, your goal is to learn how to do or use something.

- **Purpose 4: Read for pleasure:** Here reading is for enjoyment and relaxation.

Your syllabus will help you define an assignment's purpose. If, for example, your next economics class will cover the topic of inflation, read the chapter and target what you are expected to know. You may be required to learn definitions, explain causes and consequences and government intervention strategies, and apply concepts to problems. In this case, you have three purposes—understanding, critical evaluation, and practical application. If the purpose is unclear, ask your instructor.

As Key 7.4 shows, good readers link reading pace to reading purpose. Your pace in reading online materials will be discussed later in the chapter.

Key 7.4 Link reading pace to reading purpose

TYPE OF MATERIAL	READING PURPOSE	PACE
Academic readings ■ Textbooks ■ Original sources ■ Lab reports ■ Required fiction	■ Critical analysis ■ Learning/memorizing ■ Preparation for tests	Slow, especially if the material is unfamiliar or difficult
Manuals ■ Instruction and materials	Practical application	Slow to medium
Journalism and nonfiction for the general reader ■ Nonfiction books ■ Newspapers ■ Magazines	■ Understanding concepts and specific facts ■ Practical application of material	Medium to fast
Non-required fiction	Understanding general ideas, concepts, and specific facts for enjoyment	Variable, but tending toward faster speeds

Source: Adapted from Nicholas Reid Schaffzin, *The Princeton Review Reading Smart,* New York: Random House, 1996, p. 15.

Chapter 7

Spend Enough Time

For every hour you spend in the classroom each week, remember that you should spend at least two hours preparing. For example, making the most of a course load of 15 credit hours means spending 30 hours a week studying and doing homework outside of class. Check your syllabus for the dates that reading assignments are due, and give yourself enough time to complete them. (Use the time-management strategies you learned in Chapter 3.)

Expand Your Course Vocabulary

Every subject has its own specialized vocabulary (see Key 7.5 for examples from four college texts). Even if you feel like you are diving into a foreign language, know that the more you see these terms, the more you will remember and understand them.

Apply a vocabulary-building approach to learning: Understand words in context, study definitions in the end-of-text glossary, record vocabulary and definitions in your notes, drill with flash cards (see Chapter 6), and use the terms in sentences. Be prepared to define these terms correctly on short-answer tests and to use new terms on essay exams.

Key 7.5   Every text includes specialized vocabulary

BIOLOGY TEXT	CRIMINAL JUSTICE TEXT	PSYCHOLOGY TEXT	BUSINESS TEXT
actin	biometrics	experimental method	double-entry accounting
chaparral	detainee	great person theory	leverage
exoskeleton	habitual offender	homeostasis	relationship marketing
gravitropism	RICO statute	trichromats	strategic alliance
prophase	writ of habeas corpus	vestibular senses	Uniform Commercial Code (UCC)

Multiple Intelligence Strategies for Effective Reading

Briefly describe a reading problem you have.

_____

_____

Now brainstorm potential solutions to your problem, linking each solution to an intelligence. Use the right-hand column to record your ideas.

INTELLIGENCE	SUGGESTED STRATEGIES	USE MI STRATEGIES TO COME UP WITH SOLUTIONS
Verbal–Linguistic	■ Mark up your text with marginal notes while you read. ■ Use every stage of SQ3R, taking advantage of each writing opportunity (writing Q-stage questions, writing summaries, and so on).	
Logical–Mathematical	■ Cut and paste online reading material into computer files with the same ideas. ■ Connect what you read with the world at large; consider similarities, differences and causes and effects.	
Bodily–Kinesthetic	■ Take physical breaks during reading sessions—walk, stretch, exercise. ■ Pace back and forth while reciting important ideas.	
Visual–Spatial	■ Pay special attention to photos, tables, figures, and other visual aids. ■ Make charts, diagrams, or think links illustrating difficult concepts.	
Interpersonal 	■ Read with a classmate. Have one person read a section silently and then summarize key concepts aloud. Reverse the order of summarizer and listener for each section. ■ Clarify important concepts in a study group.	
Intrapersonal	■ Read in a solitary setting, and allow time for reflection. ■ Evaluate your reaction to an assignment by considering the material in light of what you already know.	
Musical	■ Play music while you read. ■ Recite reading concepts to rhythms, or write a song to depict those concepts.	
Naturalistic	■ Study in a natural setting. If you are reading materials online and are in a Wi-Fi zone, read while sitting under a tree. ■ When taking text notes, put information into categories that make sense to you.	

How Do You Customize a Text with Highlighting and Notes?

Transform your textbook into a valuable learning tool through highlighting and notes. This will help you make the most of study time as you set the stage for review.

How to Highlight a Text

Highlighting involves the use of markers, pens, or pencils to flag important passages. Use the following techniques to do this effectively:

- **Develop a system, and stick to it.** Decide in advance if you will use different colored markers for different elements, brackets for long passages, or pencil underlining. Make a key that identifies each notation.

- **Consider using a regular pencil or pen instead of a highlighter pen.** The copy will be cleaner and look less like a coloring book.

- **Read an entire paragraph before you highlight.** Don't start until you sense what is important. Your goal is to highlight key material, not the entire page.

- **Avoid overmarking.** A phrase or two per paragraph is usually enough. Enclose long passages with brackets rather than marking every line, and avoid underlining entire sentences. The less color the better.

Although these techniques will help you pull out important information, *learning* demands that you go beyond marking your book. *Experts agree that you will not learn what you highlight unless you interact with the material through surveying, questioning, reciting, and review.*

How to Take Text Notes

When you combine highlighting with marginal notes or text flags, you remind yourself what each passage is about and why it is important. This combination makes the text a personal learning tool when you study for exams. Going a step further by taking a full set of text notes is an excellent way to commit material to memory. Moreover, when you combine your text and class notes, you have a comprehensive note set that will prepare you for exams (see Chapter 9).

Taking Marginal Notes

Here are tips for taking marginal notes right on textbook pages:

- Use pencil so you can erase comments or questions that are answered as you read.

- Write your Q-stage questions in the margins right next to text headings.

- Mark critical sections with marginal notations, such as *def.* for "definition," *e.g.* "for example," or *concept* for an important concept.
- Write notes at the bottom of the page connecting the text to what you learned in class. If you don't have enough room, attach sticky notes with your comments.

Key 7.6 shows how one student chose to highlight and take marginal notes in a business textbook.

Key 7.6 Underlining and taking marginal notes help you master content

How does target marketing and market segmentation help companies sell product?

TARGET MARKETING AND MARKET SEGMENTATION

Marketers have long known that products cannot be all things to all people. Buyers have different tastes, goals, lifestyles, and so on. The emergence of the marketing concept and the recognition of consumer needs and wants led marketers to think in terms of **target markets**—groups of people with similar wants and needs. Selecting target markets is usually the first step in the marketing strategy.

Target marketing requires **market segmentation**—dividing a market into categories of customer types or "segments." Once they have identified segments, companies may adopt a variety of strategies. Some firms market products to more than one segment. General Motors (*www.gm.com*), for example, offers compact cars, vans, trucks, luxury cars, and sports cars with various features and at various price levels. GM's strategy is to provide an automobile for nearly every segment of the market.

In contrast, some businesses offer a narrower range of products, each aimed toward a specific segment. Note that segmentation is a strategy for analyzing consumers, not products. The process of fixing, adapting, and communicating the nature of the product itself is called *product positioning*.

Definitions

target market
Group of people that has similar wants and needs and that can be expected to show interest in the same products

← *GM eg*

market segmentation
Process of dividing a market into categories of customer types

GM makes cars for diff. market segments

How do companies identify market segments?

Identifying Market Segments

By definition, members of a market segment must share some common traits that affect their purchasing decisions. In identifying segments, researchers look at several different influences on consumer behavior. Three of the most important are *geographic*, *demographic*, and *psychographic variables*.

What effect does geography have on segmentation strategies?

Geographic Variables Many buying decisions are affected by the places people call home. The heavy rainfall in Washington State, for instance, means that people there buy more umbrellas than people in the Sun Belt. Urban residents don't need agricultural equipment, and sailboats sell better along the coasts than on the Great Plains. **Geographic variables** are the geographical units, from countries to neighborhoods, that may be considered in a segmentation strategy.

These patterns affect decisions about marketing mixes for a huge range of products. For example, consider a plan to market down-filled parkas in rural Minnesota. Demand will be high and price competition intense. Local newspaper ads may be

Buying decisions influenced by where people live

geographic variables
Geographical units that may be considered in developing a segmentation strategy

— good eg —
selling parkas in Minnesota

Thought
Geographical variables change with the seasons

Source: Business Essentials, 5th ed., by Ronald J. Ebert and Ricky W. Griffin, © 2005. Reprinted by permission of Pearson Education, Inc., Upper Saddle River, NJ.

TAKE ACTION
Mark Up a Page to Learn a Page

Below, the text material in Key 7.6 continues. Put pencil to paper as you highlight concepts and take marginal notes. Compare your efforts to those of your classmates (use your interpersonal intelligence) to see how each of you approached the task and what you can learn from others.

Key 7.6 Continued

effective, and the best retail location may be one that is easily reached from several small towns.

Although the marketability of some products is geographically sensitive, others enjoy nearly universal acceptance. Coke, for example, gets more than 70 percent of its sales from international markets. It is the market leader in Great Britain, China, Germany, Japan, Brazil, and Spain. Pepsi's international sales are about 15 percent of Coke's. In fact, Coke's chief competitor in most countries is some local soft drink, not Pepsi, which earns 78 percent of its income at home.

demographic variables
Characteristics of populations that may be considered in developing a segmentation strategy

Demographic Variables Demographic variables describe populations by identifying such traits as age, income, gender, ethnic background, marital status, race, religion, and social class. For example, several general consumption characteristics can be attributed to certain age groups (18–25, 26–35, 36–45, and so on). A marketer can, thus, divide markets into age groups. Table 10.1 lists some possible demographic breakdowns. Depending on the marketer's purpose, a segment can be a single classification (*aged 20–34*) or a combination of categories (*aged 20–34, married with children, earning* $25,000–$34,999). Foreign competitors, for example, are gaining market share in U.S. auto sales by appealing to young buyers (under age 30) with limited incomes (under $30,000). Whereas companies such as Hyundai *(www.hyundai.net)*, Kia *(www.kia.com)*, and Daewoo *(www.daewoous.com)* are winning entry-level customers with high quality and generous warranties, Volkswagen *(www.vw.com)* targets under-35 buyers with its entertainment-styled VW Jetta.[4]

psychographic variables
Consumer characteristics, such as lifestyles, opinions, interests, and attitudes, that may be considered in developing a segmentation strategy

Psychographic Variables Markets can also be segmented according to such **psychographic variables** as lifestyles, interests, and attitudes. Take, for example, Burberry *(www.burberry.com)*, whose raincoats have been a symbol of British tradition since 1856. Burberry has repositioned itself as a global luxury brand, like Gucci *(www.gucci.com)* and Louis Vuitton *(www.vuitton.com)*. The strategy, which recently resulted in a 31-percent sales increase, calls for attracting a different type of customer—the top-of-the-line, fashion-conscious individual—who shops at such stores as Neiman Marcus and Bergdorf Goodman.[5]

Psychographics are particularly important to marketers because, unlike demographics and geographics, they can be changed by marketing efforts. For example, Polish companies have overcome consumer resistance by promoting the safety and desirability of using credit rather than depending solely on cash. One product of changing attitudes is a booming economy and the emergence of a robust middle class.

TABLE 10.1
Demographic Variables

Age	Under 5, 5–11, 12–19, 20–34, 35–49, 50–64, 65+
Education	Grade school or less, some high school, graduated high school, some college, college degree, advanced degree
Family life cycle	Young single, young married without children, young married with children, older married with children under 18, older married without children under 18, older single, other
Family size	1, 2–3, 4–5, 6+
Income	Under $9,000, $9,000–$14,999, $15,000–$24,999, $25,000–$34,999, $35,000–$45,000, over $45,000
Nationality	African, American, Asian, British, Eastern European, French, German, Irish, Italian, Latin American, Middle Eastern, Scandinavian
Race	Native American, Asian, Black, White
Religion	Buddhist, Catholic, Hindu, Jewish, Muslim, Protestant
Sex	Male, female

Your marked-up text is uniquely yours; no one else will highlight or take text notes as you do because no one else has your knowledge, learning style, or study techniques. Therefore, you may run into problems if you buy used texts that are heavily highlighted or filled with notes. Even if the previous owner was a good student, he or she is not you—and that fact alone may make it more challenging to learn the material well.

Taking Full-Text Notes

Taking comprehensive notes on assigned readings means constructing a summary of the main ideas in your own words. Focus on the main ideas and supporting examples, and don't include any of your own ideas or evaluations at this point. Your summary should just condense the material, making it easier to focus on concepts and their relationships.

Here are suggestions for creating effective full-text summaries:

- Use your own words. If you rewrite the author's words directly, you may be just repeating concepts you do not yet understand. When studying a technical subject with precise definitions, however, you may have to use text wording.

- Try to make your notes simple, clear, and brief. Include what you need to understand about the topic, while leaving out less important details.

- Consider outlining the text so you can see how ideas relate to one another.

- Before you write, identify the main idea of a passage.

- Once an idea ends and another begins, begin taking notes from memory in your own words. Go back to the text, as needed, for information that you didn't get at first.

- Take notes on tables, charts, photographs, and captions. Visual presentations may contain information found nowhere else in the text.

- Use shorthand symbols to write quickly (see Chapter 9).

- Construct charts, tables, and diagrams to visually express written concepts.

- Devise a color-coding system to indicate levels of importance of different ideas, and then mark up your notes with these colors.

How Can You Read Online Materials Effectively?

If you grew up using the Internet or feel right at home with a computer, you may be a "digital native"[10] who is:

- More comfortable reading from a computer screen than a printed page. (Before entering college, you clocked thousands of hours reading Web sites and blogs and sending e-mails and text and instant messages.)

- A multitasker who feels able to juggle three, four, and five things at once, including reading your college assignments.

- Impatient if you have to wade through long articles or dense paragraphs and happier if the information comes in easily digestible chunks.

- Expecting information on demand—what you need, when you need it.

- Willing to jump from reading one thing to another simply because you saw something of interest that had a hypertext link.

- Accepting of blinking ads and other online distractions and convinced that you are able to ignore them.

- Unlikely to persevere with a single task without interruption for more than 20 minutes at a time.

(Even if you are just starting to use a computer, you will quickly become a screen reader and may take on many of these habits.)

When Web researcher Jakob Nielsen studied how the Internet has changed reading, he identified *F-pattern reading*. At the beginning of a document, readers using a screen read across the line—from one end to the other—much in the same way they would read a book. But as they move through the material, the width of their horizontal reading narrows as their pace quickens. By the time they reach the bottom of the document, eye movements are almost vertical as they disregard any material on the page's lower right-hand corner. "F is for fast," said Nielsen. "That's how users read content."[11]

POWERFUL QUESTIONS

Powerful questions activate this chapter's Habit for Success, so try these: In what ways do you read print and online materials differently?

What do you do when screen reading

makes it hard to focus on long passages? If you identify online reading patterns that interfere with your ability to learn, what can you do to address the problems? Hanh, the student described at the start of the chapter, couldn't remember what she read on screen. How does her difficulty differ from yours?

ask questions

© iStockphoto.com

Screen readers spring across the page, focusing on heads and subheads, key words, bullet points, variations in typeface, visuals, and color. They want to discover the meat of the material quickly and are not likely to wade through introductions or fat paragraphs in search of ideas. They are experts at skimming and scanning.

Your college success depends on being able to read both printed and on-screen material effectively. You have two goals: To improve your screen reading skills so that you learn the material and to be able to shift to a slower gear when you read a printed text.

Reading and Studying Online Material

When you are reading on-screen articles that you need for class, you need to capture important ideas so that you can come back to them. Jacob Nielsen suggests a step-by-step process, which includes aspects of SQ3R:

1. **Skim through the article** to see if it contains important ideas.

2. **Before reading in depth, save the article on your computer.** This gives you the ability to highlight and add notes, just as you would on a printed page. You can do this in a number of ways, including converting the article into a print format and then copying it into an e-mail to yourself. You can then collect e-mails on the same subject in a single file.

3. **Survey the article.** Read the title, subtitle, headings, figures, charts, and tables.

4. **Come up with questions to guide your reading** . Ask yourself what general and specific information you want to learn from the article.

5. **Read the article in depth.** You have already judged that the material is important, so take it much slower than you would normally.

6. **Highlight and take notes.** Use the program's highlighter function to call attention to material you want to come back to. Set up a color code to indicate levels of importance—for example, yellow is level 1, green is level 2, and turquoise is level 3. Take notes in comment boxes next to key ideas or add your thoughts in the text itself.

7. **Print out articles you would rather study on paper.** Make sure the printouts include your highlighting and notes.

8. **Review your notes and combine them** with the notes you took in class and on your printed text. Use your combined notes to study for exams. (Chapter 9 covers combining text and class notes.) Use the techniques you learned in the review stage of SQ3R.

Screen reading for extended periods can cause eye strain, so position the monitor to minimize glare, and give your eyes a short break every half hour. If you can change the typeface, choose one that minimizes strain such as Verdana, Trebuchet, or Georgia.

Finally, knowing your learning style will help you read more effectively on the computer. If you are a visual learner, you may want to print out materials on a regular basis. If you are a bodily-kinesthetic learner, you might want to surround yourself with your print-outs in idea stacks. If you are a musical learner, you may want to tune your computer into a music Web site and listen while you read.

Shifting Gears and Slowing Down When Reading Printed Texts

Being aware that your skills as a screen reader are different from those you need to read printed textbooks will help you shift gears when picking up a book. Textbooks require close, slow reading that may seem like walking through mud after spending hours a day on the Internet.

Textbooks provide a comprehensive framework on a topic that goes beyond the just-in-time information nuggets that the Internet tends to deliver. Often, textbooks need greater concentration than Internet pages and an undistracted focus when material is difficult. They require what developmental psychologist Maryanne Wolf calls *deep reading,* reading that goes beyond scanning words and involves comprehension and interaction with the material.[13]

Whether on a printed page or on a screen, can you accomplish the hard reading required in college, and is it worth the effort? When Michigan State University professor Nancy Bunge asked her students these questions, their answer was a resounding yes. Writing on a course evaluation about the term's reading, one student said, "The hard books were a huge challenge for me, but it's the challenge that makes them interesting to get through and worth learning."[14]

Once I was a scuba diver in the sea of [printed] words. Now I zip along the surface [of the Internet] like a guy on a Jet Ski.

Nicholas Carr, American writer in the fields of technology, business, and culture

Habit for Success

ask questions

Below are examples of how you can put this habit into action in different situations. Use the three spaces to add your own ideas for actions you can accomplish now or in the future. Be specific, and be realistic.

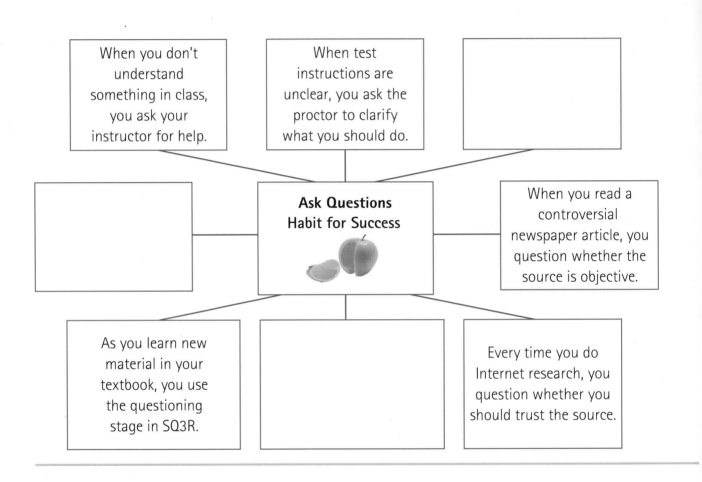

When you don't understand something in class, you ask your instructor for help.

When test instructions are unclear, you ask the proctor to clarify what you should do.

Ask Questions Habit for Success

When you read a controversial newspaper article, you question whether the source is objective.

As you learn new material in your textbook, you use the questioning stage in SQ3R.

Every time you do Internet research, you question whether you should trust the source.

Building Skills
for successful learning

Note the Important Points

How can SQ3R help you own what you read?

List and describe the five parts of SQ3R.

1. _____

2. _____

3. _____

4. _____

5. _____

Identify which part of SQ3R you think will help you the most this semester and the reason why.

_____

_____

What improves reading comprehension?

Name three actions you can take right now to improve your understanding of what you read.

1. _____

2. _____

3. _____

How do you customize a text with highlighting and notes?

Describe two methods you learned in this chapter to improve your text highlighting.

1. _____

2. _____

Describe two methods you learned in this chapter to improve your marginal notes.

1. _____

2. _____

Describe two methods you learned in this chapter to improve your full-text notes.

1. _____

2. _____

How can you read online materials effectively?

Describe how being a "digital native" can help and hurt you as you study.

_____

_____

_____

List two actions you can take to become a better screen reader.

1. _____

2. _____

Critical Thinking

Studying a Text Page

Page 217 is from the chapter "Groups and Organizations" in the sixth edition of John J. Macionis's *Sociology.*[15] Apply SQ3R as you read the excerpt. Use what you learned in this chapter to complete the questions that follow (some questions ask you to mark the page itself).

Step 1: Gather and analyze information. First gather: Skim the excerpt. Identify the headings on the page and the relationships among them. Mark primary-level headings with a #1, secondary headings with a #2, and third-level headings with a #3.

Then analyze: Which heading serves as an umbrella for the rest?

_____

_____

What do the headings tell you about the content of the page?

_____

_____

Step 2: Create useful study questions. Identify three key concepts, and then write three study questions that will help you learn them.

1. _____

   _____

2. _____

   _____

3. _____

   _____

Step 3: Read and remember. Put SQ3R to work. Use a marker pen to highlight phrases and sentences. Write marginal notes for later review. Identify where you might write "e.g." to flag an example. After reading this page thoroughly, write a short summary here:

_____

_____

_____

Step 4: Check your understanding of content. Using your own words, summarize in one sentence:

- The distinction among groups, categories, and crowds

_____

_____

- The distinction among primary and secondary groups

_____

_____

- The main idea of this passage

_____

_____

SOCIAL GROUPS

Virtually everyone moves through life with a sense of belonging; this is the experience of group life. A **social group** refers to *two or more people who identify and interact with one another*. Human beings continually come together to form couples, families, circles of friends, neighborhoods, churches, businesses, clubs, and numerous large organizations. Whatever the form, groups encompass people with shared experiences, loyalties, and interests. In short, while maintaining their individuality, the members of social groups also think of themselves as a special "we."

Groups, Categories, and Crowds

People often use the term "group" imprecisely. We now distinguish the group from the similar concepts of category and crowd.

Category. A *category* refers to people who have some status in common. Women, single fathers, military recruits, homeowners, and Roman Catholics are all examples of categories.

Why are categories not considered groups? Simply because, while the individuals involved are aware that they are not the only ones to hold that particular status, the vast majority are strangers to one another.

Crowd. A *crowd* refers to a temporary cluster of individuals who may or may not interact at all. Students sitting in a lecture hall do engage one another and share some common identity as college classmates; thus, such a crowd might be called a loosely formed group. By contrast, riders hurtling along on a subway train or bathers enjoying a summer day at the beach pay little attention to one another and amount to an anonymous aggregate of people. In general, then, crowds are too transitory and impersonal to qualify as social groups.

The right circumstances, however, could turn a crowd into a group. People riding in a subway train that crashes under the city streets generally become keenly aware of their common plight and begin to help one another. Sometimes such extraordinary experiences become the basis for lasting relationships.

Primary and Secondary Groups

Acquaintances commonly greet one another with a smile and the simple phrase, "Hi! How are you?" The response is usually a well scripted, "Just fine, thanks, how about you?" This answer, of course, is often more formal than truthful. In most cases, providing a detailed account of how you are *really* doing would prompt the other person to beat a hasty and awkward exit.

Sociologists classify social groups by measuring them against two ideal types based on members' genuine level of personal concern. This variation is the key to distinguishing *primary* from *secondary* groups.

According to Charles Horton Cooley (1864–1929), a **primary group** is a *small social group whose members share personal and enduring relationships*. Bound together by primary relationships, individuals in primary groups typically spend a great deal of time together, engage in a wide range of common activities, and feel that they know one another well. Although not without periodic conflict, members of primary groups display sincere concern for each other's welfare. The family is every society's most important primary group.

Cooley characterized these personal and tightly integrated groups as *primary* because they are among the first groups we experience in life. In addition, the family and early play groups also hold primary importance in the socialization process, shaping attitudes, behavior, and social identity.

Source: Sociology, 6th ed., by John J. Macionis, © 1997. Reprinted by permission of Pearson Education, Inc., Upper Saddle River, NJ.

Team Building

Improve Your Highlighting Skills

1. Photocopy a three- to four-page textbook section, and have everyone highlight what's important. Compare versions. Ask group members to explain why they highlighted certain material and not others and to describe how they made their choices. Learn from each other about how to think carefully before you highlight.

2. Each group member should then pledge to use, over a period of a week, two highlighting techniques learned in step 1.

3. At the end of the week, discuss the results. Have each person answer this question: "Am I a better highlighter as a result of this exercise, and am I learning more content?" Based on your experience, explain here how your highlighting has changed (or not), and how you believe any changes you've put into place will help you.

_____

_____

_____

_____

_____

_____

_____

Test Prep: Start It Now

ask questions

Make Questioning Part of Your Study Routine

A midterm is coming up in a few weeks, and it is time to start studying. Ask yourself these questions *right now* to maximize your learning:

- Have I checked my syllabus to identify exactly what will be on the test?
- Am I using SQ3R to study all the material?
- What steps will I take to maximize my learning style as I study?
- Are the highlighting and notes I've taken on the text helping me study? If not, how can I improve them?
- Do I read online materials as carefully as printed materials? If not, what steps am I taking to become a better screen reader?
- When I finish studying, am I able to summarize the material in writing or teach it to another student? If not, have I asked for help?

Now adjust your studying as a result of your answers. After the exam, assess whether these adjustments helped you learn. Write your thoughts about the experience below.

_____

_____

_____

_____

_____

_____

_____

reading across the disciplines

math, science, social science,
and literary texts

rosemary knew when she started college that she wanted to be a physical education teacher or a personal trainer, and she is doing well in her major. The problem is that she is doing poorly in everything else. "I don't see the point of studying history, American lit, or chemistry," she tells her advisor during a conference about her grades. "I'm never going to use this stuff, am I?"

In this chapter . . .

you explore answers to these questions:

HOW do you read math and science texts? p. 222

HOW do you read texts in the social sciences and humanities? p. 228

HOW do you "read" visual aids? p. 232

HOW do you read works of literature? p. 238

Habit for Success

use what you know

Using what you already know will help you learn new material and solve problems. A concept in psychology, for example, can give you insight into a character in a novel.

How Do You Read Math and Science Texts?

Getting a college education involves learning many subjects, even those that seem off track from your interests and out of your comfort zone. Rosemary doesn't realize this yet. Here is some evidence that might help Rosemary approach her work in different academic disciplines with a positive attitude:

- An art history course will help you enjoy museums and give you a feel for historical times, places, and events.
- A political science course will help you understand why it's important to vote.
- A literature course will help you think about important ideas and explore human nature.
- A biology course will help you apply the right first aid to a burn.
- An earth science course will help you understand alternative energy sources.
- A statistics course may help you determine your risk for getting a disease that runs in your family.

General Education Requirements

courses, required for graduation, in a variety of academic fields including the humanities, social sciences, math, and science.

In other words, there are dozens of reasons to take courses outside of your field. And if your college has **general education requirements,** you may have to take a wide variety of courses in order to graduate. (General education requirements are often part of a liberal arts education.) Knowing the unique features of textbooks in each field and knowing how to read visual aids that appear in many texts will help you learn.

Reasons to take math and science courses are many, from enjoying the precision of numbers and scientific experiments to wanting a career in fields that require the knowledge. Mathematical and scientific strategies can be applied to a wide range of situations, helping you develop your thinking and problem solving skills.

The whole object of education is…to develop the mind. The mind should be a thing that works.

Sherwood Anderson, American novelist and short-story writer

Math and science courses relate closely to one another, said Don Pierce, executive director of education at Heald Colleges. "Math is the empowering skill that underlies all science. Without it, you can't succeed as a scientist. The scientific process depends on your ability to analyze, interpret, and attach meaning to data."[1] For example, in beginning chemistry, you will usually have to balance chemical equations. This may involve writing an equation, drawing a diagram, or perhaps working backwards.

Key 8.1 lists just some of the math and science courses you may take, along with related careers. In a world that is being transformed by new discoveries and technologies, having a strong math and science background prepares you for tomorrow's jobs. A background in math and science will also help you manage your personal life as you create monthly budgets, choose auto insurance, understand illnesses, and more.

Being successful in math and science depends on how you approach the material. Try these strategies when you study and do homework. Get extra help at the campus tutoring center. Start early in the term, so you don't fall behind.

Grasping science concepts often requires action. What you do in the lab will reinforce your understanding of the text.

© Laima Druskis/PH College/Pearson Education

How to Approach Your Textbook

Math and science textbooks move sequentially. That is, your understanding of later material depends on how well you learned material in earlier chapters. Use the following strategies to get the most from your textbooks.

Interact with math material actively through writing. Math textbooks are problem-and-solution based. As you read, highlight important information, and take notes of examples. If problem steps are left out, as they often are, work them out on your pad or in the book. Draw sketches to help visualize the material. Try not to move on until you understand example problems and how they relate to the central ideas. Write down questions for your instructor or fellow students.

Pay attention to formulas. Math and science texts are filled with **formulas**. Focus on learning the main ideas behind each formula, and do problems to make sure that learning sticks.

Formulas
general facts, rules, or principles usually expressed in mathematical symbols.

COLLEGE COURSES	ASSOCIATED CAREERS IN DIFFERENT FIELDS

MATH

- Pre-calculus
- Calculus
- Geometry
- Algebra
- Statistics
- Symmetry
- Differential equations

- Hospital insurance manager
- Pharmacist and pharmacy technician
- Network systems analyst
- Data communication analyst
- Real estate appraiser
- Auto insurance claims adjuster
- Marketing research analyst
- Personal financial advisor
- Government tax agent
- Credit counselor

SCIENCE

- Anatomy and physiology
- Biology and microbiology
- Chemistry
- Environmental sciences
- Geology and oceanography
- Kinesiology
- Nutrition
- Physics
- Astronomy
- Computer science
- Horticulture

- Medical doctor
- Dental hygienist
- Nurse/case manager
- Nurse or nurse practitioner
- Nutritionist
- Physical or occupational therapist
- Veterinarian and veterinary technician
- Software designer and programmer
- Medical assistant
- Pharmaceutical sales representative
- Sports physiologist
- Jet engine repair specialist
- Landscaper and arborist
- Skin care specialist
- Emergency medical technician

Use memory strategies to learn science. Science textbooks are packed with vocabulary specific to the field (for example, an environmental science text may refer to the *greenhouse effect, integrated waste management,* and the *law of limiting factors*). To remember what you read, use mnemonic devices, test yourself with flash cards, and rehearse aloud or silently (see Chapter 6). Selective highlighting and writing summaries, perhaps in table form, will also help (see Chapter 7). Key 8.2—a page from *Environmental Science,* 10th edition, by Richard T. Wright—shows the kind of material you may be reading.[2]

18.1 The Solid-Waste Problem

The focus of this chapter is **municipal solid waste** (MSW), defined as the total of all the materials (commonly called trash, refuse, or garbage) thrown away from homes and commercial establishments and collected by local governments. MSW is different from hazardous waste (covered in Chapter 19) and nonhazardous industrial waste. The latter is no small matter: Industrial facilities generate and manage 7.6 billion tons of nonhazardous industrial waste annually. Included in the category are wastes from demolition and construction operations, agricultural and mining residues, combustion ash, sewage treatment sludge, and wastes generated by industrial processes. The states oversee these wastes because Congress has not delegated any authority to the EPA to regulate them, as it has for MSW and hazardous waste.

Disposal of Municipal Solid Waste

Over the years, the amount of MSW generated in the United States has grown steadily, in part because of a growing population but also because of changing lifestyles and the increasing use of disposable materials and excessive packaging. In 1960, the nation generated 2.7 pounds (1.2 kg) per person per day. In 2003, we generated a total of 236 million tons (215 million metric tons) of MSW, an average of 4.5 pounds (2 kg) per person per day. With a 2006 population of 298 million, that is enough waste to fill 89,000 garbage trucks each day. The *solid-waste problem* can be stated simply: *We generate huge amounts of MSW, and it is increasingly expensive to dispose of it in ways that are environmentally responsible and protective of human health.*

The refuse generated by municipalities is a mixture of materials from households and small businesses, in the proportions shown in Figure 18–2. However, the proportions vary greatly, depending on the generator (commercial versus residential), the neighborhood (affluent versus poor), and the time of year (during certain seasons, yard wastes, such as grass clippings and raked leaves, add greatly to the solid-waste burden). Little attention is given to what people throw away in their trash. Even if there are restrictions and prohibitions, they can be bypassed with careful packing of the trash containers. Thus, many environmentally detrimental substances—paint, used motor oil, small batteries, and so on—are discarded, with the feeling that they are gone forever.

Whose Job? Customarily, local governments have had the responsibility for collecting and disposing of MSW. The local jurisdiction may own trucks and employ workers, or it may contract with a private firm to provide the collection service. Traditionally, the cost of waste pickup is passed along to households via taxes. Alternatively, some municipalities have opted for a "pay-as-you-throw" (PAYT, as it is called) system, in which households are charged for waste collection on the basis of the amount of trash they throw away. Some municipalities put all trash collection and disposal in the private sector, with the collectors billing each home by volume and weight of trash. The MSW that is collected is then disposed of in a variety of ways, and it is at the point of disposal that state and federal regulations begin to apply.

Past Sins. Until the 1960s, most MSW was burned in open dumps. The waste was burned to reduce its volume and lengthen the life span of the dump site, but refuse does not burn well. Smoldering dumps produced clouds of smoke that could be seen from miles away, smelled bad, and created a breeding ground for flies and rats. Some cities turned to incinerators, or combustion facilities, as they are called today—huge furnaces in which high temperatures allow the waste to burn more completely than in open dumps. Without controls, however, incinerators were prime sources of air pollution. Public objections and air pollution laws forced the phaseout of open dumps and many incinerators during the 1960s and early 1970s. Open dumps were then converted to landfills.

Where Does It Go? In the United States in 2003, 55.4% of MSW was disposed of in landfills, 30.6% was recovered for recycling and composting, and the remainder (14.0%) was combusted (Fig. 18–3). Over the last

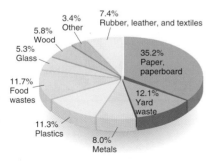

Figure 18–2 U.S. municipal solid-waste composition. The composition of municipal solid waste in the United States in 2003. (*Source:* Data from EPA, Office of Solid Waste, *Municipal Solid Waste in the United States: 2003 Facts and Figures*, April 2005.)

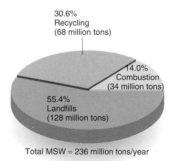

Figure 18–3 U.S. municipal solid-waste disposal. Disposal of solid waste to landfills, combustion, and recycling, 2003. (*Source:* Data from EPA, Office of Solid Waste, *Municipal Solid Waste in the United States: 2003 Facts and Figures*, April 2005.)

Math anxiety, the stress you feel when doing math, is especially common before and during exams. Use this assessment to rate your own discomfort.[3]

Fill in the blank with a number from 1 to 5 to indicate how strong your anxiety is for each item.
1—No anxiety, 2—a little, 3—some, 4—more, 5—always

I am anxious:

1. At the thought of taking a math course. _____

2. When I go into a math class. _____

3. When I open a math book. _____

4. When I study math alone. _____

5. When I do math with others watching. _____

6. When the teacher watches me do math. _____

7. When anyone in my family is discussing a math problem. _____

8. When making change at a store. _____

9. When people at work (friends) discuss math. _____

10. When my parents or friends explain a math problem to me. _____

Use the same scale to indicate how true each of the following statements is for you:

1. I have been uncomfortable with school math. _____

2. I really don't know how to understand, learn, and remember math. _____

3. I never really liked math. _____

4. I have never read a math book in school. _____

5. As far back as I can remember, I got nervous when family members or friends brought up a problem using numbers. _____

TOTAL for both scales: _____
Scoring Key: 60–75 High anxiety   40–60 Medium anxiety   15–40 Low anxiety

Place a check mark next to the symptoms you experience while studying math.

Nausea _____   Extreme nervousness _____

Can't hear the teacher _____   Negative self-talk that fills your mind _____

Inability to concentrate _____   Blank brain _____

Stomachache _____   Shortness of breath _____

Sweaty palms _____   Other (explain) _____

Many of the test anxiety strategies in Chapter 10 will help you conquer your fear of math.

Source: Gina Allred, "Anxiety in Math Class."

You may have used your math knowledge to calculate your GPA or to analyze student loan refinancing options. If you didn't have all the knowledge needed to handle these problems, think about what you *did* know that gave you a base for learning more. **The next time you face** a practical math problem, what steps will you take to use your current knowledge to find an answer?

use what you know

Studying and Homework

Doing homework in math and science requires perseverance and action.

Review materials. Review your class notes as soon as possible after each class. Have the textbook alongside, and compare the lecture information to the book. Fill in missing steps in the instructor's examples before you forget them. You may want to write the instructor's examples in the book next to the corresponding topics.

Do problems, problems, and more problems. Working through problems provides examples that will help you understand concepts and formulas. Plus, becoming familiar with a group of problems and related formulas will help you apply what you know to similar problems on other assignments and tests.

Fight frustration with action. If you are stuck on a problem, go on to another one. If you repeatedly get a wrong answer, look at the steps you've taken, and see if anything doesn't make sense. If you hit a wall, take a break to clear your head. If you have done the assigned homework but still don't feel secure, do additional problems or ask for help.

Work with others. Try to set up study groups outside of class. Do as much of your homework as you can on your own, and then meet to discuss it and work through additional problems. Be open to other perspectives, and ask others how they arrived at answers, especially if they used different approaches.

Focus on learning styles. Use strategies that activate your strengths. A visual learner might draw pictures to illustrate problems, and an interpersonal learner might organize a study group. Musical learners might create songs describing math concepts. Barbara Aaker wrote 40 songs for her students at the Community College of Denver to help musical learners retain difficult concepts. Key 8.3 presents one of her algebra songs.

By the way . . .

reading even as little as 15 minutes a day outside of your schoolwork will expose you to more than a million words of text in a year.[4]

"HOW MUCH IS THAT *X* IN THE EQUATION?"
(to the tune of "How Much Is That Doggie in the Window?")

How much is that *x* in the equation?
What value will make it be true?
To find the *x* and get the solution
The numbers attached we **undo**.

The **connector** is plus or minus seven,
To find *x* we have to **undo**.
Just write below both sides—make it even.
We **undo** to find the *x* value.

If multiply or divide is showing,
The **connector** tells what has been done.
To **undo** is where we still are going—
We're trying to get *x* alone.

Source: Reprinted with permission. Barbara Aaker, *Mathematics: The Musical*, Denver: Crazy Broad Publishing,1999.

By the way . . .

over the past year, nearly 3 out of 10 freshmen at four-year colleges explored topics in different academic fields on their own, even when the work was not required for class.[6]

The American Association for the Advancement of Science sponsors a "Dance Your Ph.D." contest to inspire doctoral students to use bodily-kinesthetic intelligence to express their projects. Watch this YouTube video (http://www.youtube.com/watch?v=_IUVkMXd_c8) showing how Lara Park, a nutritional biologist at Tufts University, uses ballet to demonstrate how a diet deficient in folate—a vitamin found in leafy greens—can make a person susceptible to colon cancer.[5]

Strive for accuracy. Complete a step of an algebra problem or biology lab project inaccurately, and your answer will be incorrect. In class, the consequences of inaccuracy are reflected in low grades. In life, the consequences could show in a patient's health or in the strength of a bridge. Check over the details of your work, and always try to get it exactly right.

How Do You Read Texts in the Social Sciences and Humanities?

Courses in the social science and humanities prepare you to be a well-rounded person, able and ready to fulfill your responsibilities to yourself, your family, and a free democracy. They also prepare you for 21st century jobs by focusing on critical thinking, civic and historic knowledge,

Multiple Intelligence Strategies for Working with Numbers

Briefly describe a math- or science-related problem you have.

_____

_____

Now brainstorm potential solutions to your problem, linking each solution to an intelligence. Use the right-hand column to record your ideas.

INTELLIGENCE	SUGGESTED STRATEGIES	USE MI STRATEGIES TO COME UP WITH SOLUTIONS
Verbal-Linguistic	▪ Whenever possible, convert numerical problems and formulas to word problems. ▪ Convert word problems into numbers to help solidify the relationship between words and the numbers they signify.	
Logical-Mathematical	▪ Use math games and puzzles. ▪ Make sure you understand every formula; then, carefully work through each step of the problem-solving process.	
Bodily-Kinesthetic	▪ Find physical representations of problems. Use pennies; cut up an apple; drive distances. ▪ For hands-on experience, take science classes with a lab.	
Visual-Spatial	▪ Draw visual representations of problems—geometrical shapes, grids, charts, matrices—and use plenty of space. ▪ Circle important items in the description of the problem.	
Interpersonal	▪ Go over homework problems with study group partners. Discuss different approaches. ▪ Schedule a time to talk with your instructor about difficult concepts.	
Intrapersonal 	▪ Find a solitary spot to read or do homework. ▪ Take quiet breaks when you hit a roadblock. Take a walk or a nap; it may help you think of a new approach.	
Musical	▪ Listen to music whenever possible. The rhythms and notes of music are based in mathematics.	
Naturalistic	▪ When you need science credits, look for courses in biological sciences and/or botany. ▪ Find patterns and categorize the information whenever possible.	

and ethical reasoning. Key 8.4 lists just some of the social science and humanities courses you may take in college and the related careers.

As you study these disciplines, look for themes and use critical thinking as the foundation for your work. Build knowledge by using what you know to learn new material.

Look for Themes

The National Council for the Social Studies (http://www.socialstudies.org) identifies 10 themes that organize the study of the social sciences and humanities. These themes provide "umbrellas" under which you can group ideas that you encounter in different classes and reading materials:

- Culture
- Time, continuity, and change
- People, places, and environment
- Individual development and identity
- Individuals, groups, and institutions
- Power, authority, and governance
- Production, distribution, and consumption
- Science, technology, and society
- Global connections
- Ideals and practices of citizenship

Thinking critically about what you read in social sciences textbooks may mean looking up words in the dictionary and comparing what you read to other publications.

Look for these themes as you read, even if they are not spelled out. For example, as you read a chapter in a political science text on presidential politics, think of the history of presidential elections, the impact of specific individuals on the presidency, how the Internet is changing electoral politics, the international implications of U.S. electoral politics, and more.

Relying on the Habit for Success of using what you know to learn new material will help you place new information under an appropriate "umbrella." This requires the kind of analysis that is fueled by critical thinking.

© Spencer Grant/PhotoEdit

COLLEGE COURSES	ASSOCIATED CAREERS IN DIFFERENT FIELDS

SOCIAL SCIENCES

- Anthropology
- Criminal justice
- Business
- Information science
- Sociology
- Social work
- Political science
- Psychology
- Archeology
- Economics
- Geography
- International relations
- Education
- Linguistics

- Lawyer
- Paralegal
- Mental health and substance abuse social worker
- Geriatric care social worker
- Elementary and high school teacher
- Online instructor
- Human resources manager
- Advertising copy writer
- Web-based journalist
- Nonprofit foundation fund-raiser
- Government staff worker
- College admissions manager
- Police officer
- College textbook marketing representative
- Labor union official
- Retirement counselor

HUMANITIES

- Art history
- Literature
- Film and theater
- Music appreciation
- World languages
- Communications
- Religion
- Philosophy
- History
- African-American studies
- Latino studies
- Women's and gender studies

- Museum curator
- Architect
- Graphic designer
- Actor/director
- Musician
- International marketing manager
- College professor
- Government official
- Tourism consultant

Learn Through Critical Thinking

Courses in the social sciences ask hard questions about what it means to be an individual, a family member, a citizen of a local community, a nation, and the world. They focus on controversial topics such as ethics, human rights and freedoms, and personal and community responsibility. They look at these topics over time and in different cultures. They show how individuals and nations can behave in ways that range from cruelty to extreme kindness.

To wade through all this, you need well-developed critical-thinking skills (see Chapter 5):

- **Use SQ3R to learn new material.** Ask questions, and don't move forward until you understand what you are reading.

- **Think of the social sciences in terms of problems and solutions.** Whether you are studying affordable housing, stock market behavior, voting rights, or health-care policy, you are analyzing social problems and searching for workable solutions.

- **Look for strong evidence and logic.** It is up to you to judge whether arguments stand up or fall apart when closely examined.

- **Never assume that you or the writer is bias free.** Bias affects everything you read, sometimes intentionally, but often unconsciously. It also seeps into your own thinking. Be aware of your assumptions and try to set them aside as you read.

- **Ask hard questions about conclusions and generalizations.** Conclusions may be based on faulty cause-and-effect logic, and generalizations may be steeped in bias.

Your personal beliefs—your definition of a family, your view of history, your understanding of how others influence how you think—may be tested in your social science courses. While this testing may be difficult at times, the payoff of greater knowledge and broader perspective is worth the effort.

In addition to reading the words and mathematical symbols and formulas in math and science texts, you will also be "reading" visual aids. Visual aids are also found in social sciences and humanities texts.

How Do You "Read" Visual Aids?

Visual aids present data in tables, charts, drawings, maps, and photographs. Their purpose is to show, clarify, or summarize information in a form that is easy to read and understand. A table or chart can present information more concisely than if the information were presented in paragraph form. PowerPoint and other software programs make visual aids easy to create.

As you will see in Chapter 9, visual aids are also important study tools. When you translate words in a text into a table or chart, you simplify the information and engage in active learning.

Visual Aids
tables, charts, drawings, maps, and photographs that present information.

What Visual Aids Show

Visual aids highlight statistical comparisons that show the following:

- **Trends over time.** The number of computers with Internet connections per household in 2010 as compared with the number in 2002

real people

use what they know to learn and solve problems

Laban Seyoum

Political science graduate student, Southern Connecticut State University

n many ways, Laban Seyoum's story is common to many immigrants who came to this country to find a better life.

Born in Ethiopia (now Eritrea), Laban grew up in the middle of a civil war, saw his father falsely imprisoned by a brutal military dictator, faced deportation, and spent two long years traveling to the United States to find freedom.

Laban arrived in the United States when he was 18 and worked for two years in different part-time jobs before starting college at Southern Connecticut State University (SCSU) in 2003. The striking contrast between the education he was used to in Africa and the education he encountered here forced him to learn new skills and redefine what it means to be educated.

"In Ethiopia, I was trained to memorize," Laban explained. "The professor would give a well-structured lecture, and then once a month there would be an exam, which would require nothing more than a recitation of the class notes. American education teaches analytical thinking, and memorizing dates and facts is only a part of it."

Stop and Think

- Rather than using what he knew to learn new material, Laban had to "unlearn" basic approaches to education. Have you ever been in a situation where going forward required that you first take a few steps back?

Laban struggled most with reading. Although English is the language of instruction in Ethiopia, he didn't like to read and would fall asleep over his books. That changed when he realized that pursuing a major in political science depended on keeping up with the latest news.

"I read newspapers for at least a half hour a day. I also read short stories. Nothing complicated," said Laban. "My purpose was not to dissect the stories or analyze the news but to tolerate reading and make it a habit."

Laban had other purposes as well. He recited material aloud to eliminate his accent and improve his grammar. "As my reading improved, so did my ability to understand concepts and read faster. My writing also got better," he said.

Laban followed the advice of an English professor and began copying sentences, word for word, from newspapers and books. "As I copied from Winston Churchill, I became comfortable with sentence structure. I am a better writer today because of this tedious work."

Stop and Think

- Laban learned to love reading by reading what he loved. Apply this principle to yourself. What would inspire you to become a better reader and connect with your coursework?

By the time he was in graduate school, Laban had come a long way. He was able to connect new information to what he knew and link information from different sources to solve problems. He is happy he has come so far, since he needs solid reading and writing skills in his planned career in politics. A passionate advocate who worked during the 2008 presidential election and served as a congressional intern in 2009, Laban is determined to improve himself every day. "The U.S. has given me an enormous opportunity," he said, "and I'm going to live up to it."

Think about Laban and Think about Yourself

- Whether you were born abroad or in the United States, what obstacles have you had in your education, and how did you overcome them?

- American students build new knowledge on what they know and use critical thinking to connect ideas. How can this habit give you an advantage in the global marketplace?

© Seth Wenig/AP Images

President **Barack Obama** started his career as a community organizer in Chicago. As a senator of Illinois, he put his knowledge of the law to work. When he ran for president, he used what he knew about building grassroots support and strong teams. His success is linked, in part, to his ability to inspire people and build an organization.

use what you know

- **Relative rankings.** The size of the advertising budgets of four major companies
- **Distributions.** Student performance on standardized tests by geographic area
- **Cycles.** The regular upward and downward movement of the nation's economy as defined by periods of prosperity and recession

Knowing what to look for in visual aids, including tables and charts, will help you learn to "read" their information.

Tables

You will encounter *data tables* and *word tables*. Data tables present numerical information—for example, the number of students taking a standardized test in 50 states. Word tables summarize and consolidate complex information, making it easier to study and evaluate. Look at Key 8.1 in this chapter for an example of a word table. Key 8.5, which shows the top study-abroad destinations for U.S. college students, is a data table.[7]

Charts

Variables
Factors or conditions that are subject to change.

Also known as graphs, *charts* show statistical comparisons in visual form. They present **variables**, which are numbers that can change, often along vertical—top to bottom—and horizontal—side to side—axes. You will find pie, bar, and line charts in your texts.

- **Pie charts** present data as wedge-shaped sections of a circle to show the relative size of each item as a percentage of the whole.
- **Bar charts** consist of horizontal bars of varying lengths to show relative as well as absolute quantities. Whereas pie charts compare individual parts with the whole, bar charts compare items with one another.
- **Line charts** show trends. The horizontal axis often shows a span of time, and the vertical axis frequently represents a specific measurement such as dollars.

Key 8.6 uses data from a National Endowment for the Arts report, "To Read or Not to Read: A Question of National Consequence," to show examples of a bar and a line chart.[8] The bar chart shows the percentage of U.S. college freshmen who read little or nothing for pleasure. The line chart shows the average annual spending on books per household between 1985 and 2005. Key 8.7 is a pie chart showing the regions of the world from which foreign students in the United States originate.[9]

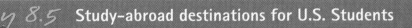
	NUMBER OF STUDENTS		NUMBER OF STUDENTS
1. Britain	32,705	11. Japan	5,012
2. Italy	27,831	12. Argentina	3,617
3. Spain	24,005	13. Greece	3,417
4. France	17,233	14. South Africa	3,216
5. China	11,064	15. Czech Republic	3,145
6. Australia	10,747	16. Chile	2,824
7. Mexico	9,461	17. Ecuador	2,813
8. Germany	7,355	18. Austria	2,810
9. Ireland	5,785	19. New Zealand	2,718
10. Costa Rica	5,383	20. India	2,627

Source: "Top 2007–08 Destinations for U.S. Students," In Karin Fischer, "For American Students, Study-Abroad Numbers Continue to Climb, but Financial Obstacles Loom." *The Chronicle of Higher Education,* November 21, 2008, p. A24. New York: Institute of International Education, 2008.

Key 8.6　Sample bar and line charts

Percentage of U.S. College Freshmen Who Read Little or Nothing for Pleasure

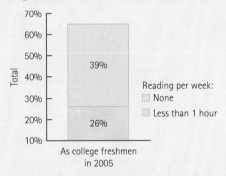

Source: University of California, Los Angeles, Higher Education Research Institute

Average Annual Spending on Books, by Consumer Unit
Adjusted for Inflation

The Consumer Price Index, 1982–1984 (less food and energy), was used to adjust for inflation.
Source: U.S. Department of Labor, Bureau of Labor Satistics

In National Endowment for the Arts, "To Read Not To Read: A Question of National Consequence, Research Report #47 (Washington DC: Office of Research and Analysis, NEA, November 2007). (available on the web at *www.nea.gov/research/ToRead.PDF*)

Read this excerpt from Frank Schmalleger's *Criminal Justice Today*, 10th edition.[10]

The Comprehensive Drug Abuse Prevention and Control Act of 1970

By 1970, America's drug problem was clear, and legislators were anxious to return to a more punitive approach to controlling drug abuse. Under President Richard Nixon, legislation designed to encompass all aspects of drug abuse and to permit federal intervention at all levels of use was enacted. Termed the Comprehensive Drug Abuse Prevention and Control Act of 1970, the legislation still forms the basis of federal enforcement efforts today. Title II of the law is the **Controlled Substances Act (CSA)**. The CSA sets up five schedules that classify psychoactive drugs according to their degree of psychoactivity and abuse potential:[38]

Controlled Substances Act (CSA)

Title II of the Comprehensive Drug Abuse Prevention and Control Act of 1970, which established schedules classifying psychoactive drugs according to their degree of psychoactivity.

Psychological Dependence

A craving for a specific drug that results from long-term substance abuse. Psychological dependence on drugs ins marked by the belief that drugs are needed to achieve a feeling of well-being.[iii]

Physical Dependence

A biologically based craving for a specific drug that results from frequent use of the substance. Physical dependence on drugs is marked by a growing tolerance of a drug's effects, so that increased amounts of the drug are needed to obtain the desired effect, and by the onset of withdrawal symptoms over periods of prolonged abstinence.[iv]

- Schedule I controlled substances have no established medical usage, cannot be used safely, and have great potential of abuse.39 Federal law requires that any research employing Schedule I substances be fully documented and that the substances themselves be stored in secure vaults. Included under this category are heroin, LSD, mescaline, peyote, methaqualone (Quaaludes), psilocybin, marijuana,[40] and hashish, as well as other specified hallucinogens. Penalties for first-offense possession and sale of Schedule I controlled substances under the federal Narcotic Penalties and Enforcement Act of 1986 include up to life imprisonment and a $10 million fine. Penalties increase for subsequent offenses.
- Schedule II controlled substances are drugs with high abuse potential for which there is a currently accepted pharmacological for medical use. Most Schedule II substances are also considered to be addicitive.[41] Drugs that fall into this category include opium, morphine, codeine, cocaine, phencyclidine (PCP), and their derivatives. Certain other stimulants, such as methylphenidate (Ritalin) and phenmetrazine (Preludin), and a few barbiturates with high abuse potential also come under Schedule II. Legal acess to Schedule II substances requires written nonrefillable prescriptions, vault storage, and thorough record keeping by vendors. Penalties for first-offense possession and sale of Schedule II controlled substances include up to 20 years' imprisonment and a $5 million fine under the federal Narcotic Penalties and Enforcement Act. Penalties increase for subsequent offenses.
- Schedule III controlled substances have lower abuse potential than do those in Schedules I and II. They are drugs with an accepted medical use but that may lead to a high level of **psychological dependence** or to moderate or low **physical dependence**.[42] Schedule III substances include many of the drugs found in Schedule II but in derivative or diluted form. Common low-dosage antidiarrheals, such as opium-containing paregoric, and cold medicines and pain relievers with low concentrations of codeine fall into this category. Anabolic steroids, whose abuse by professional athletes has been subject to scrutiny, were added to the list of Schedule III controlled substances in 1991. Legitimate access to Schedule III drugs is through a doctor's prescription (written or oral), with refills authorized in the same manner. Maximum penalties associated with first-offense possession and sale of Schedule III controlled substances under federal law include five years' imprisonment and fines of up to $1 million.
- Schedule IV controlled substances have a relatively low potential for abuse (when compared to higher schedules), are useful in established medical treatments, and involve only a limited risk of psychological or physical dependence.[43] Depressants and minor tranquilizers such as Valium, Librium, and Equanil fall into this category, as do some stimulants. Schedule IV substances are medically available in the same fashion as Schedule III drugs. Maximum penalties associated with first-offense possession and sale of Schedule IV substances under federal law include three years in prison and fines of up to $1 million.
- Schedule V controlled substances are prescription drugs with a low potential for abuse and with only a very limited possibility of psychological or physical dependence.[44] Cough medicines (antitussives) and antidiarrheals containing small amounts of opium, morphine, or codeine are found in Schedule V. A number of Schedule V medicines may be purchased through retail vendors with only minimal controls or upon the signature of the buyer (with some form of identification required). Maximum federal penalties for first-offense possession and sale of Schedule V substances include one year in prison and a $250,000 fine.

Source: Schmalleger, Frank, *Criminal Justice Today,* 10th edition, © 2009, pp. 583–584. Reprinted by permission of Pearson Education, Inc., Upper Saddle River, NJ.

Convert the important information from this excerpt into a word table. Use this template (copy it onto a separate page or recreate it in a computer document if you need more space):

CHARACTERISTICS OF THE COMPREHENSIVE DRUG ABUSE PREVENTION AND CONTROL ACT OF 1970

	SCHEDULE I CONTROLLED SUBSTANCES	SCHEDULE II CONTROLLED SUBSTANCES	SCHEDULE III CONTROLLED SUBSTANCES	SCHEDULE IV CONTROLLED SUBSTANCES	SCHEDULE V CONTROLLED SUBSTANCES
Description					
Drugs in category					
Penalties for abuse					

How can sorting material from verbal descriptions and converting them into tables (tapping your naturalistic and visual-spatial intelligence) help you study for exams?

_____

_____

Key 8.7   Sample pie chart

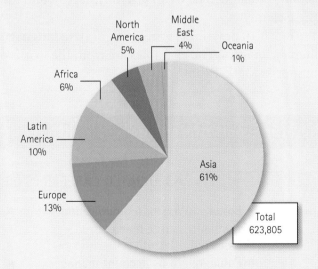

Foreign Students in the U.S. by Region of Origin, 2007–8

- North America 5%
- Middle East 4%
- Oceania 1%
- Africa 6%
- Latin America 10%
- Europe 13%
- Asia 61%
- Total 623,805

Source: Aisha Labi, "As World Economies Struggle, Competition Heats Up for Students from Abroad," *Chronicle of Higher Education*, November 21, 2008, p. A22. Copyright 2008, *The Chronicle of Higher Education*. Reprinted with permission.

How Do You Read
Works of Literature?

Even if you're not an English major, you will probably take one or more literature courses. These courses may be a required, or they may interest you. Whatever the reason, studying literature broadens your education and life in a number of ways:

- It exposes you to the world's greatest writers and writing.
- It allows you to experience other times and cultures.
- It helps you understand how others react to the problems of daily life.
- It gives you insight into your own thinking as you ask yourself how you would react to different situations.
- It gives you an avenue for lifelong enjoyment.

Key 8.8 lists just some of the literature courses you may take in college and related careers. Notice that the list includes careers that, on the surface, have nothing to do with literature. They are there because studying literature requires careful, critical thinking, which is the foundation for success in many fields.

Understanding Literary Elements

Literature courses ask you to look at different literary elements to find meaning on various levels. Although you might think that analyzing a book in depth will prevent you from enjoying it, the opposite is true. The process will help you see things that you never knew were there and increase your appreciation.

Novels and short stories tell stories through twists and turns in plots, the actions of characters, writing style, imagery, and more. Key 8.9 summarizes these elements.

Key 8.10 describes forms of **figurative language** that are at the heart of literary imagery. The examples are from the works of the great American humorist Mark Twain.

Figurative Language
words or phrases that describe one thing in terms of something else.

Key 8.8 Literature courses prepare you for different careers

COLLEGE COURSES	ASSOCIATED CAREERS IN DIFFERENT FIELDS	
- 20th century American literature - Modern European literature - 19th century romantic poetry - Greek and Roman drama - Contemporary theater	- Editor in Web-based publishing - Human resource manager - Sales representative - Public relations account manager - Internet-based librarian - Actor/director/producer	- Paralegal - Teacher - Government official - Writer/journalist - Community organizer - Filmmaker

LITERARY ELEMENT	DESCRIPTION	ADDITIONAL INFORMATION
Setting	Where and when the action occurs, including: ■ Location (the country or supernatural world in which the plot takes place) ■ Climate and season ■ Economic and social environment ■ Historical period	As you read about different historical contexts, remember that authors are writing about conditions and attitudes that may or may not still exist. Know that authors do not necessarily agree with what they describe.
Plot	The events and actions that take place	Plot includes such elements as: ■ *Exposition*—introductory material with story elements ■ *Foreshadowing*—suggestions of what will occur ■ *Conflict*—interactions that define the plot. ■ *Crisis*—the plot turning point. ■ *Climax*—what happens as a result of the crisis. ■ *Resolution*—events that conclude the action
Characters	Personalities, thoughts, and actions of the people who move the plot forward	You may discover a *protagonist*—a person who struggles toward someone or something—and an *antagonist*, who struggles against someone or something. The struggle may be internal or external. It may involve an attempt to achieve hopes and goals, to overcome problems, to defeat others who stand in the way of a goal, to change society, and more.
Theme	The work's central message revealed through the interplay of character and plot.	Such universal ideas as love, hate, relationships, war, and power are explored. Some themes are directly stated (explicit), others are implied. You have to dig through plot and character to uncover meaning.
Point of view	The author's perspective on the material he or she is presenting	This is often revealed though the voice of a *third-person narrator*, an objective observer who moves the story along without comment. When authors use a *first-person narrator*, information is presented through a main character.
Style	How the author uses language to communicate thoughts and feelings	Is the style sparse and bare, like that used by Ernest Hemingway, in *For Whom the Bell Tolls*? Is it descriptive, as in *Great Expectations* by Charles Dickens? Is it romantic with a focus on the intensity of feelings as in *Wuthering Heights* by Emily Bronte?
Imagery	Figures of speech used to create pictures in the reader's mind	See Key 8.10

FIGURE OF SPEECH	DEFINITION	EXAMPLES FROM MARK TWAIN
Metaphor	A comparison between two or more things that are not similar, **without** using the words *like* or *as* in the comparison.	"Put all your eggs in the one basket and—WATCH THAT BASKET."
Simile	A direct, explicit comparison between two things that lack similarity. The word *like* or *as* structures the comparison.	"Soap and education are not as sudden as a massacre, but they are more deadly in the long run."
Hyperbole	A gross, deliberate exaggeration for emphasis.	"Tomorrow night I appear for the first time before a Boston audience—4,000 critics."
Understatement	An understatement for emphasis or effect.	"Good breeding consists in concealing how much we think of ourselves and how little we think of the other person."
Personification	When a human trait is given to an inanimate object, animal, or idea.	"Habit is habit, and not to be flung out of the window by any man, but coaxed down-stairs a step at a time."
Analogy	A comparison of similar traits between dissimilar things.	"The fact that man knows right from wrong proves his *intellectual* superiority to the other creatures; but the fact that he can *do* wrong proves his *moral* inferiority to any creature that *cannot*."
Irony	The use of words in the opposite way than their intended meaning.	"An experienced, industrious, ambitious, and often quite picturesque liar."

Using Critical Thinking to Evaluate Literature

Use critical-reading skills to evaluate the material. Start with overview questions.

- What is the goal of the work? What are its themes? What do they mean to you?
- Has the work changed your thoughts, attitudes, or feelings in any way?
- Did you personally identify with any of the characters?
- Did the work give you greater understanding of a different time or culture?

Now raise critical-thinking questions that focus on the various literary elements:

- **Character.** How do characters reveal who they are? How are the main characters similar or different? How do a character's actions change the course of the story?

Chapter 8

TAKE ACTION
Connect Courses in Different Disciplines to Your Own Success

Identify the subject you are thinking of majoring in and any career areas that interest you:

_____

_____

Now, list five courses you are likely to take in college that are *unrelated* to your major (some of these may be required courses):

Course #1: _____

Course #2: _____

Course #3: _____

Course #4: _____

Course #5: _____

Engage your interpersonal intelligence and talk to someone—an instructor, a fellow student, an advisor—about how these courses may help you with your major and in your career. List three ways that you came up with together:

1. _____

2. _____

3. _____

- **Plot.** How would you evaluate the power of the story? Did it hold your interest?
- **Setting.** How does the setting relate to the actions of the major and minor characters?
- **Point of view.** How are the author's views expressed through characters' actions?
- **Style.** How would you describe the writing style? How does it compare to other works you have read?
- **Imagery.** How does the author use imagery as part of the theme?

This analysis will help you appreciate literature on many levels. Every time you analyze a work, you peel away layers of meaning to reveal artistry you may not see in a casual reading.

I was like a sponge. It was learn, learn, learn.

Robin Griffin, full-time worker who took courses to prepare for the next step in her ca

Habit for Success

use what you know

Below are examples of how you can put this habit into action in different situations. Use the three spaces to add your own ideas for actions you can accomplish now or in the future. Be specific, and be realistic.

When reading a novel, think about what you know about the historical context.

Analyze a strange sound your car is making based on your experience with cars and knowledge of the manual.

Use What You Know Habit for Success

Use what you know about working with people when you meet members of a new study group.

Think about how a study topic has touched your life. For example, if you've been through a recession, recall your experience.

Learn a new hobby or sport that builds on existing skills—for example, use what you know about volleyball to learn badminton.

Building Skills
for successful learning

Note the Important Points

How do you read math and science texts?

Name three approaches that will help you read and comprehend math and science texts.

1. _____

2. _____

3. _____

How do you read texts in the social sciences and humanities?

Name three approaches that will help you read and comprehend social science texts.

1. _____

2. _____

3. _____

How do you "read" visual aids?

Describe three types of charts and the information they often present.

1. _____

2. _____

3. _____

How do you read works of literature?

Briefly describe each of the following elements that help you understand a literary work.

1. setting _____

2. plot _____

3. characters _____

4. theme _____

5. point of view _____

6. writing style _____

7. imagery _____

Critical Thinking

applying learning to life

Get the Most from Your Textbook

From a math, science, or social science textbook, choose a chapter that you are about to cover in class. Do the following to maximize your understanding:

1. Read the chapter now, before its material is covered in class. Take notes. Check this box when you have read it through: ☐

2. Identify and work through one challenging concept or formula. Develop a plan to learn it. Base your plan on what will help most—memory techniques, study groups, practice with problems, asking your instructor for help, and so forth.

Note the concept or formula here:

_____

Briefly describe your plan:

_____

_____

Check the box when you have put your plan into action, and indicate whether it helped. Work done? ☐

How did your plan help?

_____

_____

_____

Team Building

collaborative solutions

Take a Study Group Approach to Quantitative Learning

Choose one or two people from one of your math, science, or social science classes—fellow students with whom you feel comfortable. Use problems from your assigned text.

1. Choose one problem, and work on it separately. After finishing the problem, come together to share your methods. Discuss how you approached the problem. What steps did you each take to solve it? What strategies did you use? How did you check to see if your procedures were correct?

2. Now pick a different problem on which to work together. After solving it, discuss your problem-solving process. Did you learn more or less by working together, as compared with working alone? Were you able to solve the problem faster by working together than when you worked alone? Did you gain a better understanding of the problem by working together?

Test Prep: Start It Now

Question What You Know to Prepare for a Test

Your first big test in your intro to psychology course is around the corner, and you are gearing up for a big push. You know that your instructor asks questions that tie in other fields, so you decide to prepare yourself by taking a mock test. The subject—socioeconomic and gender differences in coping with stress—will be on the exam. You start your preparation by reading this excerpt from your text, *Understanding Psychology*, 8th edition by Charles G. Morris and Albert A. Maisto. [11]

Socioeconomic and Gender Differences in Coping with Stress
Who experiences the most stress?

Consider the impact of socioeconomic status on stress and coping. In poor neighborhoods, addressing even the basic tasks of living is stressful. Housing is often substandard and crowded; there are fewer stores, and they offer lower quality goods; crime and unemployment rates are likely to be high; and schools have lower teacher—student ratios, high staff turnover, and more part-time teachers. In short, poor people have to deal with more stress than people who are financially secure (N. Adler et al., 1994; G. W. Evans & English, 2002; Gutman, McLoyd, & Tokoyawa, 2005). Moreover, some data indicate that people in low-income groups cope less effectively with stress and that, as a result, stressful events have a stronger impact on their emotional lives (Hammack, Robinson, Crawford, & Li, 2004). People in lower income groups are significantly more depressed, anxious, hopeless, and hostile. As we will see, those negative emotions are associated with worse physical and mental health (Gallo & Matthews, 2003). Psychologists have offered possible explanations for these data. People in lower socioeconomic classes often have fewer means for coping with hardship and stress (Gallo & Matthews, 2003). Low-income people also have fewer people to turn to and fewer community resources to draw on for support during stressful times (Ghate & Hazel, 2002). These factors help explain why stress often takes a greater toll on people in lower socioeconomic classes.

Are there gender differences in coping with stress? At present, the answer seems to be "yes"—at least under some circumstances. One study of the victims of Hurricane Andrew found that although men and women were affected equally when stress was measured physiologically, women reported experiencing more stress than men (T. Adler, 1993). In another study of 300 dual-income couples, women and men felt equally stressed by the state of their marriage, their jogs, and how well their children were doing. However, the women in this study experienced greater stress than men when problems developed in long-term relationships than the men were (R. C. Barnett, Brennan, & Marshall, 1994). Women and men also appear to respond differently to the stress caused by an automobile accident, with woman experiencing more stress both immediately after the accident and several months later (Bryant & Harvey, 2003). Some research indicates that when faced with equally stressful situations, men and women generally use quite similar coping strategies (L. S. Porter & Stone, 1995). However other research suggests the opposite—that in at least some circumstances, men and women use rather different coping strategies (Anshel, Porter, & Quek, 1998; Bellman, Forster, Still, & Cooper, 2003; Narayanan, Shankar, & Spector, 1999; Ptacek, Smith, & Dodge, 1994). For example, studies (Hussong, 2003; Nolen-Hoeksema, 1999) have found that when men are down or depressed, they are more likely than women to turn to alcohol; when women are blue, sad, or mad, they are more likely to ruminate about the problem, revisiting negative emotions and the events that led up to them in their minds (see "on the cutting Edge: Tend and Befriend: A Female Response to Stress?").

Source: Morris, Charles G., Maisto, Albert A., *Psychology: An Introduction,* 12th edition, © 2005. Used by permission of Pearson Education, Inc., Upper Saddle River, NJ.

Chapter 8

Now ask yourself these questions. Your goal is to link what you know in other areas to material you are learning. Write your answers on a separate piece of paper or on a computer file.

1. What is your personal experience with stress differences? Do the men you know react to stress differently than your female friends and family? Describe these differences.

2. Think about novels you read. Can you point to differences in the stress reactions of main characters that support or dispute the findings described in this excerpt? Cite and describe an example.

3. Think about current events that put people in stressful situations. Can you identify anything you've read recently that supports or disputes the findings described in this excerpt? Describe two examples.

4. Finally, evaluate whether this exercise stretched your thinking. In which of the courses you are now taking would questioning and linking to what you know improve how you learn?

active listening and note taking

taking in and recording information

javier bristled when he heard his sociology instructor say that
young people often stick with friends because their parents
disapprove. Javier likes his friends for who they are, not because
he's trying to rebel. When the instructor moved to another topic,
Javier was still annoyed and wanted to raise his hand to say so.
As he thinks about how he would word his comment, he blocks
everything out and stops taking notes. Only when he hears the
instructor talking about "a test next Thursday" does he realize
that he missed a lot.

In this chapter . . .

you explore answers to the following questions:

HOW can you become a better
listener?   p. 250

WHAT note-taking system should
you use?   p. 254

HOW can you make the most of class
notes?   p. 260

HOW do you combine class and text notes
to create a master set?   p. 265

HOW can you take notes faster?   p. 269

listen actively

Consider what others say as you try to understand different perspectives and new ideas. Listen for ideas that diverge from your own thinking—and include them in your notes.

How Can You Become a Better Listener?

As Javier discovered, the act of hearing isn't the same as the act of listening. *Hearing* refers to sensing spoken messages from their source. *Listening* involves a complex communication process in which the listener understands the speaker's intended message. With effort, you can improve your listening skill.

Know the Stages of Listening

Listening is made up of four stages that build on one another: sensation, interpretation, evaluation, and reaction. These stages take the message from the speaker to the listener and back to the speaker (see Key 9.1).

You can become a better listener by managing listening challenges (maximizing the sensation stage) and switching from a passive to an active mode (maximizing the interpretation and evaluation stages).

Asking questions is a key component of listening. This student is taking a moment to check his understanding of a concept with a classmate.

© Andrew Lichtenstein/Corbis

Manage Listening Challenges

Classic studies have shown that, immediately after listening, you are likely to recall only half of what was said. Four factors explain why:[1]

Listen a hundred times; ponder a thousand times; speak once.

Key 9.1 The listening process moves messages along a listening loop

SPEAKER DELIVERS MESSAGE TO LISTENER

Reaction	Evaluation	Interpretation	Sensation
Listener provides feedback to speaker through questions and comments.	Listener judges message against personal values and needs.	Listener attaches meaning to message.	Listener hears message when ears pick up sound waves.

Divided Attention

Although you are capable of listening to more than one message at the same time, you may not completely hear or understand any of them. Learning to focus your attention—even as it is pulled in different directions—is a big challenge. Your goal is to reduce **distractions** so you can concentrate.

To minimize *internal distractions*, try to be relaxed, comfortable, and clear headed for every class. Get enough sleep, eat enough to avoid hunger, and minimize stress by getting your assignments done. In addition, try to set personal problems aside until after class.

You can minimize *external distractions* by sitting near the front of the room and moving away from talkers. Bring a sweatshirt that you can put on or take off if the room temperature is unpredictable.

Distractions
internal or external interference that gets in the way of listening.

Shutting Out the Message

No instructor can force you to listen. That responsibility is yours. If you think that a subject is difficult or boring, you may tune out and miss information that prepares you for what comes next. If you focus on a narrow point and shut out the rest of the message, it can be tough to refocus.

Active Listening and Note Taking

251

How do you avoid these listening lapses? Start by realizing that instructors often present material that is not in the text and then test you on it. If you try to listen to the entire message and take comprehensive notes, you will be better prepared for exams. If you miss something, try to refocus quickly instead of worrying. After class, look at a classmate's notes to fill in the gaps.

The Rush to Judgment

Like Javier, you may stop listening when you hear something you don't like. Your prejudices may also interfere. If for whatever reason you do not like your instructors or their ideas, you may decide that they're not worth listening to. Anyone whose words have been ignored because of race, ethnic background, gender, sexual preference, or disability understands the power of prejudice to shut down listening.

For example, an instructor who is known to take a particular political point of view may find that students who oppose that view tend to shut down in class. A student who is uncomfortable about an instructor's sexual orientation or culture of origin may make assumptions about what the instructor says during lecture. The ultimate result of situations like this is that students lose the opportunity to learn new information, think it over critically, and gain something valuable from it.

Make sure you don't lose your opportunity to learn. Before you decide to tune out, consider these points:

- Being educated involves evaluating other points of view—even those different from your own. Be open to the possibility that your instructor may say something worth considering.

- You are under no obligation to like every instructor. However, academic integrity requires that you listen respectfully and with an open mind.

POWERFUL
QUESTIONS

listen actively

Think about what goes through your mind while you listen to instructors with whom you disagree. Do you stop listening, engage in an internal argument, or try to figure out how to respond? Do you try to see things from the instructor's perspective?

Come up with actions you are willing to take so that you can listen effectively the next time this occurs.

Hearing and Vision Problems and Learning Disabilities

If you have hearing problems, listen to a recorded lecture. Find out if digitalized recordings are available for downloading onto your computer or MP3 player, or ask your instructor if it is okay to record a lecture. Being able to see also helps you concentrate on what you hear. So if you need glasses for reading or distance vision, make sure you bring them.

The Real People profile on page 256 introduces you to Ismael Valenzuela, a veteran who suffered a mild traumatic brain injury in Iraq. Vets with injuries like this may have trouble listening. They should find out if their college has special services for veterans.

Become an Active Listener

On the surface, listening seems passive: You sit back as someone else speaks. In reality, effective listening is an active process that asks a lot of you.

Be on time. Start by showing up a few minutes before class is scheduled to begin. Instructors often make important announcements at the start of class and may summarize the last lecture. Have your notebook open when the instructor begins.

Set purposes for listening. Many instructors state what they will cover at the start of the class. A marketing instructor might say, for example, "Today, we're going to discuss web advertising." Writing the purpose in your notebook will help you focus. Following what comes next requires preparation: Before class, read assignments (syllabi include due dates; see example on page 101), and review notes from previous classes so you are up to speed.

Focus on understanding. Rather than taking notes on everything, record information only when you can say to yourself, "I get it!" If you miss material, leave some space and return later. Your instructor may repeat the point, or another comment may help you piece it together.

Ask questions. Even if you understand the material, ask yourself: What topic is this material part of? What is the bigger idea? How does it relate to the material covered in the last class? Questions link what you are learning to what you already know. Jot down questions for your instructor, and come back to them at a break point or during a class discussion.

Pay attention to verbal signposts. The **verbal signposts** instructors use may signal what they consider important. An idea described as "new and exciting" or "classic" is more likely to be on a test than one described as "interesting" (see Key 9.2).

Over time, you will also recognize your instructor's nonverbal speaking style. For example, you may realize that when she looks at her notes, she is probably about to say something important, or when he asks multiple questions about a topic, he is repeating for emphasis.

Verbal Signposts
spoken words or phrases that connect ideas and signal what is important.

SIGNALS POINTING TO KEY CONCEPTS	SIGNALS OF SUPPORT
A key point to remember . . .	A perfect example, . . .
Point 1, point 2, etc. . . .	Specifically, . . .
The impact of this was . . .	For instance, . . .
The critical stages in the process are . . .	Similarly, . . .

SIGNALS POINTING TO DIFFERENCES	SIGNALS THAT SUMMARIZE
On the contrary, . . .	From this you have learned, . . .
On the other hand, . . .	In conclusion, . . .
In contrast, . . .	As a result, . . .
However, . . .	Finally, . . .

Know what helps and hinders listening.   Ralph G. Nichols, a pioneer in listening research, defined the characteristics of successful and unsuccessful listeners by studying 200 freshmen at the University of Minnesota over a nine-month period. Measure yourself against his findings using the self-assessment in the green box on the next page.[3]

Your success in retaining information is linked to taking notes that become study tools. The note-taking systems described next will help you create notes you will turn to many times throughout the term.

What Note-Taking System Should You Use?

Note taking can be a challenge, especially when difficult concepts give you trouble or you can't keep up with the instructor's pace. These problems may leave you wondering how important notes are, especially since you have your text and other assigned materials to study. Don't be fooled: *Note taking involves you in the learning process in ways you cannot do without.*

Class notes provide a record of what went on and are tools for studying. Also, because you can't write *everything* down, note taking encourages you to

On a scale of 1 to 10—10 being the best and 1 being the worst—rate yourself in each category.

Characteristics of a good listener (10)	Characteristics of a poor listener (1)	How do you rate?
I make a conscious decision to work at listening and consider difficult material a challenge.	I don't care about the listening process and tune out difficult material.	
I fight distractions by concentrating harder.	I give into distractions and stop listening.	
I continue to listen to difficult or dry material, hoping to learn something interesting.	I give up when I lose interest.	
I withhold judgment until I hear everything.	I focus on my own thoughts as soon as a speaker says something controversial.	
I keep focused by recognizing organizational patterns, transitional language, and summary statements.	I get sidetracked by random comments.	
I adapt my note-taking style to the style and organization of the speaker.	I always take notes in the same way, no matter the speaker's style.	
I ignore negative reactions and force myself to listen.	I let an initial emotional response disrupt listening.	
I use extra time to evaluate, summarize, and question what I hear and anticipate what comes next.	I think about other things and often miss a lot.	

think critically and evaluate what is worth remembering. Ask yourself questions to decide whether to include material in your notes:

- Is this information important for my success in the course and in my career?
- Do I recognize its connections to what I already know?
- Do I want to learn it for myself?

You will benefit most from a note-taking system that feels comfortable to you and makes the most sense for the course content and the style of the instructor.

Take Notes in Outline Form

When a lecture seems well organized, it makes sense to use an informal outline to show how ideas and supporting details relate and to indicate levels of importance. Key 9.3 demonstrates how an informal outline uses consistent indentations and dashes to show these relationships.

By the way . . .

if you graduate from a four-year college, you are likely to earn $800,000 more over your lifetime than you would if you only had a high school diploma.[4]

Ismael Valenzuela

Two tours of duty in Iraq changed Ismael Valenzuela in ways he never imagined when he joined the Marines.

Surviving close combat, watching a friend die, and being exposed to a constant barrage of explosions and small-arms fire helped him understand what he wanted from life and what he had to do to get it. What he wanted after returning to civilian life at age 33 was to go back to school and study astronomy and engineering. A resident of New York City, his goal was to attend the Borough of Manhattan Community College. He had tried community college in El Paso, Texas, when he was younger, but he wasn't ready. "A big piece of the puzzle was still missing," he explained. Time and the Marine Corps made him serious and willing to listen to others.

Stop and Think

How have your own life experiences readied you for the challenge of college? Do you think tough times—like going to war—help you define your goals and work to get them?

The person whom Ismael listened to most was Dr. Eugenio Barrios, BMCC's director of admissions. He took Ismael under his wing because he saw in him a maturity forged in war. "Their desire is there," he said of Ismael and other veterans who were enrolled at BMCC.

"There is a word in Spanish for that: *las ganas.* They have that very strong will to succeed."

Having missed BMCC's application deadline, Ismael was forced to wait to start school. He got into fights, drank too much, and wrestled mental health problems that he brought back with him from Iraq. With the help of a Veterans Administration psychiatrist and Dr. Barrios, he made it to the start of classes.

Ismael now faced new struggles because he had not scored well on his BMCC placement exams. He thought about the time in Iraq when he was knocked unconscious for 10 minutes after his Humvee flipped over. But even if his fuzziness was linked to a mild brain injury or to post-traumatic stress disorder following seven years in the Marines, he wasn't about to make excuses for his scores. Rather, he took the words of Dr. Barrios to heart: To succeed, he had to bring everything he learned in Iraq to his schoolwork.

Stop and Think

Do you think that Ismael's ability to listen to Dr. Barrios was a sign of his growing ability to consider different views? What can you do to improve how you listen in difficult situations?

Iraq war verteran and student at the Borough of Manhattan Community College[5]

Up to the challenge, Ismael studies three times harder than other students and sees himself making progress, although he has already hit bumps on the road. He failed his first math class but is now passing all his courses. "I don't know how many times I just want to throw the books," he said. "But I am super-motivated. That is one of the things keeping me sane."

Ismael's goal is to one day return to the Marine Corps as a pilot.

Think about Ismael and Think about Yourself

Cleveland State University has "vets only" courses to help returning vets adjust to college. Says Professor John Schupp, who spearheaded the program, "In the military world it's the team. The squadron must survive. When you come to school, it's all personal—my books, my grades, my stuff, my notes." Even if you didn't serve in the military, how can working with others—in study groups or class projects—help you become a better listener in the classroom?

© Peter Kramer/AP Images

Bobbi Brown's success as an entrepreneur started with her willingness to consider her mother's perspective. When she was confused about what she wanted to do with her life, her mother told her to imagine it was her birthday and think about what she would most like to do. Bobbi's answer: Go play with makeup at a department store. Bobbi later founded a makeup business that is a multimillion-dollar success.

list
act

Civil Rights Legislation: 1860–1968

—Post-Civil War Era
  —Fourteenth Amendment, 1868: equal protection for all citizens
  —Fifteenth Amendment, 1870: constitutional rights of citizens regardless
    of race, color, or previous servitude
—Civil Rights Movement of the 1960s
  —National Association for the Advancement of Colored People (NAACP)
    —Established in 1910 by W.E.B. DuBois and others
    —Legal Defense and Education fund fought school segregation
  —Martin Luther King Jr., champion of nonviolent civil rights action
    —Marched on Washington, D.C.: 1963
    —Awarded NOBEL PEACE PRIZE: 1964
    —Led voter registration drive in Selma, Alabama: 1965
  —Civil Rights Act of 1964: prohibited discrimination in voting, education,
    employment, and public facilities
  —Voting Rights Act of 1965: gave the government power to enforce desegregation
  —Civil Rights Act of 1968: prohibited discrimination in the sale or rental of
    housing

When an instructor's presentation is disorganized, an outline may not be the best in-class strategy. Focus instead on taking down whatever information you can as you try to connect key topics. After class, do your best to restructure your notes and, if possible, rewrite them. If you are unclear about how ideas link, review the concept in your text or ask for help.

Guided Notes

Sometimes instructors distribute guided notes, usually in the form of an outline, to help you follow the lecture. However helpful this handout is, it should not replace your own notes, especially since guided notes usually lack detail. When you get guided notes on paper or on the board or overhead projector, copy them into your notebook or computer file, leaving space for additional information. When you receive these notes online but will not have your computer in class, be sure to take a printed copy with you.

Use the Cornell Note-Taking System

The *Cornell note-taking system*, also known as the *T-note system*, was developed by Walter Pauk at Cornell University.[6] It consists of three sections:

- **Notes,** the largest section, on the right (see Key 9.4). Skip lines between topics so you can see where sections begin and end.

Key 9.4 **The Cornell system has space for notes, comments, and a summary**

Label a sheet of paper with the date and title of the lecture.   *October 3, 200x, p. 1*

UNDERSTANDING EMPLOYEE MOTIVATION

Cue Column	Notes
Why do some workers have a better attitude toward their work than others?	Purpose of motivational theories —To explain role of human relations in motivating employee performance —Theories translate into how managers actually treat workers
	2 specific theories
Some managers view workers as lazy; others view them as motivated and productive.	—Human resources model, developed by Douglas McGregor, shows that managers have radically different beliefs about motivation. —Theory X holds that people are naturally irresponsible and uncooperative —Theory Y holds that people are naturally responsible and self-motivated
Maslow's Hierarchy	—Maslow's Hierarchy of Needs says that people have needs in 5 different areas, which they attempt to satisfy in their work. —Physiological need: need for survival, including food and shelter
self-actualization needs (challenging job) esteem needs (job title) social needs (friends at work) security needs (health plan) physiological needs (pay)	—Security need: need for stability and protection —Social need: need for friendship and companionship —Esteem need: need for status and recognition —Self-actualization need: need for self-fulfillment Needs at lower levels must be met before a person tries to satisfy needs at higher levels. —Developed by psychologist Abraham Maslow

Two motivational theories try to explain worker motivation. The human resources model includes Theory X and Theory Y. Maslow's Hierarchy of Needs suggests that people have needs in 5 different areas: physiological, security, social, esteem, and self-actualization.

Create the cue column by drawing a vertical line about 2 1/2 inches from the left side of the paper. End the line about 2 inches from the bottom of the sheet

Create the summary area by starting where the vertical line ends (about 2 inches from the bottom of the page) and drawing a horizontal line across the paper.

- **Cue column,** to the left of your notes. Leave it blank while you take notes, and fill it in later as you review. You might insert key words or comments to highlight ideas or clarify meaning. You might add examples or diagrams. You might raise questions to answer as you study.

- **Summary,** at the bottom of the page. Use this section to summarize critical points in your own words.

Key 9.4 shows how the Cornell system is used in a business course and gives you instructions to create the format yourself.

Create a Think Link

A *think link,* also known as a *concept map* or *word web,* is a visual form of note taking that uses shapes and lines to link ideas and supporting details. The visual design makes connections easy to see, and shapes and pictures extend the material beyond words.

To create a think link, start by circling or boxing your topic, in the middle of a sheet of paper. Next, draw a line from the topic, and write the name of one major idea at the end of the line. Circle that idea also. Then, jot down specific facts related to the idea, linking them to the idea with lines. Continue the process, connecting thoughts to one another with circles, lines, and words. Key 9.5 on the next page is a think link on the sociological concept called stratification.

Examples of think link designs include stair steps showing connected ideas that build toward a conclusion and a tree with trunk and roots as central concepts and branches as examples. In some situations a think link may be difficult to construct in class, such as if your instructor talks quickly. In this case, transform your notes later when you review.

Use Other Visual Note-Taking Strategies

Several other note-taking strategies will help you organize information and are especially useful to visual learners. These strategies may be too involved to complete in class, so save them for when you take text notes or combine class and text notes.

- **Time lines.** Use a time line to put information in chronological order. Draw a vertical or horizontal line, and connect each item to the line, in order, noting dates and event descriptions.

- **Tables.** Use the columns and rows of a table to organize information as you condense and

Inside Tips from
Carol, Career Coach

Your ability to take good notes is directly related to your ability to follow up action items after a business meeting. Without careful notes, you can forget what was said and mistake what you have to do next. Note-taking in the world of work is associated with being thorough and conscientious. The higher you go in an organization, the more important this skill becomes.

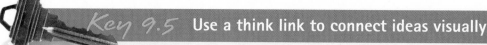
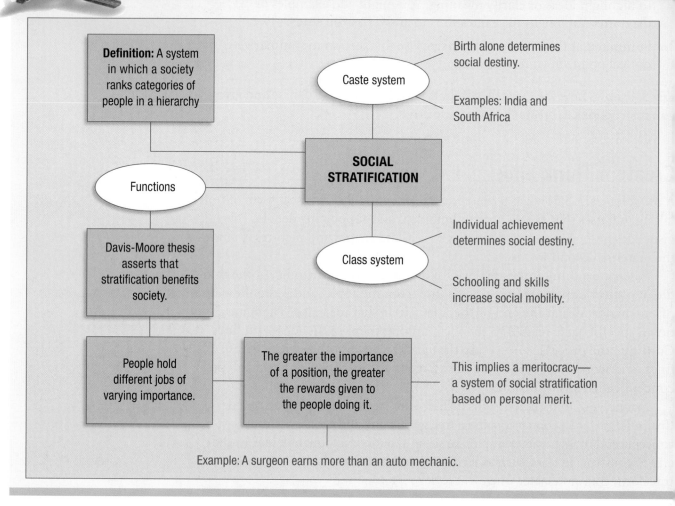

Definition: A system in which a society ranks categories of people in a hierarchy

Caste system

Birth alone determines social destiny.

Examples: India and South Africa

SOCIAL STRATIFICATION

Functions

Davis-Moore thesis asserts that stratification benefits society.

Class system

Individual achievement determines social destiny.

Schooling and skills increase social mobility.

People hold different jobs of varying importance.

The greater the importance of a position, the greater the rewards given to the people doing it.

This implies a meritocracy— a system of social stratification based on personal merit.

Example: A surgeon earns more than an auto mechanic.

summarize your class and text notes. The Take Action exercise in Chapter 8 shows you how to turn a block of text into a word table.

- **Hierarchy charts.** You can use a hierarchy chart to show levels within a government bureaucracy, levels of scientific classification of animals and plants, and more.

How Can You Make the Most of Class Notes?

Taking good class notes improves with practice—practice preparing, practice doing, and practice reviewing.

Prepare for Note Taking

Showing up for class on time is only the beginning. How else can you prepare?

More than anything else you do, completing reading assignments before class prepares you to take effective notes. Check your syllabi for assignment due dates, and then plan your reading time.

To get a sense of how each lecture relates to your reading assignment, compare the lecture topic listed on the syllabus with the topic in the text. If the lecture material is not in the text, you know you have a different listening and note-taking challenge than if the material is in the text. Why? Because hearing material for the first time is more difficult than hearing what is familiar.

Coming to class fully prepared also gives you note-taking flexibility. Say, for example, your instructor defines a word on the board, but before you can copy the definition, she presents an example that you want to hear. If you read the text before class and know that the definition is there, you can listen carefully to the example.

Review what you know.   Take 15 minutes before class to review your notes from the previous class and reading assignment notes for that day. This will give you the context to follow the lecture from the start. Without this preparation, you may find yourself flipping back in your notebook instead of listening to new information.

Before your instructor begins, write down one or two questions to put yourself in an active listening mode. If you know nothing about the topic, think about why learning it is important. If your questions are not answered during the lecture, *ask them.* This shows the instructor that you are involved with the material.

Gather your supplies.   Use a separate notebook for each course, and start a new page for each class. If you use a binder, punch holes in handouts and insert them immediately after your notes for that day. If you take notes on a laptop, open the file containing your class notes right away.

Choose the best note-taking system.   Select a system from those discussed earlier that will work best in each class. Consider these factors when making your choices:

- **The instructor's style.** You'll have a pretty good idea of this after a few classes. In the same term, you may have an instructor who is organized and speaks slowly, another who jumps from topic to topic and talks rapidly, and a third who goes off on tangents in response to questions. Your challenge is to adapt your note taking to each situation.

- **The course material.** You may decide that an informal outline works best for a highly structured lecture but that a think link is right for a looser presentation. Try one note-taking system for several classes, and then adjust if necessary.

- **Your learning style.** A visual-spatial learner might prefer think links or the Cornell system; a thinker type might be comfortable with outlines; an interpersonal learner might use

Focused, active listening is the foundation of good notes. You can only write down and understand what you have clearly heard.

© William Thomas Cain/Liaison/Getty Images

the Cornell system and fill in the cue column in a study group. You might even find that one system is best in class and another in review sessions.

Gather support.   In each class, set up a support system with one or two students so that you can look at their notes when you're absent or confused about something you heard.

TAKE ACTION
Prepare to Listen and Take Notes in Your Hardest Class

Get set to take in and record information in your most difficult class.

Course name and date of next class:

_____

Consult your syllabus, and then list everything you have to read before the next class (include pages from text and supplemental sources):

_____

_____

List three listening strategies you can use to minimize distractions during the class:

1. _____

2. _____

3. _____

Which note-taking system is best suited for the class? Why?

_____

_____

Write the names and contact information of two classmates whose notes you can borrow if you miss a class or are confused about material:

1. _____

2. _____

Briefly describe a note-taking problem that you have in class.

_____

_____

Now brainstorm potential solutions to your problem, linking each solution to an intelligence. Use the right-hand column to record your ideas.

INTELLIGENCE	USE MI STRATEGIES TO TAKE EFFECTIVE NOTES	USE MI STRATEGIES TO COME UP WITH SOLUTIONS
Verbal-Linguistic 	■ Rewrite your class notes in an alternate style to see connections more clearly. ■ Combine class and text notes to get a complete picture.	
Logical-Mathematical	■ When combining notes into a master set, integrate the material into a logical sequence. ■ Create tables that show relationships.	
Bodily-Kinesthetic	■ Think of your notes as a crafts project that enables you to see "knowledge layers." Use colored pens to add texture. ■ Study with your notes spread in sequence around you to see knowledge building from left to right.	
Visual-Spatial	■ Take notes using colored pens or markers. ■ Rewrite lecture notes in think-link format, focusing on what's most important.	
Interpersonal 	■ Try to schedule a study group right after class to discuss your notes. ■ Review class notes with a partner. Compare notes to see what the other missed.	
Intrapersonal	■ Schedule quiet time soon after class to review and think about your notes. ■ As you review, decide whether you understand the material or need help.	
Musical	■ To improve recall, recite concepts in your notes to rhythms. ■ Write a song that includes material from your class and text notes. Use the refrain to emphasize what is important.	
Naturalistic	■ As you create a master note set, notice similarities and differences in concepts by organizing material into natural groupings.	

Record Information Effectively During Class

Use these suggestions to record what is important in a format that is easy to review:

- Date and identify each page. When you take several pages of notes, write 11/27A, 11/27B, for example, to keep track of page order. Add the lecture topic (11/27A—Bird Migration Patterns) to make it easy to gather all your notes.

- If the instructor jumps from topic to topic during a single class, start a new page for each topic.

- Record whatever your instructor emphasizes by paying attention to verbal and nonverbal cues.

- Write down all key terms and definitions.

- When a concept is difficult, record examples, applications, and links to other material.

- Write down all questions your instructor raises, since they may be on a test.

- Be organized but not fussy. You can improve your notes later.

- Write quickly but legibly, perhaps using shorthand (see suggestions later in the chapter).

- Leave one or more blank spaces between points so that when you review you can see where one topic ends and another begins. (This won't work with a think link.)

- Draw pictures and diagrams to illustrate ideas.

- Use a star or underlining to indicate important material. (Highlighting takes too much time.)

- Flag important material in a consistent way—with indenting, spacing, or underlining—so you can find it later.

- If you have trouble understanding a concept, record as much as you can, leaving space, and then flag the margin with a large question mark. After class, try to clarify your questions in the text or with a study partner, or ask your instructor for help.

Key 9.6 will prepare you to take notes during class discussions.

Review and Revise Your Notes

Because your class notes may be incomplete in some places, confusing in others, and unreadable in still others, it is critical to review and revise them soon after class. Fill in gaps while you still remember what went on, clarify shorthand and messy handwriting, and use empty spaces on the page to raise questions. Reviewing and revising your class notes prepares you for the vital step of combining class and text notes.

Listen to everyone; you never know when something important will be said.

Use a think link to connect ideas that come from different perspectives.

Take good notes during discussion:

Listen for threads that weave through comments. They may signal an important point.

Listen for encouraging comments from the instructor, such as "You make a great point."

Take notes when the instructor rephrases and clarifies a point.

How Do You Combine Class and Text Notes to Create a Master Set?

Studying from a single, comprehensive set of notes is more efficient than flipping back and forth between multiple sets. Furthermore, studying from either text or class notes alone is not enough. Your instructor may present material in class that is not in the text or gloss over topics that the text covers in depth. So take the time to combine your class and text notes into a **master note set** that reflects everything you need to know.

Master Note Set
combined text and class notes that make studying easier.

Take a Step-by-Step Approach

Step 1: Act quickly while the material is fresh. If possible, use a computer.

Step 2: Reduce your notes to focus on what's important. Your goal is to create a key terms and concepts summary that covers the material in your class and text notes. To do this, look for common threads that appear in both note sets. Pay special attention to information in summary charts or tables and to examples that bring the material together. Go back to your text, if necessary, to clarify confusing information, and then summarize it here. As you begin to study, move back and forth between the full set and the reduced set. Key 9.7 shows a comprehensive outline and a reduced key-term outline of the same material.

Step 3: Recite what you know.   As you approach exam time, use your bare-bones notes as cues for reciting everything you know about a topic. Recite out loud, write your responses on paper, make flash cards, or work with a study partner to ensure that you know the material in depth and that you can produce what you know on a test.

Step 4: Think critically.   Use strategies like these when you study from your combined notes:

- Brainstorm and write down examples from other sources that illustrate central ideas. Write down new ideas or questions that come up as you review.
- Think of ideas from readings or lectures that support or clarify your notes.
- Consider what in your class notes differs from your reading notes and why.
- Apply concepts to end-of-text problems, to problems posed in class, or to real-world situations.

Step 5: Review and review again.   Continue to review your key-word summary until you know the material inside out. "Few of us are gifted with the kind of memory that allows us to reproduce something new and difficult after one exposure," explain study-skills experts James and Ellin K. Deese.[7] Try to vary your review methods—focusing on active involvement. Recite the material to yourself, have a Q&A session with a study partner, or take a practice test. Summarize your notes in writing from memory after you review.

Step up your efforts before a test. Schedule longer review sessions, call a study group meeting, and review more frequently. Shorter sessions of intense review interspersed with breaks may be more effective than long hours of continuous studying.

A word of warning about comparing notes with study group partners: Don't be surprised if each of you has a different take on what went on in class, especially if the material was difficult or the presentation confusing. When this happens, work together to reconstruct critical information and, if necessary, bring in other perspectives.

Different Views of Freedom and Equality in the American Democracy

I. U.S. democracy based on 5 core values: freedom and equality, order and stability, majority rule, protection of minority rights, and participation.

    A. U.S. would be a "perfect democracy" if it always upheld these values.

    B. U.S. is less than perfect, so it is called an "approaching democracy."

II. Freedom and Equality

    A. Historian Isaiah Berlin defines freedom as either positive or negative.

        1. Positive freedoms allow us to exercise rights under the Constitution, including right to vote.

        2. Negative freedoms safeguard us from government actions that restrict certain rights, such as the right to assemble. The 1st Amendment restricts government action by declaring that "Congress shall make no law . . ."

    B. The value of equality suggests that all people be treated equally, regardless of circumstance. Different views on what equality means and the implications for society.

        1. Equality of opportunity implies that everyone has the same chance to develop inborn talents.

            a. But life's circumstances—affected by factors like race and income—differ. This means that people start at different points and have different results. E.g., a poor, inner-city student will be less prepared for college than an affluent, suburban student.

            b. It is impossible to equalize opportunity for all Americans.

        2. Equality of result seeks to eliminate all forms of inequality, including economic differences, through wealth redistribution.

    C. Freedom and equality are in conflict, say text authors Berman and Murphy: "If your view of freedom is freedom from government intervention, then equality of any kind will be difficult to achieve. If government stays out of all citizen affairs, some people will become extremely wealthy, others will fall through the cracks, and economic inequality will multiply. On the other hand, if you wish to promote equality of result, then you will have to restrict some people's freedoms—the freedom to earn and retain an unlimited amount of money, for example."*

KEY-TERM OUTLINE OF THE SAME MATERIAL

Different Views of Freedom and Equality in the American Democracy

I. America's 5 core values: freedom and equality, order and stability, majority rule, protection of minority rights, and participation.

    A. "Perfect democracy"

    B. "Approaching democracy"

II. Value #1—Freedom and equality

    A. Positive freedoms and negative freedoms

    B. Different views of equality: equality of opportunity versus equality of result

    C. Conflict between freedom and equality centers on differing views of government's role

*Larry Berman and Bruce Allen Murphy, *Approaching Democracy: Portfolio Edition,* Upper Saddle River, NJ: Prentice Hall, 2005, pp. 6–8.

TAKE ACTION
Combine Class and Text Notes

Following are two presentations on the same topic: The first is an excerpt on hate crimes from a sociology textbook, and the second presents class notes based on a lecture. After you read both, complete the following:

List three key facts found in the class notes but not in the text:

1. _____

2. _____

3. _____

What does this tell you about the importance of combining your notes when you study?

_____

On paper or in a computer file, combine both note sets into a comprehensive set. Be creative as you try one of the note-taking systems presented earlier. If you are a visual learner, try a think link.

Excerpt on hate crimes from *Sociology,* 10th edition, by John J. Macionis

The term **hate crime** refers to *a criminal act against a person or a person's property by an offender motivated by racial or other bias.* A hate crime may express hostility toward someone's race, religion, ancestry, sexual orientation, or physical disability. The federal government records about 10,000 incidents of hate crimes each year.

Most people were stunned by the brutal killing in 1998 of Matthew Shepard, a gay student at the University of Wyoming, by two men filled with hate toward homosexuals. The National Gay and Lesbian Task Force reports that one in five lesbians and gay men is physically assaulted and that more than 90 percent are verbally abused because of sexual orientation (cited in Berrill, 1992:19–20). Victims of hate-motivated violence are especially likely to be people who contend with multiple stigmas, such as gay men of color. Yet hate crimes can victimize anyone: A recent study found that about 25 percent of the hate crimes based on race targeted white people (Jenness & Grattet, 2001).

By 2002, forty-five states and the federal government had enacted legislation that increased penalties for crimes motivated by hatred. Supporters are gratified, but opponents charge that such laws punish "politically incorrect" thoughts.[8]

	NOTES FROM SOCIOLOGY CLASS ON HATE CRIMES

What are hate crimes?
  —also called bias crimes
  —defined in a 1990 federal law as an offense "in which the defendant's conduct
    was motivated by hatred, bias, or prejudice, based on the actual or perceived
    race, color, religion, national origin, ethnicity, gender, or sexual orientation
    of another individual or group of individuals."
      —Congress passed 2nd law in 1994 that focused on "crimes of violence
        motivated by gender." These crimes are considered felonies.
          —The same law labeled offenses motivated by bias against people with
            disabilities as hate crimes.
          —Examples: Matthew Shepard was murdered in 1998 because he was gay;
            James Byrd Jr. was murdered in 1999 because of his race.
Controversy over whether hate crimes should be punished more severely than crimes not
motivated by bias.
  —One side says they should
      —motive has always been considered in weighing criminal responsibility
      —hate crimes inflame the public more than non-hate crimes, and punishment
        should be given with that in mind
      —hate crime victims often have greater injury than victims of other crimes
  —Critics disagree
      —difficult to separate hard-core racism from impulsive acts, especially
        if the offender is young
      —hate-crime laws are a potential threat to free-speech guarantees in that
        courts may convict people because of their attitudes and words, not
        their actions.

How Can You Take Notes Faster?

When you use **shorthand** in instant and text messaging, it helps you write
faster. You can use the same notations in class to record important ideas.
Because you are the only reader, you can abbreviate words any way you want.
Use these tips, and the notations on the next page, to create shorthand.

1. Use standard abbreviations in place of complete words.

2. Remove vowels from the middle of words: prps = purpose, lwyr = lawyer,
   cmptr = computer.

3. Substitute word beginnings for entire words: info = information, subj =
   subject.

4. Form plurals by adding s to shortened words: prblms = problems.

Shorthand
rapid handwriting
during note taking
that uses symbols,
abbreviations, and
shortened words.

w/	with		cf	compare, in comparison to
w/o	without		ff	following
ur	you are		Q	question
→	means; resulting in		gr8	great
←	as a result of		pov	point of view
↑	increasing		<	less than
↓	decreasing		>	more than
∴	therefore		=	equals
b/c	because		b&f	back and forth
≈	approximately		△	change
+ or &	and		2	to; two; too
y	why		afap	as far as possible
NO. or #	number		e.g.	for example
i.e.	that is,		c/o	care of
cos	change of subject		lb	pound

5. Abbreviate proper nouns such as places, people, companies, scientific substances, events, and so on: DC = Washington, D.C., H2O = water, Moz. = Wolfgang Amadeus Mozart.

6. If a word or phrase is repeated, write it out once, and then abbreviate it. For example, if you listen to a lecture on genetic links to breast cancer, start by writing "breast cancer gene 1," and then use BRCA1 as you continue.

If your notes aren't comprehensive, legible, or focused, think critically about how to improve them. Can't read them? Get more sleep, improve your handwriting, or use a pen that doesn't leak. Lots of confusing gaps? You might have been distracted, not figured out how to deal with a disorganized instructor, or not read the assignment. Brainstorm solutions from the strategies in this chapter. With effort, your notes will become a dependable learning tool.

College is a refuge from hasty judgment.

Robert Frost, American poet and Pulitzer Prize winner (1874–1963)

Habit for Success

listen actively

Below are examples of how you can put this habit into action in different situations. Use the three spaces to add your own ideas for actions you can accomplish now or in the future. Be specific, and be realistic.

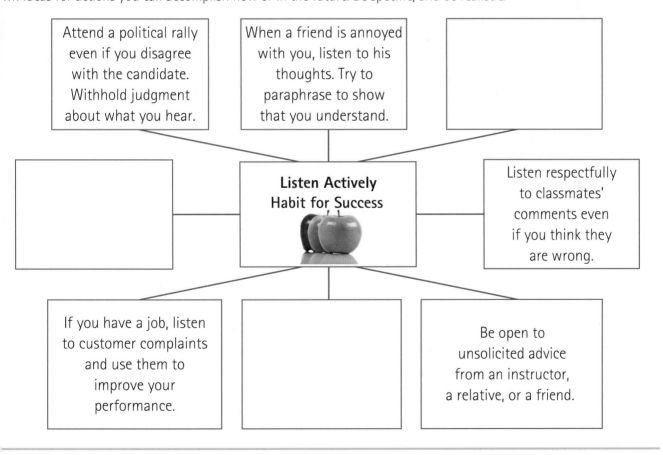

Attend a political rally even if you disagree with the candidate. Withhold judgment about what you hear.	When a friend is annoyed with you, listen to his thoughts. Try to paraphrase to show that you understand.	

Listen Actively Habit for Success

Listen respectfully to classmates' comments even if you think they are wrong.

If you have a job, listen to customer complaints and use them to improve your performance.

Be open to unsolicited advice from an instructor, a relative, or a friend.

Note the Important Points

How can you become a better listener?

What do you do that makes it harder to listen in class?

_____

What steps will you take to improve or replace habits that cause listening problems?

_____

What note-taking system should you use?

What do you consider one advantage of taking notes in each format?

Outline form: _____

Cornell T-system: _____

Think Link: _____

Which system are you likely to use in your two toughest classes?

Class #1: _____

Class #2: _____

How can you make the most of class notes?

Name two actions you will take to prepare to take better notes.

Action #1: _____

Action #2: _____

Name two actions you will take to effectively record information during class.

Action #1: _____

Action #2: _____

How do you combine class and text notes to create a master set?

List the steps you should take to create a master note set:

_____

How can you take notes faster?

Create two personal shorthand symbols to speed up your note taking.

1. _____

2. _____

Critical Thinking
applying learning to life

Identify Optimum Listening and Note-Taking Conditions

Think of a recent class in which you were able to <u>listen effectively</u> and take notes.

Describe the environment (course title, type of classroom setting, and so forth):

_____

_____

Describe the instructor's style (lecture, group discussion, Q&A):

_____

_____

Describe your level of preparation and attitude toward the class:

_____

_____

Describe your note-taking style and the effectiveness of your notes as study tools:

_____

_____

Describe any listening barriers:

_____

_____

Now think of a recent class in which you found it <u>hard to listen</u> and take notes.

Describe the environment (course title, type of classroom setting, and so forth):

_____

_____

Describe the instructor's style (lecture, group discussion, Q&A):

_____

_____

Describe your level of preparation and attitude toward the class:

_____

_____

Describe your note-taking style and the effectiveness of your notes as study tools:

_____

_____

Describe any listening barriers:

_____

Examine the two situations. Identify two conditions that are crucial for effective listening and note taking:

_____

_____

Describe one way to improve your listening and note taking in the more difficult situation:

_____

_____

_____

Team Building

collaborative solutions

Create a Note-Taking Team

In this course or another, come together with two or three classmates to review the quality and style of each other's class notes. Your goal is to strengthen your personal note-taking techniques.

1. Pass around the class notes you took on a specific day. Try to choose a day when a lot of new material was covered and when student comments were important. Allow as much time as needed to review one another's work. (Reread your own notes as part of this step.)

2. Make a list of the strengths and weaknesses of each note set. As you read, think back to what you considered important in class and how you included that material in your own notes.

3. Next, discuss each other's evaluations. Consider choice of note-taking system, effectiveness of short-hand, comprehensiveness of notes (material included and omitted), usefulness of the notes as a study tool, etc. Think about what techniques worked well, and consider ways to use them.

4. Finally, have each person choose one new technique to start using right away. In a week, reconvene to assess your progress.

Test Prep: Start It Now

Search for Barriers to Active Listening

Choose a day when you took notes in class, and contact a classmate who was also there. Exchange copies of your notes from that day so that you can each experience the class from a different perspective. Read each other's notes as you try to identify listening barriers that got in the way of hearing what the instructor said.

Classmate's name: _____

Date of class notes: _____

Consider what may have obstructed your listening. Your partner should do the same. Then rewrite your notes, including useful ideas and supporting details from your classmate's notes.

Answer the following questions:

What, if anything, was missing from your notes that you gained from reading your classmate's notes?

_____

_____

What did you learn about the material from that day's class from reading your classmate's notes?

_____

_____

Name any listening barrier(s) that affected your note-taking ability on that day.

_____

Name any changes you plan to make in your note-taking strategy following this exercise.

_____

_____

_____

You now have a better understanding of that day's class, an understanding of your listening behavior in a specific situation, and an improved set of notes. Refer to these and the rest of your notes regularly in the time leading up to this test. Consider meeting again with this classmate to review notes for other important classes.

Time for a change: take steps to improve a habit for success

For this exercise, refer back to the results of the assessment you took in Chapter 1 on page 19.

First: Write the third of your three *strongest* Habits for Success here (a different strong habit from the ones you explored on pages 93 and 186)._____

_____

Why does it work for you? Name a result of this habit that helps you solve problems and move toward important goals._____

_____

Now: Write the third of your three *least developed* Habits for Success here (a different habit from the ones you explored on pages 93 and 186)._____

_____

_____

Why do you want to develop this habit—in other words, what positive effect do you think it will have on your ability to solve problems and achieve goals? _____

_____

_____

Focus on this challenging habit more carefully. Name two specific, short-term actions you can take to power up this habit. (Refer to the actions you listed in Chapter 1's Take Action exercise on page 14 if they connect to this habit.)

1. _____

2. _____

Name a support person, and describe your plan for communicating your progress and getting encouragement (for example, have your person call, e-mail, or text you on a regular basis to check up on particular actions you've committed to taking).

Remember, the way to make a habit stick is to do it over and over again over a period of at least 21 days. *Right now,* commit to checking your progress on a regular basis over the next three weeks, using whatever method you prefer.

Describe the method you will use to track your habit development.

What will you use? (example: date book, electronic planner, cell phone alarm, e-mail alert)

When and how often will you use it? (example: every day at bedtime, every other day when I get up, twice a week after a particular class)

It's time for a change—put your plan in motion *today.* You will revisit your progress in Chapter 12.

Revisit Your Progress
Look back at the Time for a Change exercise at the end of Chapter 6 on page 186. Take a moment to describe how you have developed this habit, including how consistently you perform your chosen actions, how well you document your progress, the helpfulness of your support system, and whether you are satisfied with your progress. If you are not satisfied, describe how you will adjust your actions in order to move ahead.

_____

_____

_____

_____

Quick review of your end of Chapter 3 habit: Briefly describe the status of your progress on the habit from page 93.

_____

_____

_____

_____

_____

test taking I

test preparation and objective tests

ryan is panicked. He never imagined that tests in college would be much harder than tests in high school or that he needed to learn new test-taking strategies. A multiple-choice question is a multiple-choice question, right? Wrong. To his surprise, his first tests included questions that looked manageable but weren't. He was thrown off by the way questions were worded, by answers that required more than memorized facts, and by how much he had to know. He failed two of his three early tests and worries that he is headed toward the same result at finals time.

In this chapter . . .

you explore answers to the following questions:

HOW can preparation improve test performance?   p. 282

HOW can you work through test anxiety?   p. 287

WHAT general strategies add to test success?   p. 290

HOW can you master objective test questions?   p. 292

HOW can you learn from test mistakes?   p. 300

© Shutterstock

take responsible risks

Taking calculated risks allows you to test your limits and take action that moves you ahead. With the risk of every test comes the opportunity to grow.

How Can Preparation Improve Test Performance?

Ryan doesn't realize it, but he is lucky. He learned early in the term that he needs help. He can improve his performance if he starts now to develop his test-taking skills. As you will see in this chapter, test taking is about preparation, persistence, and strategy. It is also about conquering fears, focusing on details, and learning from mistakes.

You prepare for exams by attending class; staying on top of assignments; completing readings, papers, and projects; and participating in class discussions. Add the following tactics to your test-prep routine.

Identify Test Type and Coverage

Before you start studying, find out all you can about the test:

- **Topics that will be covered.** Will it cover everything since the course began, or will it have a narrower focus?

- **Material you will be tested on.** Will the test cover only what you learned in class and in the text, or will it also include outside readings?

- **Types of questions.** Will the questions be objective (multiple choice, true/false, sentence completion), subjective (essay), or a combination?

- **How the test will be graded.** Will partial credit be given for certain questions? Do you need to show your work (on math and science tests)? Are some sections worth more than others?

A winning effort begins with preparation.

Joe Gibbs, Super Bowl Champion football coach

Your instructors may answer these questions in class. They may explain the test format and topics. They may hint about possible questions, either directly ("I might ask a question on....") or indirectly ("One of my favorite theories is..."). How else can you find answers?

Use SQ3R to identify what's important. Often, the questions you write and ask yourself as you read may be part of the test. Textbook study questions are also good candidates.

Listen for clues at review sessions. Many instructors hold review sessions before midterms and finals. Bring your own questions, and listen to what others ask. They may deal with topics you thought you knew but need help with.

Meet with or e-mail your instructor. Spending a few minutes talking about the test one-on-one may clarify misunderstandings and help you focus on what to study.

Talk to people who already took the course. Ask about test difficulty, whether tests generally cover assigned readings or class notes, and question type. If you learn that the instructor focuses on specific facts, for example, incorporate a flash-card drill into your study routine. If she emphasizes broad concepts, focus on the big picture.

Examine old tests, if the instructor permits. Some instructors make old tests available in class, online, or in the library. If you get a test from another source, such as a sorority or fraternity, ask the instructor if it's okay to look at it. Old tests will help you answer questions like:

- Do tests focus on examples and details, general ideas and themes, or a combination?
- Are the questions straightforward or confusing and sometimes tricky?
- Will you be asked to integrate facts from different areas in order to draw conclusions?
- Will you be asked to apply principles to new situations and problems?

Your notes are a key study tool. If you stay focused in class and take comprehensive notes, you will make your life easier at test prep time.

© Geri Engberg Photography

Remember that not all tests are created equal—a quiz is less important than a midterm or final and may need less preparation. Give each quiz or test the amount of study time that makes sense for its value. After taking the first exam in a course, you will have a better idea of what to expect.

Create a Study Schedule and Checklist

To choose what to study, go through your notes, texts, handouts, and other materials, and set aside what you don't need. Then look at the materials that remain. Your goal is to focus on what is likely to be on the exam.

Next, use the time-management and goal-setting skills from Chapters 2 and 3 to prepare a schedule. Consider your study materials, the number of days until the test, your ongoing responsibilities, and the time you can study each day. Use a checklist to slot specific tasks into each study session, but be flexible. If studying a topic takes longer than you planned, rearrange your time to get everything done. The following Take Action exercise will help you organize.

TAKE ACTION
Organize for Test Success

Complete this checklist for your next exam to define your study goals, get organized, and stay on track. Make extra copies to use with other important exams, and start filling them out as soon as exams are announced.[1]

Course: *Instructor:*

Date, time, and place of test:

Type of test (is it a midterm or a minor quiz?):

Information from instructor (types of questions, test length, effect on final grade, etc.):

Topics to be covered, in order of importance:

1. _____

2. _____

3. _____

4. _____

5. _____

Study schedule, including study materials (texts, class notes, homework problems, and so on) and the dates and times you plan to complete each:

MATERIAL	STUDY DATE AND TIME
1. _____	_____
2. _____	_____
3. _____	_____
4. _____	_____
5. _____	_____

Materials to bring to the test (textbook, sourcebook, calculator, computer):

_____

_____

Special study arrangements (study group meetings, instructor conference, tutoring), including scheduled times:

_____

_____

Study-routine adjustments to maximize your strongest intelligences (for example, interpersonal learners could study with others, musical learners could create learning tunes, bodily-kinesthetic learners could listen to lectures on an MP3 player while walking to class):

_____

_____

Life-management issues (such as rearranging work hours to study with a classmate):

_____

_____

_____

_____

Prepare Through Careful Review

A thorough, active review is the best way to set yourself up for test success. SQ3R (see Chapter 7) provides an excellent review structure for reading materials. For combined class and text notes, active involvement is key (see Chapter 9) as you use these strategies:

- **Go through your key terms and concepts outline, and recite what you know about a topic.** Reading is not enough. To learn and retain information, you need to express content in your own words and apply it to problems.

- **Use critical thinking.** Think about examples that illustrate concepts, experiences that demonstrate points, and different opinions. Use what you know to solve problems.

- **Don't stop until you really know the material.** Take a practice test, do question-and-answer sessions with a study partner, answer your SQ3R questions in writing one more time, and apply concepts to new material.

Take a Pretest

Use end-of-chapter text questions or questions from the text Web site to create your own pretest. If your course doesn't have an assigned text, create questions from your notes and outside readings. Use old homework problems to target topics.

The best questions test your understanding and ability to apply what you have learned. Take pretests under test-like conditions—in a quiet place, with no books or notes to help you (unless the exam is open book), and with a clock to tell you when time is up.

Prepare Physically

To work at your best under pressure, get as much sleep as you can the night before the exam. You will work better, since sleep improves memory. Eat a light, well-balanced meal with plenty of protein. When time is short, grab a quick-energy snack such as a banana, orange juice, a peanut butter sandwich, or a granola bar—and *never* skip breakfast.

Make the Most of Last-Minute Cramming

If learning is your goal, **cramming** is not the answer since information rarely sticks in your brain after the exam (Chapter 6 explains why cramming doesn't work). However, nearly every student crams, especially during midterms and finals. When you have to do it, these hints will help you make the most of it:

- **Focus on crucial concepts.** Summarize the most important points and try to resist reviewing notes or texts page by page.

Cramming

studying intensively and around the clock right before an exam.

- **Create a last-minute study sheet.** On a single sheet of paper, write down key facts, definitions, formulas, and so on. If you prefer visual notes, use think links to map out ideas and examples. You can also put items on flash cards and review them right before the test.

- **Don't oversleep.** To avoid missing the test, set several alarms in different places, far enough away that you have to get out of bed to turn them off.

- **Arrive early.** Review your study sheet until you are asked to clear your desk.

After your exam, evaluate how cramming affected your work. Did it help, or did it load your mind with random details? Did it increase or decrease your anxiety? Then evaluate how cramming affects your recall. You probably won't remember much within a few days. This can work against you in advanced courses that build on this knowledge and in careers that require it. Think ahead about how you can start studying earlier to prepare for your next exam.

How Can You Work Through Test Anxiety?

A certain amount of stress can be a good thing. You are alert, ready to act, and geared up to do your best. Some students, however, experience incapacitating stress before and during exams, especially midterms and finals.

Test anxiety can cause sweating, nausea, dizziness, headaches, and fatigue. It can reduce concentration and cause you to forget everything you learned. Sufferers may get lower grades because their performance does not reflect what they really know.

Test Anxiety debilitating physical and psychological symptoms that interfere with doing your best work before and during a test.

POWERFUL
QUESTIONS

Identify your specific test-taking fears, and write out your plan to overcome them. If test anxiety isn't a problem, what do you think contributes to your pretest calm?

Now, respond to this statement:

"Putting myself out there for a test helps me learn to take responsible academic risks, especially if I view my test performance as a sign of progress toward a long-term goal."

take responsible risks

Have a Positive Attitude

Solid preparation is the best way to reduce anxiety. Having a positive attitude also helps:

- **See tests as opportunities to learn.** Stop thinking of tests as contests to win or lose. Instead, think of them as checkpoints that tell you what you are learning.

- **Understand that tests measure performance, not personal value.** Whether you get an A or an F, you are the same person.

- **Practice relaxation.** Minimize stress by breathing deeply, closing your eyes, visualizing getting a good grade, and finishing with time to spare.

- **Shut out negative vibrations and stress from others.** Try to avoid studying with people who are also anxious because you may pick up their fears. If you arrive early for a last-minute review, sit far away from others who are discussing the test.

- **Practice positive self-talk.** Tell yourself that you can do well and that it is normal to feel anxious, particularly before an important exam.

- **Don't expect to be perfect.** Perfection is not possible, so ease up on yourself.

- **Remind yourself of your goals.** Connecting the test to your long-term goals will help you calm down as you focus on what's important.

Test Anxiety and the Returning Student

If you're returning to school after years away, you may worry about taking exams. Give yourself a boost of confidence by focusing on what experience has taught you, including the ability to handle work and family pressures. Without knowing it, you may have developed many of the time-management, planning, organizational, and communication skills you need for test success.

In addition, life experiences give meaning to abstract classroom ideas. For example, workplace relationships may help you understand social psychology concepts, and refinancing your home mortgage may help you grasp the importance of economic cycles.

Inside Tips from Sarah, Self-Management Coach

Children aren't the only ones who are calmed and motivated by special objects. You may have one or more objects that hold special meaning for you—a photograph, a stone or crystal, a wristband, a piece of jewelry, a hat. Why not see if your special object can be a comfort or inspiration at test time? Bring it along. Use it to get focused when you take your seat and to calm yourself during the test if anxiety strikes.

real people

take responsible risks

Carla Baku

Stanford University English major[4]

Carla Baku had no idea what it would take to get through college (no one in her family had attended). After high school, she signed up for a course at a community college near her home in Eureka, California, but quit after a few sessions. Other people may have stopped there, but other people aren't Carla Baku.

Ten years later she decided to give college another try, despite her fears, the need to care for four young sons, and an unsupportive husband. "It was a fight from the beginning...twice a week I had to orchestrate my departure with some serious strategizing." Carla juggled her schedule, prepared dinners, traded babysitting with neighbors, and got to class.

"I was panic stricken," she said. Slowly, the joy of learning overwhelmed fear. I finished that class with an A and knew that, whatever it took, I was going to get a college education."

Stop and Think

What personal and family risks did Carla take when she enrolled in college after so much time off? What risks are you taking to get an education?

Carla's path continued through twists and turns—and took a lot more time. In the years following her early success, she divorced her abusive husband, got a job that would support her family, and became a certified domestic violence counselor.

Fast forward 14 more years. Now remarried to someone who backed her dream, Carla finally finished her community-college requirements at California's College of the Redwoods and wanted to transfer to a four-year school to study writing, journalism, and poetry. Realizing that she needed a full scholarship to attend full time, she started applying. When she was awarded a Jack Kent Cooke Foundation Undergraduate Transfer Scholarship, she was determined to go to the best school near her home.

That was Stanford University, but to get in, she had to take the SATs for the first time at the age of 50. "I sat there with a whole lot of [teenagers who were younger than my children], all of us clutching our No. 2 pencils, hoping for the best."

Stop and Think

If you were in Carla's place, how would you handle being so different from everyone around you? How could you focus on your goals in the face of fear?

At Stanford, Carla is 30 years older than her classmates, but she embraces the generation gap and learns from her younger peers who also learn from her. "I am living proof that if one is tenacious and willing to work hard, if one is willing to throw themselves into the void of the unknown, the universe will rise up to meet you in the most wonderful and unexpected ways," she said. "Coming to Stanford has helped me see that the most crippling limits we encounter are often the limits we put on ourselves."

Think about Carla and Think about Yourself

- Consider this statement: Taking risks means overcoming "limits we put on ourselves." What does it mean to you?
- Carla also said that "a single life...has a vast influence for good or ill in the universe." With this in mind, and considering the risks you are willing to take, answer the question posed by poet Mary Oliver: "What will you do with your one wild and precious life?"

After attempting to climb K2, the world's second tallest mountain, **Greg Mortenson** was sheltered in the Pakistani village of Korphe until he returned to health. In appreciation, he promised to build the town's first school—a commitment that grew when he created the Central Asia Institute, which built more than 100 schools across rural Pakistan and Afghanistan.

take responsible risks

What General Strategies Add to Test Success?

The following strategies will help you do your best on every test.

Choose the Right Seat

Choose a seat that puts you in the right frame of mind and minimizes distractions. If possible, sit near a window, next to a wall, or in the front row so you can look off into the distance without looking at another student's work. Most students can focus better if they do not sit near friends.

Write Down Key Facts

Before you look at the test, write down information, including formulas, rules, and definitions, that you don't want to forget. Use the back of the question sheet so your instructor knows that you made these notes after the test began.

Begin with an Overview

Spend a few minutes at the start looking over the questions so you know how many there are in each section, what types, and their point values. Then schedule your time. For example, if a two-hour test has two sections of equal value—an essay section with four questions and a short-answer section with 60 questions—you might spend an hour on the essays (15 minutes per question) and an hour on the short answers (one minute per question).

Take level of difficulty into account as you schedule. This means that if you think you can get through the short-answer questions in 45 minutes and sense that the essays will take longer, you can budget an hour and a quarter for the essays.

Read Test Directions

Reading test directions carefully can save you trouble. Although a history test of 100 true/false questions and two essays may look straightforward, the directions may tell you to answer 80 of the 100 questions and to write only one essay.

If the directions tell you that some questions or sections are weighted more heavily than others, it's smart to spend more time on them (the short-answer questions, for example, may be worth 30 points compared with 70 points for the essays).

Mark Up the Questions

As you work, circle qualifiers, such as *always, never, all, none, sometimes,* and *very*; verbs that communicate specific instructions; and concepts that are tricky or need special attention. On multiple-choice exams, you may want to write one or two words next to the choices you reject indicating why they are wrong before marking the correct answer on the answer sheet.

Take Special Care on Machine-Scored Tests

Use the right pencil (usually a #2), and mark your answer in the correct space, filling it completely. The computer may misread stray pencil marks or partially erased answers, so be neat. Use a straight edge to focus on the correct line for each question. Periodically, check the answer number against the question number to make sure they match. If you mark the answer to question 4 in the space for question 5, not only will your response to question 4 be wrong, but your responses to all subsequent questions will also be off by a line. When you plan to return to a question and leave a space blank, put a small dot next to the number on the answer sheet.

Work from Easy to Hard

Begin with the easiest questions, and answer them quickly without sacrificing accuracy. This will boost your confidence and leave the bulk of time for the harder questions. Mark tough questions as you reach them, and return to them after answering the questions you know.

Watch the Clock

Some students are so concerned about time that they rush through the test and have time left over. If this happens to you, spend the remaining time checking your work instead of leaving early. You may be able to correct mistakes, change answers, or add information. If, on the other hand, midway through the test you realize that you are behind, re-evaluate to determine the best use of the remaining time. Whatever you do, be flexible.

© iStockphoto.com

Take a Strategic Approach to Questions You Can't Answer

When you encounter questions you do not understand or cannot answer, what can you do?

- If your instructor is in the room, ask for clarification. Sometimes a simple rewording will help you realize that you know how to answer it.

- Skip the question and come back to it later. Let your subconscious mind work on it.

When you receive your exam, resist the temptation to jump right in. Taking time to survey the directions and questions is essential to your success.

- Use what you know about the topic to build connections that may lead to the answer.
- Try to remember where the material was covered in your notes and text. Creating this visual picture may jog your memory about content as well.
- If it's a short answer or essay question, put yourself out there and start writing. The act of writing about related material may help you recall the information you need. You may want to freewrite your thoughts on scrap paper, think about what you've written, and then write your final answer on the test.

Master the Art of Intelligent Guessing

When you are unsure of an answer on a short-answer test, you can leave it blank or guess. The best advice is to guess, as long as you are not penalized for incorrect answers. Take advantage of what you know to figure out what you don't know.

When you check your work at the end of the test, decide whether you would guess the same way again. Because your first instincts are usually best, chances are that you will leave your answers alone. However, you may notice something that changes your mind—a qualifier that affects meaning, for example—or you may recall additional facts.

Maintain Academic Integrity

Cheating as a strategy to pass a test or get a better grade robs you of the opportunity to learn, which, ultimately, is your loss. Cheating also jeopardizes your future if you are caught. You may be reprimanded—or even expelled—if you violate your school's code of academic integrity.

Cheating has gone high-tech, with students using their cell phones, MP3 players, graphing calculators, and Internet-connected laptops to share information with other test takers or search the Internet. Because high-tech cheating can be hard to detect in large rooms, some instructors ban all electronic devices. Leave at home or turn off what your instructors don't allow.

How Can You Master Objective Test Questions?

Every type of test question has a different way of finding out how much you know. For **objective questions**, you choose or write a short answer, often making a selection from a limited number of choices. Multiple-choice,

Following are six situations that provide cheating *opportunities*. On a scale of 1 to 5, 1 being the least likely and 5 being the most likely, assess whether you would cheat in each situation. There's no need to write your responses. Just think of what you would do in each case. Be honest with yourself.

1. You can see the answers of the person sitting next to you, who is a good student.
2. Your instructor doesn't want the class to look at any of his previous tests, but a friend offers you a copy of the test from the same class last term.
3. Your instructor doesn't have a clue about technology, so it would be easy to Twitter, IM, or e-mail for help with tough questions.
4. Your instructor allows you to answer essay questions on your laptop. You have a Wi-Fi connection, so you can search the Internet for information.
5. A friend shows you how to write test facts on the inside of a water bottle label and then re-glue the label back on the bottle.
6. You hear about some YouTube videos that demonstrate cheating methods that are virtually detection-proof.

What did you learn from your answers? If you believe that you are likely to cheat, think about what could happen if you are found out and how much you will never learn. Finally, think about what cheating may mean for your future.

ill-in-the-blank, matching, and true/false questions fall into this category. **Subjective questions** also require you to plan, organize, draft, and refine a response. All essay questions are subjective (see Chapter 11).

Key 10.1 shows real test questions from Western civilization, macroeconomics, Spanish, and biology college texts published by Pearson Education. Included are multiple-choice, true/false, fill-in-the-blank, matching, and essay questions. Analyzing these questions will help you gauge what to expect when you take your exams. (Essay questions are examined in Chapter 11.)

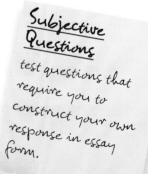

Objective Questions

test questions that ask you to select the correct answer from a limited number of choices or write in a word or phrase.

Multiple-Choice Questions

Multiple-choice questions are the most popular type of question on standardized tests. Use the following strategies to answer them correctly:

Read directions carefully. For example, while most test items ask for a single answer, some give you the option of marking several correct choices.

Read each question and try to think of the answer before looking at the choices. Then read the choices and choose one. If an answer you thought of matches a choice, it is most likely correct.

Underline key words and phrases. Break complicated questions into small sections that are easy to understand. Focus especially on qualifiers such as *always*, *never*, *tend to*, *most*, *often*, and *frequently*. Look also for negatives "Which of the following is *not* …").

Subjective Questions

test questions that require you to construct your own response in essay form.

■ MULTIPLE-CHOICE QUESTION

India's first leader after independence was:

A. Gandhi   B. Bose   C. Nehru   D. Sukharno   *(answer: C)*

■ FILL-IN-THE-BLANK QUESTION

East Pakistan became the country of _____ in 1971.

A. Burma   B. East India   C. Sukharno   D. Bangladesh   *(answer: D)*

■ TRUE/FALSE QUESTION

The United States initially supported Vietnamese independence.   T   F   *(answer: false)*

■ ESSAY QUESTION

Answer one of the following:

1. What led to Irish independence? What conflicts continued to exist after independence?

2. How did Gandhi work to rid India of British control? What methods did he use?

■ MULTIPLE-CHOICE QUESTION

If the labor force is 250,000 and the total population 16 years of age or older is 300,000, the labor-force participation rate is

A. 79.5%   B. 83.3%   C. 75.6%   D. 80.9%   *(answer: B)*

■ FILL-IN-THE-BLANK QUESTION

Mike has just graduated from college and is now looking for a job, but has not yet found one. This causes the employment rate to _____ and the labor-force participation rate to _____.

A. increase; decrease   C. stay the same; stay the same

B. increase; increase   D. increase; stay the same   *(answer: C)*

■ TRUE/FALSE QUESTION

The Consumer Price Index somewhat overstates changes in the cost of living
because it does not allow for substitutions that consumers might
make in response to price changes.   T   F   *(answer: true)*

■ ESSAY QUESTION

During a press conference, the Secretary of Employment notes that the unemployment rate is 7.0%. As a political opponent, how might you criticize this figure as an underestimate? In rebuttal, how might the Secretary argue that the reported rate is an overestimate of unemployment?

(Possible answer: The unemployment rate given by the secretary might be considered an underestimate because discouraged workers, who have given up the job search in frustration, are not counted as unemployed. In addition, full-time workers may have been forced to work part-time. In rebuttal, the secretary might note that a portion of the unemployed have voluntarily left their jobs. Most workers are unemployed only briefly and leave the ranks of the unemployed by gaining better jobs than they had previously held.)

■ MATCHING QUESTION

You are learning new words and your teacher asks you to think of an object similar to or related to the words he says. His words are listed below. Next to each word, write a related word from the list below.

el reloj   el cuaderno   el pupitre   una computadora

el televisor   la tiza   el lápiz   la mochila

1. el escritorio   _____   4. la pizarra   _____

2. el bolígrafo   _____   5. el libro   _____

3. la videocasetera   _____

(answers: 1 el pupitre; 2. el lápiz; 3. el televisor; 4. la tiza; 5. el cuaderno)

■ ESSAY QUESTION

Your mother always worries about you and wants to know what you are doing with your time in Granada. Write a short letter to her describing your experience in Spain. In your letter, you should address the following points:

1. What classes you take

2. When and where you study

3. How long you study every day

4. What you do with your time (mention three activities)

5. Where you go during your free time (mention two places)

■ MULTIPLE-CHOICE QUESTION

What units are bonded together to make a strand of DNA?

A. chromatids   B. cells   C. enzymes   D. nucleotides   E. proteins   *(answer: D)*

■ TRUE/FALSE QUESTION

Errors never occur in DNA replication, because the DNA polymerases edit out mistakes.   T   F

(answer: false)

■ FILL-IN-THE-BLANK QUESTION

In a normal DNA molecule, adenine always pairs with _____ and cytosine always pairs with _____.

(answers: thymine; guanine)

■ MATCHING QUESTION

Match the scientists and the approximate time frames (decades of their work) with their achievements.

Column 1   Column 2

____ 1. Modeled the molecular structure   ____ A. George Beadle and Edward Tatum,
         of DNA   1930s and 1940s

____ 2. Generated X-ray crystallography   ____ B. James Watson and Francis Crick, 1950s
         images of DNA

____ 3. Correlated the production of one   ____ C. Rosalind Franklin and Maurice Wilkins,
         enzyme with one gene   1950s

(answers: 1–B; 2–C; 3–A)

Sources: [*Western Civilization* test items] Margaret L. King, *Western Civilization: A Social and Cultural History*, 2nd ed., Upper Saddle River, NJ: Pearson Education, Inc., 2003. Questions from *Instructor's Manual and Test Item File* by Dolores Davison Peterson. Used with permission. [*Macroeconomics* test items] Arthur O'Sullivan and Steven M. Sheffrin, *Macroeconomics: Principles and Tools*, 3rd ed., Upper Saddle River, NJ: Pearson Education, Inc., 2003. Questions from *Test Item File 2* by Linda Ghent. Used with permission. [*Mosaicos* test items] Matilde Olivella de Castells, Elizabeth Guzmán, Paloma Lupuerta, and Carmen García, *Mosaicos: Spanish as a World Language*, 3rd ed., Upper Saddle River, NJ: Pearson Education, Inc., 2002. Questions from *Testing Program* by Mark Harpring. Used with permission. [*Biology* test items] David Krogh, *Biology: A Guide to the Natural World*, 2nd ed., Upper Saddle River, NJ: Pearson Education, Inc., 2002. Questions from *Test Item File* edited by Dan Wivagg. Used with permission.

Make sure you read every word of every answer. Instructors may include answers that are correct, except for a single word.

If you don't know the answer, eliminate answers that you know or think are wrong. If you can leave two possible answers, you will have a 50–50 chance of choosing correctly. To guess right, ask questions like these about each of the choices:

- **Is the choice accurate on its own terms?** If there's an error in the choice—for example, a term that is incorrectly defined—the answer is wrong.

- **Is the choice relevant?** An answer may be accurate but unrelated to the question.

- **Are there any qualifiers?** Absolute qualifiers—such as *all, only,* and *always*—often make a statement false while conservative qualifiers—*generally, often, rarely, usually,* and *sometimes*—often make a statement true. For example, the statement "Normal children *always* begin talking before the age of 2" is untrue (some normal children start talking later). Analysis has shown that choices containing conservative qualifiers are often correct.

- **Do the choices give clues?** Does a puzzling word remind you of a word you know? Do any parts of an unfamiliar word—its prefix, suffix, or root—ring a bell?

When questions are linked to a reading passage, read the questions first. This will help you focus on the information you need to answer the questions.

True/False Questions

Be sure to read *every* word to avoid jumping to an incorrect conclusion. Common problems in reading too quickly include missing negatives (*not, no*) and absolute and conservative qualifiers that would change your response. You will lose full credit if you mark a statement as true when only part of it is true.

Here are some examples of the kinds of true/false questions you might encounter in an introductory psychology course (the correct answer follows each question):

Are the following questions true or false?
1. Alcohol use is clearly related to increases in hostility, aggression, violence, and abusive behavior.   *(true)*
2. Marijuana is harmless.   *(false)*
3. Simply expecting a drug to produce an effect is often enough to produce the effect.   *(true)*
4. Alcohol is a stimulant.   *(false)*

Source: Gary W. Piggrem and Charles G. Morris, *Test Item File for Understanding Psychology,* 3rd ed., 1996. Reprinted by permission of Pearson Education, Inc., Upper Saddle River, NJ.

Here are examples of the kinds of multiple-choice questions you might encounter in an introductory psychology course (the correct answer follows each question):

1. Arnold is at the company party and has had too much to drink. He releases all of his pent-up aggression by yelling at his boss, who promptly fires him. Arnold normally would not have yelled at his boss, but after drinking heavily he yelled because
   a. parties are places where employees are supposed to be able to "loosen up"
   b. alcohol is a stimulant
   c. alcohol makes people less concerned with the negative consequences of their behavior
   d. alcohol inhibits brain centers that control the perception of loudness   *(answer: C)*
2. Which of the following has not been shown to be a probable cause of or influence in the development of alcoholism in our society?
   a. intelligence
   b. culture
   c. personality
   d. genetic vulnerability   *(answer: A)*
3. Geraldine is a heavy coffee drinker who has become addicted to caffeine. If she completely ceases her intake of caffeine over the next few days, she is likely to experience each of the following *except*:
   a. depression
   b. lethargy
   c. insomnia
   d. headaches   *(answer: C)*

Source: Gary W. Piggrem and Charles G. Morris, *Test Item File for Understanding Psychology,* 3rd ed., 1996. Reprinted by permission of Pearson Education, Inc., Upper Saddle River, NJ.

Matching Questions

Matching questions ask you to match the terms in one list with the terms in another list. For example, the directions may tell you to match a communicable disease with the microorganism that usually causes it. The following strategies will help you handle these questions.

Understand the directions.   They will tell you whether each item can be used only once or more than once.

Work from the column with the longest entries.   The left-hand column usually contains terms to be defined or questions to be answered, while the right-hand column usually contains definitions or answers. Entries on the right are generally longer than those on the left. Reading the items on the right only once will save time as you work to match them with the shorter phrases on the left.

Start with the matches you know.   On your first run-through, mark the matches you know with a penciled line. Finalize your choices when you complete all the items. If you can use an answer only once, you may have to change answers if you reconsider a choice.

Finally, tackle the matches you're not sure of.   On your next run-through, focus on the more difficult matches. Think back to your class lectures and study sessions, and visualize text notes. If one or more phrases seem to have no correct answer, look at your easy matches, considering the possibility that one or more are wrong.

Fill-in-the-Blank Questions

Fill-in-the-blank questions, also known as sentence-completion questions, ask you to supply one or more words or phrases with missing information to complete the sentence.

Be logical.   Insert your answer; then reread the sentence from beginning to end to be sure it makes sense and is factually and grammatically correct. Consider thinking of the right answer *before* looking at the choices and then finding the choice that most closely matches.

Note the length and number of the blanks.   If two blanks appear right after one another, the instructor is probably looking for a two-word answer. If a blank is longer than usual, the correct response may be long. However, if you are certain of an answer that doesn't seem to fit the length of the blanks, trust your knowledge.

Pay attention to how blanks are separated.   When there is more than one blank in a sentence and the blanks are widely separated, treat each one separately. Answering each as if it were a separate sentence-completion question makes it more likely that you will get at least one correct.

Think outside the box.   If you can think of more than one correct answer, take the risk of putting them both down. Your instructor may be impressed by your initiative.

If you are unsure, make an educated guess.   Have faith that, after hours of studying, the correct answer is somewhere in your mind and that your guess is not completely random.

Here are examples of fill-in-the-blank questions you might encounter in an introductory astronomy course (correct answers follow questions):

1. A _____ is a collection of hundreds of billions of stars.   *(galaxy)*
2. Rotation is the term used to describe the motion of a body around some _____.   *(axis)*
3. The solar day is measured relative to the sun; the sidereal day is measured relative to the

   _____.   *(stars)*
4. On December 21, known as the _____ _____, the sun is at its

   _____ _____.   *(winter solstice; southernmost point)*

Source: Eric Chaisson and Steve McMillan, *Astronomy Today,* 3rd ed., 1999. Reprinted by permission of Pearson Education, Inc., Upper Saddle River, NJ.

Briefly describe a problem you have with answering objective test questions.

_____

_____

Now brainstorm potential solutions to your problem, linking each solution to an intelligence. Use the right-hand column to record your ideas.

INTELLIGENCE	SUGGESTED STRATEGIES	USE MI STRATEGIES TO COME UP WITH SOLUTIONS
Verbal–Linguistic	■ Read carefully to understand every word of every question. ■ Do language-oriented questions first, saving extra time for questions involving visual or quantitative elements.	
Logical–Mathematical	■ Focus on quantitative and/or objective questions first, saving extra time for more subjective work such as essays. ■ Use logic to narrow choices in multiple-choice and matching questions.	
Bodily–Kinesthetic	■ Select a seat in the test room where you feel comfortable. ■ Take brief breaks to stretch your muscles at your seat.	
Visual–Spatial 	■ Focus on the length and number of the blanks in fill-in-the-blank questions. ■ Create think links to connect ideas and analyze different possibilities.	
Interpersonal	■ Replay study group conversations in your mind to remember facts. ■ Think through an answer by imagining you are explaining it to someone.	
Intrapersonal	■ If you hit a difficult question, take a deep breath and focus on what you know about the topic. ■ Visualize answering every question correctly.	
Musical	■ Remember the rhymes and tunes you created to help you learn. Recite them to yourself to recall an answer.	
Naturalistic	■ Instructor and weather permitting, take your exam outdoors.	

The purpose of a test is to see how much you know, not merely to get a grade. Embrace this attitude to learn from your mistakes.

How Can You Learn
from Test Mistakes?

As painful as test mistakes can be, they are valuable learning tools. With exam in hand, use the following strategies to learn the material you got wrong and to reduce the likelihood of making the same errors again. (If your instructor posts grades but does not hand exams back, ask to see your paper.)

Try to Identify Correctable Problems

- Was the problem in the way you studied? Did you focus on memorizing material instead of understanding and applying it? Did you misunderstand or fail to learn key material? Did you skip part of the text or miss classes in which ideas were covered?

- Did your answer lack specific information? Did you need better support for your thesis? Was your analysis incomplete or not very strong?

- Were you surprised by the questions? For example, did you expect them a to be from the text instead of coming from the text and a supplemental reading?

- Were you careless? Did you misread the question or directions? Did you blacken the wrong box on the answer sheet? Did you skip a question? Did you write illegibly?

- Did test anxiety throw you off balance?

Work to Improve

Rework the questions you got wrong. Based on instructor feedback, try to rewrite an essay, recalculate a math problem, or redo questions following a reading selection. If you discover a pattern of careless errors, be more careful and save time to double-check your work.

Talk to your instructor. Discuss the specific mistakes you made. Asking for a review will leave a positive impression. If you are not sure why you were marked down on an essay, ask what you could have done to improve your grade. If you feel that an essay was unfairly graded, ask your instructor to read it again.

Rethink the way you studied. Use the varied techniques in *Keys to Effectiv Learning* to study more effectively so that you can show yourself and your instructor what you are capable of doing. Start early in the term to make positive adjustments.

TAKE ACTION
Learn from Your Mistakes

Look at an exam on which your performance fell short. If possible, choose one that contains different types of objective and subjective questions. With the test and answer sheet in hand, use critical thinking and your logical-mathematical intelligence to answer the following questions:

1. Identify the types of questions on which you got the most correct answers (for example, matching, essay, multiple choice).

_____

2. Identify the types of questions on which you made the greatest number of errors.

_____

3. Analyze your errors to identify patterns. Did you misread the instructions or ignore qualifiers that changed meaning? What did you find?

_____

_____

4. List two steps you will take to avoid these problems as you prepare for and take your next exam:

ction 1: _____

ction 2: _____

f you fail a test, don't throw it away. Use it as a way to review difficult material, especially if you will be tested on it again. You might also want to keep . as a reminder that you can improve with hard work and determination.

Tests are a fact of life in college, so how you prepare for and take them and valuate how you did has a major impact on your sense of accomplishment nd happiness in college. When you accept tests as a fact of college life, you ill be more comfortable and well on your way to being able to show what ou know to your instructors.

The college undergraduate is a lot of things, many of them as familiar, predictable and responsible as the bounce of a basketball, and others as startling (and occasionally disastrous) as the bounce of a football.

John Sloan Dickey (1907–1991), American diplomat, scholar, and college

Habit for Success

take responsible risks

Below are examples of how you can put this habit into action in different situations. Use the three spaces to add your own ideas for actions you can accomplish now or in the future. Be specific, and be realistic.

You ask to join a study group with top students because of how much you will learn from them.

You know that a course will be a challenge, but you register because you are committed to working hard.

Take Responsible Risks Habit for Success

You guess on some objective test questions because you believe you are prepared to guess right.

You risk looking unprepared in front of your instructor when you ask for help with basic concepts that will be on the test.

You risk having friends misunderstand your motives when you sit away from them during a test.

Building Skills
for successful learning

Note the Important Points

How can preparation improve test performance?

List three specific actions you will take to prepare for every exam.

1. _____

2. _____

3. _____

How can you work through test anxiety?

What is test anxiety? _____

_____

Identify three actions you can take to reduce anxiety before and during a test.

1. _____

2. _____

3. _____

What general strategies add to test success?

List, in order of importance, three steps you will take during exams to improve your performance.

1. _____

2. _____

3. _____

How can you master objective test questions?

For each question type, name one specific helpful strategy.

Multiple-choice questions _____

_____

True/false questions _____

_____

Matching questions _____

_____

Fill-in-the-blank questions _____

_____

How can you learn from test mistakes?

What benefit can you gain if you view tests as learning opportunities?

_____

_____

_____

Critical Thinking

Analysis of How You Perform on Tests

First, look at the potential problems listed here. Circle the ones you think affect your performance. Use the blank spaces to add additional problems.

Incomplete preparation   *Confusion about directions*

Fatigue   *Test anxiety*

Feeling rushed during the test   _____

Weak understanding of concepts   _____

Poor guessing techniques   _____

Now brainstorm ways to minimize your two most significant problems. Include strategies you learned in this chapter:

Problem 1: _____

_____

Solutions: _____

_____

Problem 2: _____

_____

Solutions: _____

_____

Team Building

collaborative solutions

Benchmark to Improve Your Test-Preparation Habits

Benchmarking is a business practice in which companies evaluate how other companies perform and then change their methods to reflect the "best practices." You can use benchmarking right now to learn how others prepare for exams and to adopt the best practices that will work for you:

Step 1: Form a study group with two or three others in one of your courses. Ask each group member to record everything he or she does to prepare for the next exam. Among the items on the lists may be:

- Making a study checklist and posting it on my bulletin board
- Spending two hours a day studying at the library in the week before the exam
- Learning what to expect on the test
- Getting a partner to drill me on multiple-choice questions from old tests
- Using SQ3R to review material
- Recording information on an MP3 player and listening to it between classes
- Having a pretest breakfast with a study group
- Getting to sleep by midnight the night before the exam

Step 2: After the exam, come together to compare preparation routines and identify differences.

Step 3: On separate paper or in a computer file, write down what you learned from the habits of your study mates that may help you prepare for upcoming exams.

Note here the most important change you plan to make based on what you learned:

_____

_____

_____

_____

Test Prep: Start It Now

Place Responsible Risk Taking at the Center of Your Education

Getting the most out of your college involves risk—putting yourself on the line in challenging courses. List two courses you plan to take in the next year that are difficult but necessary for your success. (Consult the course catalog for specific course titles.)

Course 1: _____

Course 2: _____

Now list three steps you will take to reduce the fear you are likely to have before big exams in these courses. As you think, consider the words of neuroscientist Dr. Gregory Berns: "*Fear prompts retreat....It makes it impossible to concentrate on anything but saving your skin...*"[5]

Action 1: _____

_____

Action 2: _____

_____

Action 3: _____

_____

test taking II

*getting results on essay tests
and graded projects*

gail is a good writer and does well on assignments that she works on over a few days or weeks. However, during a timed essay test, she can hardly put sentences together. Feeling like she is working against the clock, she can't imagine taking the time to outline or plan her ideas, so she writes whatever comes into her mind as soon as she finishes reading the question. As a result, her responses jump from idea to idea and are often scattered and confusing. Gail is frustrated because no matter how well she knows the material, she just can't get that knowledge across on a test.

In this chapter . . .

you explore answers to the following questions:

HOW can you do your best work on essay tests? p. 310

HOW can you deliver an effective team presentation? p. 320

Habit for Success

be flexible

Be ready and able to adjust your actions to fit changing situations. When the unexpected happens during a test or presentation, your success depends on your willingness to shift gears.

How Can You Do Your Best Work on Essay Tests?

The power to improve is in Gail's hands because essay tests are open-ended. That is, it is up to her—and to you, when you take essay exams—to decide how to answer each question. To improve your performance, focus on three areas:

- **Detail management.** As eager as you may be to get started and avoid running out of time, focus first on test directions and questions.
- **Time management.** Your time-management skills will help you parcel out your work in the limited time you have and perform effectively under pressure.
- **Writing skill.** Even though you are operating in a shorter time frame, you still need to work through a basic writing process.

Read the Directions and Questions Carefully

Pay attention to test directions. Your essay may need to be a certain length, for example, or use a specified format (for example, you may have to write a business letter). The directions will also tell you whether you need to answer all or some of the questions and, if only some, how many.

Next, read each question carefully, using critical thinking to identify exactly what the question is asking. As you read, focus on *action verbs*, which tell you how your instructor wants you to answer (see Key 11.1). Underline these verbs and use them as a guide. Finally, decide which question or questions to tackle (if there's a choice).

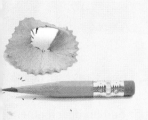

More than anything, focus on effort, not outcome. Take pride in the energy you put into [your studying]. The results will take care of themselves.

Fred Siegel, dean of freshmen, George Washington University

Key 11.1   Focus on action verbs on essay tests

ACTION VERB	DEFINITION	EXAMPLES FROM DIFFERENT DISCIPLINES
Analyze	Break into parts and discuss each part separately.	Analyze how children were viewed in such Romantic novels as *Jane Eyre* and *Wuthering Heights*.
Compare	Explain similarities and differences.	Compare public perception and treatment of Vietnam War veterans with the perception and treatment of veterans of the Iraq War.
Contrast	Distinguish between items being compared by focusing on differences.	Contrast how the body reacts to live vs. killed vaccines.
Criticize	Evaluate the issue, focusing on its problems or deficiencies.	Criticize how Freud's theory of human nature failed to consider women as equal to men.
Define	State the essential quality or meaning.	Define three basic beliefs shared by the Jewish, Christian, and Islamic religions.
Describe	Paint a picture; provide the details of a story or the main characteristics of a situation.	Describe the symptoms of posttraumatic stress syndrome in an wounded soldier.
Diagram	Present a drawing, chart, or other visual.	Diagram the forces that affect the speed of an automobile on the open road.
Discuss	Examine completely, using evidence and often presenting both sides of an issue.	Discuss how the American family has changed in the past decade.
Enumerate/list/ identify	Specify items in the form of a list.	Identify the stages in development of a human embryo.
Evaluate	Give your opinion about the value or worth of something, usually by weighing positive and negative effects, and justify your conclusion.	Evaluate the effect of the death penalty as a deterrent to crime.

(continued)

ACTION VERB	DEFINITION	EXAMPLES FROM DIFFERENT DISCIPLINES
Elaborate on	Start with information presented in the question, and then add new material.	Elaborate on the view that human development continues throughout the life span.
Explain	Make the meaning of something clear, often by discussing causes and consequences.	Explain how wind energy is converted to electricity.
Illustrate	Supply examples.	Illustrate three different approaches to handling discipline problems in a third-grade classroom.
Interpret	Explain your personal views and judgments.	Interpret the results of the latest scientific studies on the effects of statin drugs on the incidence of heart attacks.
Justify	Discuss the reasons for your conclusions or for the question's premise.	Justify the the economic bailout of financial institutions in 2008 and 2009.
Outline	Organize and present main and subordinate points.	Outline two basic approaches to writing a business e-mail.
Prove	Use evidence and logic to show that something is true.	Prove that A = B.
Refute	Use evidence and logic to show that something is not true or how you disagree with it.	Refute this statement: Left to themselves, free markets will correct problems that threaten their stability and growth.
Relate	Connect items mentioned in the question, showing, for example, how one item influenced the other.	Relate the rise in Jewish immigration to the U.S. in the early 20th century to the persecution of Jews in Russia and Poland.
Review	Provide an overview of ideas and establish their merits and features.	Review three trends that are currently influencing fashion design.
State	Explain clearly, simply, and concisely.	State the history of lunar exploration.
Summarize	Give the important ideas in brief, without comments.	Summarize four popular Internet marketing strategies.
Trace	Present a history of the way something developed, often by showing cause and effect.	Trace the history of the civil rights movement from Martin Luther King to Barack Obama.

Chapter 1

Answering essay questions effectively depends on understanding action verbs, said Kim Flachmann, professor of English at California State University at Bakersfield. "It may help to copy these words in the margin. Between the performance words are the content words—what you're being asked about."[1]

Map Out Your Time

Use the techniques you learned in Chapter 10 to schedule the available time.

- Look at how much time you have, how many essays you need to write, and how hard the questions seem.

- Decide how much time to devote to each. You may want to note your time frames on the corner of your test page or exam booklet so you can keep track.

- Remember that things don't always go as planned. If your work on an essay takes longer than expected, be flexible and reduce the time you use to answer other essays.

Inside Tips from Carol, Career Coach

When you show what you know on tests and presentations for different courses, you broaden your knowledge and become more comfortable with a wide variety of subjects. This prepares you for the world of work, where you will need to function effectively in different areas in addition to performing your own tasks well. For example, in addition to being a proficient wordsmith, an editor in a publishing company needs to be comfortable with budgeting, design, marketing, and human resource management.

Use a Shortened Version of the Writing Process

The basic process of writing has four steps: planning, drafting, revising, and editing. (See Appendix B at the end of this text for an overview of the writing process.)

Plan

The biggest advantage you can give yourself is to take time to plan. Always think through and organize your answer before you begin to write. The result will be a better essay and reduced stress. Instead of scrambling for ideas as you write, you will be carrying out an organized plan.

Think carefully about what the question is asking and what you know about the topic. On scrap paper, create an informal outline or a think link to map out your ideas and supporting evidence.

Even when time is short, you will benefit from planning your essay in whatever way works best for you. This student creates an outline before she begins to write.

© Michael Newman/PhotoEdit

Then come up with a **thesis statement** that defines your content and point of view. If necessary—and if you have the time—reorganize your outline or think link into an exact writing roadmap.

When you are asked to apply concepts to new ideas and situations, take a deep breath and try to link what you know with what you are being asked. You might also go a step further, says Professor Flachmann. "I always tell students to try to find a unique way into the question that not everybody is going to use. For example, if you are asked the cause of World War II, you may want to state and compare them to the causes of World War I. That's the way to get a higher grade and use your best critical thinking skills."[2]

To answer the third essay question in the box below, one student created the planning outline shown in Key 11.2. Notice how abbreviations and short-hand help the student write quickly. Writing "Role of BL in IC" is much faster than "Role of Body Language in Interpersonal Communication (see Chapter 9 for shorthand strategies).

Here are some examples of essay questions you might encounter in an interpersonal communication course. In each case, notice the action verbs from Key 11.1.

1. Summarize the role of the self-concept as a key to interpersonal relationships and communication.
2. Explain how internal and external noise affects the ability to listen effectively.
3. Describe three ways that body language affects interpersonal communication.

Draft

Your first draft on an exam is usually the one you hand in, because there is rarely any time for revision. If you take time in the planning stage, you will have enough material for a complete answer. Use the following guidelines:

- State your thesis, getting to the point quickly. Then move to the evidence that backs it up. Spend the bulk of your time developing your thesis, supporting evidence, and logic.

- Pay attention to how you organize your ideas and how you support them with evidence. Try to structure your essay so that each paragraph presents an idea that supports the thesis. Key 11.3 identifies commonly used organizational methods.

- Use clear language and tight logic to link ideas to your thesis and to create transitions between paragraphs.

- Look back at your outline periodically to make sure you cover everything.

- Wrap it up with a short, to-the-point conclusion.

Roles of BL in IC
1. To contradict or reinforce words
   — e.g., friend says "I'm fine"
2. To add shades of meaning
   — saying the same sentence in 3 diff. ways
3. To make lasting 1st impression
   — impact of nv cues and voice tone greater
     than words
   — we assume things abt person based on posture,
     eye contact, etc.

Revise

Although you may not have the time or opportunity to rewrite your entire answer, you can certainly improve it with minor deletions or additions in the margin. If you find a hole in your work—an idea without support, for example, or some unnecessary information—add the new material in the margins and cross out what you don't need. When adding material, you can indicate with an arrow where it fits or note that inserts can be found on separate pages. If you have more than one insert, label each to avoid confusion (Insert #1, Insert #2, etc.).

As you check over your essay, ask yourself these questions:

- Have I answered the question?
- Does my essay begin with a clear thesis statement, and does each paragraph start with a strong topic sentence that supports the thesis?
- Have I provided strong support in the form of examples, statistics, and other relevant facts to prove my argument?
- Is my logic sound and convincing? Does every sentence communicate my point?
- Have I covered all the points in my original outline?
- Is my conclusion an effective wrap-up?

ORGANIZATIONAL STRUCTURE	WHAT TO DO	EXAMPLE
Arrange ideas by time.	Describe events in order or reverse order.	In chronological order, describe the events that led to the declaration of war in Europe in 1939.
Arrange ideas according to importance.	Start with the idea that carries the most weight, and move to less important ideas. Or move from the least to the most important ideas.	In order of importance, describe five factors that led to Hitler's rise in Germany after World War I.
Arrange ideas by problem and solution.	Start with a problem, and then discuss solutions.	Describe the failed plot, at the highest level of the German military command, to kill Hitler.
Arrange ideas to present an argument.	Present one or both sides of an issue.	Present reasons why President Roosevelt decided against bombing the railroad tracks that led to the concentration camps and what his critics said about the decision.
Arrange ideas in list form.	Group a series of items.	List the Allied military leaders from the United States, Great Britain, and France and their roles in the war effort.
Arrange ideas according to cause and effect.	Show how events, situations, or ideas cause subsequent events, situations, or ideas.	Show the relationship between the U.S. involvement in World War II and the end of the economic depression.
Arrange ideas through the use of comparisons.	Compare and contrast the characteristics of events, people, situations, or ideas.	Compare the leadership styles of President Roosevelt and English Prime Minister Winston Churchill.
Arrange by process.	Go through the steps in a process: a "how-to" approach.	Describe the process by which U.S. manufacturing facilities began producing armaments for war.
Arrange by category.	Divide topics into categories, and analyze each in order.	Discuss the success of the air and sea assaults on Europe.

Edit

Check for mistakes in grammar, spelling, punctuation, and usage. The correct use of language leaves a good impression and reduces problems that may lower your grade.

Key 11.4 shows the student's completed response to the essay on body language including the word changes and inserts she made while revising the draft.

QUESTION: Describe three ways that body language affects interpersonal communication.

Body language plays an important role in interpersonal communication and helps shape the impression you make. Two of the most important functions of body language are to contradict and reinforce verbal statements. When body language contradicts verbal language, the message ~~conveyed~~ *delivered* by the body is dominant. For example, if a friend tells you that she is feeling "fine," but her posture is slumped, and her facial expression troubled, you have every reason to wonder whether she is telling the truth. If the same friend tells you that she is feeling fine and is smiling, walking with a bounce in her step, and has direct eye contact, her body language is telling the truth.

, especially when you meet someone for the first time

her eye contact minimal,

accurately reflecting and reinforcing her words.

The nonverbal cues that make up body language also have the power to add shades of meaning. Consider this statement: "This is the best idea I've heard all day." If you were to say this three different ways—in a loud voice while standing up; quietly while sitting with arms and legs crossed and looking away; and while ~~maintening~~ *maintaining* eye contact and taking the receiver's hand—you might send three different messages.

Finally, the impact of nonverbal cues can be greatest when you meet someone for the first time. When you meet someone, you tend to make assumptions based on nonverbal behavior such as posture, eye contact, gestures, and speed and style of movement.

Although first impressions emerge from a combination of nonverbal cues, tone of voice, and choice of words, nonverbal elements (cues and tone) usually come across first and strongest.

In summary, nonverbal communication plays a ~~crusial~~ *crucial* role in interpersonal relationships. It has the power to send an accurate message that may ~~destroy~~ *belie* the speaker's words, offer shades of meaning, and set the tone of a first meeting.

TAKE ACTION
Write to the Action Verb

This exercise will help you focus on action verbs as you answer essay questions.

■ Start by choosing a topic you learned about in this text—for example, the brain's memory storage systems (see pages 162–164). Write your topic here:

_____

_____

■ Put yourself in the role of instructor. Write an essay question on this topic, using one of the action verbs in Key 11.1 to frame the question. For example, "Analyze the role of rehearsal in keeping information in long-term memory."

_____

_____

■ Now choose two other action verbs from Key 11.1. Use each one to rewrite your original question.

1. _____

_____

2. _____

_____

Finally, use your logical-mathematical intelligence to analyze how each new verb changes the question's focus. Describe the change here for each new question.

1. _____

_____

2. _____

_____

think flexibly

Abigail Holtz

Transferred to Tufts University from art school

Even as a sophomore in high school, Abby Holtz knew that her educational path would be different.

After being in high school for just a year and a half, she felt boxed in and bored. Her GPA was high, but she wasn't happy.

Fashion was Abby's love. Instead of watching the board in calculus class, she drew clothing designs. She took sewing lessons in the afternoon and created real clothing out of many of her own designs.

She had to follow her fashion-design dreams. Her parents were not thrilled at first, but they allowed her to pursue her passion as long as she supplemented her fashion courses with academic ones. Abby passed the California High School Proficiency Exam to get an equivalency diploma and enrolled at both the Academy of Art University in San Francisco and Las Positas Community College. She was on her way.

Stop and Think

Wanting something as much as Abby did requires flexibility and the ability to build a plan of action. Have you ever had a dream and built a plan to reach it? Was being flexible important to reaching your goal?

Abby spent a year at art school before she figured out the environment wasn't right for her. She didn't like her classes and couldn't relate to her peers. She loved drawing, but the school didn't challenge her.

Fortunately, at community college, Abby found other subjects that interested her, especially economics. She continued studying there as she searched for a university where she could transfer. At the same time she moved out of her parents' house and took an additional job to support herself.

Although it was a very emotional time in her life, Abby learned invaluable lessons. While most of her friends were carefree and enjoying their senior year of high school, she was experiencing the "real world" and learning what it meant to be an adult.

Stop and Think

When Abby realized she made a mistake, what role did flexibility play in how she moved ahead? Do you think being flexible is more difficult when you have chosen the wrong path?

Abby chose to attend Tufts University in Medford, Massachusetts, and major in economics. Although she didn't plan to work in finance, she believed that a foundation in economics would give her an important perspective and enhance her critical-thinking skills, two things that would serve her well in any profession.

After graduation, she joined Archetype Solutions, a technology company involved in the mass customization of clothing. As the company's operations and account manager, she works with everything from supply chain management to accounting to design to marketing and brand development.

Abby looks back at her journey and has no regrets. She followed her passions without fearing mistakes. She believes that her path built her confidence and taught her lifelong lessons.

Think about Abby and Think about Yourself

What activity do you enjoy but have not considered as part of your career plan? Would you ever think of changing your mind and making it your career? If your answer is yes, or even maybe, map out your dream. How will flexibility enable you to reach your goal?

© Chris Pizzello/AP Images

Danica McKellar, a child actress on *The Wonder Years*, made the difficult transition into adult acting roles, including one on *The West Wing*. But Danica had other passions and the flexibility to pursue them. A mathematics major in college, she later wrote books to help middle-school girls develop an interest in math, helped to develop an influential mathematical physics theorem called The Chayes-McKeller-Winn Theorem, and participates in several charitable organizations.

be flexible

A final word about neatness: If your instructor can't make sense of what you write, your grade is likely to drop. If your handwriting is a problem, try printing or skipping every other line, and be sure to write on only one side of the page. You might also ask if it is possible to take the test on a computer.

How Can You Deliver an Effective Team Presentation?

With the importance of collaboration in school and in the workplace, many instructors assign team presentations that are delivered to the class. These presentations require planning, research, thought about individual and group content, and focus on delivery. Because team presentations are often graded, learning the basics is important to your academic success.

Team projects, also called group projects, reflect the wisdom of this Japanese proverb: "*None of us is as smart as all of us.*" The ability to collaborate is one of the most important skills you will learn in college. Being part of a group has significant benefits as well as a few drawbacks:

- **Benefits.** Teams tap into the varied academic, creative, and practical strengths and skills, as well as intelligences, of different people. A well-functioning group pools these human assets in order to deliver an excellent product on schedule. The product would not have been possible had one person worked alone.

- **Drawbacks.** When you work in a team, you are no longer in total control of project quality and timing. This is a problem if one or more team members slack off. You may also encounter people who are difficult (or impossible) to work with as well as logistical problems like getting everyone together at the same time.

Instructors often assign large projects to student groups. Members share the work, support each other in the learning process, and receive individual grades for their efforts. Knowing what to expect will calm your nerves.

Before presentation time, know the setup you will use. This student has a podium, microphone, and notes available to him as he speaks to his classmates.

© iStockphoto.com

Stages of a Team Project

Although every team project is different, it usually involves the following elements:

Instructor assigns the project. Group presentations are usually described in the class syllabus and can be a significant portion of your course grade. The syllabus may indicate the project theme but leave specific topic choice to each group. Your instructor will spell out what is expected, so be sure to listen carefully and ask questions.

The success of a team project often depends on the ability of group members to work together. Define how flexible you are willing to be to promote team success.

What actions will you take if one member refuses to pull his load? Will you encourage the team to speak to the student, or will you approach your instructor? If time is short, are you likely to complete the unfinished work yourself because team success depends on it?

be flexible

Instructor may divide the class into groups or give students the option of creating their own groups. If you are in the position to pick your own team, choose partners as if your grade depended on it—because it does. Choose classmates for their ability, their conscientiousness, and their easy personality, not because they are your friends or are popular. Your whole experience in the group will be affected by this decision.

Have your first team meeting. The goal is to talk about the assignment as a whole and outline the project parts, making sure that everyone is on the same page and there are no misunderstandings of the goal or responsibilities. You should leave this meeting with:

- A comprehensive vision of the goal to be accomplished
- A clear definition of each member's roles and responsibilities
- A schedule of interim and final deadlines linked to future meetings

Whether or not there is an "official" team leader, it is likely that at least one person will take on this role. The team leader has organizational and scheduling responsibility and depends on group support. (See the discussion in Chapter 4 of the responsibilities of study group leaders and participants.)

Start individual work. You complete your part of the project on your own, but the role your work plays in the end result should always be on your mind. If the group is presenting the project in front of the class, think also of the presentation.

- **Plan.** Brainstorm your topic, determine your thesis, write an outline, do research, and adjust your thesis and outline, if necessary.

Multiple Intelligence Strategies for Team Projects

Briefly describe a problem you have with participating on a team project. (If you have not yet participated in a team project, choose any teamwork or group work situation.)

_____

_____

Now brainstorm potential solutions to your problem, linking each solution to an intelligence. Use the right-hand column to record your ideas.

INTELLIGENCE	SUGGESTED STRATEGIES	USE MI STRATEGIES TO COME UP WITH SOLUTIONS
Verbal–Linguistic	■ During your first meeting, focus on the action verbs to define the project's focus. ■ Take extensive notes during all team meetings to capture ideas.	
Logical–Mathematical	■ Take notes on 3-by-5 cards, and organize them by topic. ■ Create a sequential outline before you begin your first draft.	
Bodily–Kinesthetic	■ Visit places that hold needed resources or that are related to your topic—companies, libraries, etc. ■ After a brainstorming session, take a physical activity break to think about your top three ideas. Be open to new thoughts.	
Visual–Spatial	■ Incorporate colorful visual aids into your presentation. ■ Whenever the group comes together, use a think link to map out concepts and support.	
Interpersonal 	■ Between group meetings, bounce ideas off other group members via e-mail. ■ Be a peer editor to other group members. Read each other's drafts and give feedback.	
Intrapersonal	■ Think about the feelings the project raises in you and why. ■ Schedule enough time for research and analysis so you can make needed adjustments.	
Musical 	■ Play relaxing music while you plan your first draft. ■ If you have creative freedom, write and perform a song during your presentation.	
Naturalistic	■ Have one meeting outside to inspire ideas. ■ Look for relationships among ideas that, on the surface, appear different.	

- **Draft your thoughts.** Dive into the details. Your main challenges are to organize your material, integrate your research into your work, use logic to connect evidence to main ideas, and choose the right words and tone to express your thoughts (see the research and writing appendices at the end of the text).

- **Integrate visual aids.** If your presentation includes tables, charts, maps, photographs, or other visual aids, now is the time to create and integrate them. If you import graphics from Web sites into your presentation, be sure to cite your sources.

Gather for a second meeting (or more if necessary).　When you and other group members are finished with your drafts, share your work. If possible, send your drafts via e-mail before the meeting, so people will have time to read them and offer comments and ideas. Then fit the presentation pieces together according to the outline created at the first meeting. Expect that your work—and everyone else's—will need adjustment, so don't be discouraged by the need for more work. You are not working alone, so this give and take is part of the process.

Have a final group meeting.　At this final stage, focus on:

- Putting the project pieces together (usually the team leader's responsibility)
- Polishing the writing
- Planning your delivery (if your team is required to present the project to the class)

Practice Your Performance

Up until now, your team has worked together to create the project material. If your project is final when written, your work ends here. However, if you have to make a class presentation, these suggestions will help:

- **Know everyone's role as well as your own.** Generally, one person will spearhead the presentation while others play supporting roles, although for some presentations team members have fairly equal project segments. Make sure you know what you are supposed to do and when. The success of the project depends on everyone working together.

- **Know the parameters.** How long does each team or team member have? Where will you be speaking? Be aware of where your classmates will be and available props (for example, a podium, table, whiteboard, "smart classroom" setup with a computer linked to a projector). If you are using electronic equipment, test it before the presentation.

- **Focus on your nonverbal behavior.** Your body position, voice, and clothing contribute to the impression you and other group members make. The goal is to look and sound good and to appear relaxed. Try to make eye contact with classmates, and walk around if you are comfortable doing so.

- **Practice ahead of time.** In your last meeting prior to the presentation, do a test run. If possible, practice in the room where you will speak. Gather some friends to act as your audience. Make an audio or video recording and evaluate your performance.

- **Be yourself.** Take deep breaths. Smile. Know that you can speak well and that your audience wants to see you succeed. Envision your own success.

- **Give your team members support.** Give them your full attention, and try to help if they need your expertise or seem flustered. You are in this together.

- **Be prepared for questions.** Your instructor or classmates may ask questions when the presentation is over. Your team leader may decide who should answer a question, so be prepared. Listen carefully to each question, think before you speak, and jot down ideas. Answer only part of a question if that's all you can do. Your goal is to emphasize what you know rather than what you do not know.

On a scale of 1 to 10, with 1 being the lowest and 10 being the highest, rate yourself on your team presentation ability *right now.* Then indicate where you want to be at the end of this course.

Team Presentation Skill	Rating Now	Rating Goal
Comfort with speaking in front of others	_____	_____
Ability to use effective body language and voice during presentation	_____	_____
Ability to stick to your own role	_____	_____
Ability to stick to a time limit	_____	_____
Comfort with using visual aids and technology	_____	_____
Ability to relax under pressure	_____	_____
Willingness to help others handle material	_____	_____
Being able to handle questions from your instructor and classmates	_____	_____

Working with a Virtual Team

Virtual Teams
teams in which members work together by using e-mail, social networking, instant messaging, and other technologies.

If you are taking an online class, your may be working with group members whom you have never met face to face. Technology enables you to be part of **virtual teams** that may be as effective as face-to-face teams.

Your communication tools include e-mail, chat rooms, instant messaging, text messages, social networking sites, blogs, and more. Use the edit function in your word processing program to give and receive feedback on written work. And, of course, pick up the phone to call team members when real-time conversations are needed. Many phones have three-way call capability, so three people can gather on a "conference" call.

Whether you are working online or face to face, the success of any group project depends on clear, regular communication. The bonus of working so closely with a team is that your ties to one or more members are likely to extend beyond the project. Your teammates may become friends and people you can rely on for help throughout the course.

TAKE ACTION
Be Part of a Virtual Team

You may already have communicated virtually to get work done. Describe two situations in which you worked with fellow students via the Internet.

1. _____

2. _____

Now identify two actions you can take to improve your technological skills—for example, becoming better at using the "track changes" function to comment on electronic documents.

1. _____

2. _____

Identify two ways you can improve your interpersonal skills as a virtual team member—for example, writing e-mails that encourage rather than tear down other work.

1. _____

2. _____

Finally, describe the difference, for you, between working virtually versus face to face. What strategies do you think work best for each? How do you feel about each, and why? Which do you prefer? Focus on how each mode engages your interpersonal and intrapersonal intelligence.

_____

_____

_____

_____

_____

Most successful people begin with two beliefs: the future can be better than the present, and I have the power to make it so.

David Brooks, political and cultural commentator and journalist

Habit for Success

be flexible

Below are examples of how you can put this habit into action in different situations. Use the three spaces to add your own ideas for actions you can accomplish now or in the future. Be specific, and be realistic.

As you outline an essay question answer, you realize that you mixed up an important idea. Instead of freezing, you immediately start over.

A team member wants your project assignment. You suggest to the group that a switch be made.

**Be Flexible
Habit for Success**

After two class sessions, you realize that the instructor is not right for you. You look at the course catalog and switch sections.

As you revise an essay test question, you see a gaping hole. You insert additional material on a separate page.

You lose your part-time job and wonder how you will pay school expenses. You keep applying for jobs online until you land one.

Building Skills
for successful learning

Note the Important Points

How can you do your best work on essay tests?

Identify, in sequence, the four crucial steps you should take to answer essay test questions.

1. _____

2. _____

3. _____

4. _____

List and explain three different organizational plans for writing an essay.

1. _____

_____

2. _____

_____

3. _____

_____

How can you deliver an effective team presentation?

List and describe at least four stages that are part of preparing for a team presentation.

1. _____

2. _____

3. _____

4. _____

Describe three methods you can use to practice your team performance.

1. _____

2. _____

3. _____

Define a virtual team. Are you part of one, or do you think you will be? Explain.

_____

_____

_____

_____

_____

Critical Thinking

Team Research

Join with three other classmates and decide on two narrow research topics that interest all of you and that you can investigate quickly. The first topic should be current and in the news—for example, building fuel-efficient cars, body piercing, or the changing U.S. family. The second topic should be more historical—for example, the polio epidemic in the 1950s, the Irish potato famine, or South African apartheid.

Working alone, team members should use the college library and the Internet to research both topics (see Appendix A at the end of this text for research guidelines). Set a research time limit of no more than one hour per topic. The goal should be to collect a list of sources for later investigation. When everyone is finished, the group should come together to discuss the research process. Among the questions group members should ask each other are:

- How did you "attack" and organize your research for each topic?

- What research tools did you use to investigate each topic?

- How did the nature of your research differ from topic to topic? Why do you think this was the case?

Finally, discuss what you learned that might improve the way you collaborate for a team presentation. Write your findings here:

_____

_____

_____

_____

_____

_____

_____

_____

Team Building

Tap the Diversity of Your Presentation Team

Working successfully with others requires that you first be able to identify the talents and skills that are important to team success. Complete this exercise to pinpoint the different strengths people bring.

Step 1: Come together with three classmates. Working in a face-to-face or virtual group, have each person list the academic, personal, social, and emotional qualities that he or she thinks are needed in a team presentation. Some examples to get you thinking:

- leadership
- good writer
- calmness in the face of problems
- flexibility
- ability to handle deadlines

Step 2: Now compare your lists. Think about the qualities that others included and that you did not. Choose three qualities that you now consider top priority for the success of a team. List them here, and explain why you now consider them essential:

Quality #1: _____

_____

_____

Quality #2: _____

_____

_____

Quality #3: _____

_____

_____

Test Prep: Start It Now

be
flexible

Develop Flexible Strategies for Test Success

You have just studied strategies for taking essay tests. Think about four that will help improve your performance on upcoming tests. Write these strategies here:

1. _____

2. _____

3. _____

4. _____

Over the next month—or as soon as you have exams with essay questions—evaluate whether these strategies worked well, whether they had little or no impact, or whether they actually caused problems. Write your evaluation here:

_____

_____

_____

_____

Focus on the strategies that did *not* work well. How can being flexible help you rework them, or use them differently, so they become a tool for success? Describe how you would change, or change the way you use, one particular strategy.

_____

_____

_____

_____

moving toward success

putting habits to work

In this chapter . . .

you explore answers to the following questions:

HOW do the habits for success keep you moving ahead?   p. 334

HOW can you apply each habit toward positive change?   p. 335

HOW will the habits power your successful future?   p. 348

You made it! You've explored all 11 Habits for Success that will support your efforts now and in the future. The features and exercises throughout *Keys to Effective Learning* have reinforced your habit use in the context of the chapters. This final chapter gives you the opportunity to expand this use to different areas—both in and out of school—and to check in on your progress in making the habits a part of your life.

First we make our habits, and then our habits make us.

Charles C. Noble, writer

How Do the Habits for Success Keep You Moving Ahead?

As you have seen, the Habits for Success are an amazing collection of action-promoting strategies that fuel success. They encourage you to perform at your best by acting intelligently and appropriately in any situation "As Aristotle said, 'We are what we repeatedly do. Excellence, then, is not an ac but a habit,'" quotes Professor Art Costa, whose research led to the development of the habits, and adds this: "Only by routinely practicing [the Habits fo Success] can we assure ourselves that we are thinking clearly, confronting problems intelligently, and making wise decisions."[1]

Professor Costa's research uncovered five characteristics common to people who are regular habit users:

1. **Inclination:** They tend to use and return to behavioral patterns that work

2. **Value:** They value the behaviors that work rather than other, less useful ones.

3. **Sensitivity:** They notice when it is possible, and appropriate, to use certai behaviors.

4. **Capability:** They have the basic skills and ability to carry out the behaviors.

5. **Commitment:** They make a continual effort to evaluate how they did and to improve thei performance.[2]

Students of all ages and stages of life continue to learn at college—and beyond.

© Patrick White/Merrill Education

Activate these characteristics and they, in turn, will encourage you to rely on the habits even more. They will help you stay in motion, never stop learning, solve problems, work well with others, know that the power to reach your goals is in your hands, and much more. (Key 12.1 recaps all 11 habits.)

Through the features in each chapter, you have gotten to know each habit. Take time now to expand your understanding of how you can use them in a wide variety of situations.

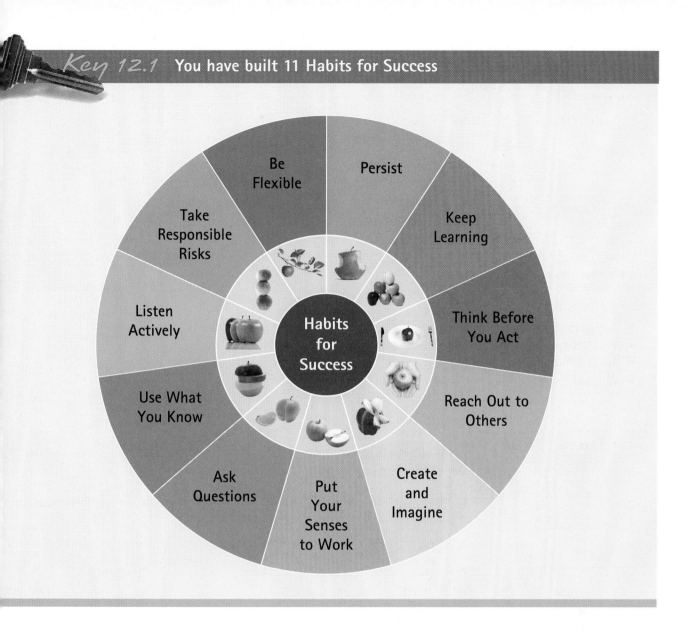

How Can You Apply Each Habit Toward Positive Change?

Start by taking a moment to think about how you currently use the habits. After you complete this self-assessment, compare it with the similar one you completed on page 19 in Chapter 1 to evaluate changes and growth.

At their heart, the Habits for Success are problem-solving tools, ready for you to apply to the problems that inevitably arise in school, work, and

First, rate each based on how much you think you have and use that habit right now—from 1 (I don't have it at all) to 10 (I live this habit).

_____ Persist		_____ Ask questions
_____ Keep learning		_____ Use what you know
_____ Think before you act		_____ Listen actively
_____ Reach out to others		_____ Take responsible risks
_____ Create and imagine		_____ Be flexible
_____ Put your senses to work		

Next, underline what you consider to be your three strongest habits. Then, (circle) what you consider the three habits that you most need to develop.

Questions to ponder:

- Are your strongest and weakest habits the same as they were in Chapter 1? Why or why not?
- What habit have you improved the most?
- What habit needs the most work?
- What other reflections do you have on your experience of building the Habits for Success?

personal situations. Professor Costa reminds problem solvers of two steps in applying the habits to any situation:

1. First, work to choose the habit or habits that will be most effective in the situation.

2. Then ask questions that help you decide *how* to apply the habit or habits you chose.

Think about these steps—and return to them again and again—as you use the habits in other contexts.

Now that you've updated your view of your habit development, turn your attention to how you can use each habit. The following grids will help you expand your use of the habits to other academic subjects as well as parts of your life:

- Other chapters from this text
- A course you are taking now
- The workplace
- Your personal life

You may have already applied the habits to some of these situations. This will encourage you to think more about other ways to use them. So start brainstorming, and know that the more you put the Habits for Success into action, the more they become part of who you are.

PERSIST. Stick to whatever you are doing until you complete it. Keep moving ahead.

Original location: Chapter 1, "Habits for Success"

Apply it! Describe how you would use this habit…

When managing your time (Chapter 3)	
When preparing for an objective test (Chapter 10)	
When working to remember material (Chapter 6)	
In the classroom—or for homework—of a course you're taking now	
In the workplace	
In your personal life	

KEEP LEARNING. Be a lifelong learner, always seeking to know more. See problems and circumstances as valuable opportunities to learn and grow.

Original location: Chapter 2, "Learning Styles"

Apply it! Describe how you would use this Habit...

When taking notes on reading materials (Chapter 9)	
When trying to understand a textbook chapter (Chapter 7)	
When setting long-term goals (Chapter 4)	
In the classroom—or for homework—of a course you're taking now	
In the workplace	
In your personal life	

THINK BEFORE YOU ACT. Manage impulsive behavior by creating a plan of action and defining your specific goals before beginning.

Original location: Chapter 3, "Time and Money"

Apply it! Describe how you would use this habit...

When trying to stay healthy and keep your energy up (Chapter 4)	
When preparing for an essay test (Chapter 11)	
When planning how to talk to an instructor about a grade (Chapter 1)	
In the classroom—or for homework—of a course you're taking now	
In the workplace	
In your personal life	

REACH OUT TO OTHERS. Learn to ask for help and give help when you can. Experience the power of achieving a goal as part of a team.

Original location: Chapter 4, "Setting and Reaching Goals"

Apply it! Describe how you would use this habit...

When working through reading material for a tough course (Chapter 8)	
When thinking through a problem (Chapter 5)	
When challenged by your learning weaknesses (Chapter 2)	
In the classroom—or for homework—of a course you're taking now	
In the workplace	
In your personal life	

CREATE AND IMAGINE. Come up with new, original, and clever ideas, solutions, and techniques.

Original location: Chapter 5, "Critical and Creative Thinking"

Apply it! Describe how you would use this habit…

When managing your income and expenses (Chapter 3)	
When creating a master note set from class and reading notes (Chapter 9)	
When coming up with questions for the Q part of SQ3R (Chapter 7)	
In the classroom—or for homework—of a course you're taking now	
In the workplace	
In your personal life	

PUT YOUR SENSES TO WORK. Note—and then look past—what you see and hear. Open your sensory pathways to all kinds of information you can use in your life.

Original location: Chapter 6, "Memory"

Apply it! Describe how you would use this habit...

When working with a study group (Chapter 4)	
When listening to an instructor's lecture (Chapter 9)	
When studying for a final exam (Chapter 10)	
In the classroom—or for homework—of a course you're taking now	
In the workplace	
In your personal life	

ASK QUESTIONS. Use questions to fill in the gaps between what you know and what you don't know. Use questions to identify problems before they stop you in your tracks.

Original Location: Chapter 7, "Reading and Studying"

Apply it! Describe how you would use this habit…

When working on a project for a presentation (Chapter 11)	
When thinking through a decision (Chapter 5)	
When considering strategies that focus on your learning strengths (Chapter 2)	
In the classroom—or for homework—of a course you're taking now	
In the workplace	
In your personal life	

USE WHAT YOU KNOW. Build on past knowledge and experiences to learn new material and solve problems.

Original location: Chapter 8, "Reading Across the Disciplines"

Apply it! Describe how you would use this habit…

When reading and researching online (Chapter 7)	
When reading through math or science materials (Chapter 8)	
When thinking about how to handle a stressful situation (Chapter 4)	
In the classroom—or for homework—of a course you're taking now	
In the workplace	
In your personal life	

LISTEN ACTIVELY. Consider what others have to say, and work to understand perspectives that differ from yours. Consider new ideas.

Original location: Chapter 9, "Active Listening and Note Taking"

Apply it! Describe how you would use this habit...

When in a discussion group in class (Chapter 6)	
When taking class notes (Chapter 9)	
When choosing a time management tool (Chapter 3)	
In the classroom—or for homework—of a course you're taking now	
In the workplace	
In your personal life	

TAKE RESPONSIBLE RISKS. Challenge your limits, but do it wisely. When you have thought through a risk and the likelihood of success is strong, dive in.

Original location: Chapter 10, "Test Taking I"

Apply it! Describe how you would use this habit…

When applying for a grant or scholarship (Chapter 3)	
When making a personal connection with an instructor (Chapter 1)	
When faced with a health crisis (Chapter 4)	
In the classroom—or for homework—of a course you're taking now	
In the workplace	
In your personal life	

BE FLEXIBLE. Be ready and able to adjust your actions and change your mind to fit a changing situation.

Original location: Chapter 11, "Test Taking II"

Apply it! Describe how you would use this habit…

When getting up to speed on the technology at your school (Chapter 1)	
When studying a subject outside of your comfort zone (Chapter 2)	
When memorizing information for a test (Chapter 6)	
In the classroom—or for homework—of a course you're taking now	
In the workplace	
In your personal life	

How Will the Habits Power
Your Successful Future?

Although everyone has a unique view of success, many people would include living with integrity, achieving in the workplace, and performing at your personal best in their definition of a successful life. The Habits for Success will help you achieve these goals.

Living With Integrity. As you use Habits for Success in your daily life, you build qualities that characterize a **person of integrity**. For example:

- Persisting develops your focus and commitment.
- Listening to other points of view develops your respect for others.
- Thinking before you act develops your ability to follow through on promises.

In other words, the habits give you tools for living according to your values and principles, empower you to work with others, and help you continually learn from mistakes.

Achieving Workplace Success. Habits for Success equip you with tools that every employer wants. You will be valued—and rewarded—because you are a good listener, because you can manage your impulses, because you are flexible, because you are a team player, because you value learning, and more.

Person of Integrity
a committed, trustworthy person, consistently true to personal values and to his or her word.

Students who are also parents may find flexibility one of their most important habits. This student manages to get some work done while caring for her infant.

© David Young-Wolff/PhotoEdit

Reaching Your Personal Best. Your *personal best* is simply the best that you can do. It may not be the best you have ever done. It may include mistakes, for nothing significant is ever accomplished without making mistakes and taking risks. It may shift from situation to situation. As long as you aim to do your best, though, you invite growth.

Aim for your personal best in everything you do. As you continue to learn, take classes, and do your highest quality work, you will strengthen your skills and set yourself up for success with people from all backgrounds, cultures, ages, and stages. As you use your habits to find intelligent approaches to problems, you will join people everywhere who aspire to be their best, do their best, and create the best for the world in which they live.

Shoot for the moon. Even if you miss it you will land among the stars.

Les Brown, author and motivational speaker

You are only beginning your lifelong career as a learner and a doer. You will continue to discover the best ways to harness the skills you developed in this course. The opportunity to make a difference for yourself and others has never been greater. With the Habits for Success and your drive to solve problems and achieve goals, you can take action that will change your life for the better.

Time for a change: take steps to improve a habit for success

Revisit Your Progress

Look back at the Time for a Change exercise at the end of Chapter 9 on page 277. Take a moment to describe how you have developed this habit, including how consistently you perform your chosen actions, how well you document your progress, the helpfulness of your support system, and whether or not you are satisfied with your progress. If not, describe how you will adjust your actions in order to move ahead.

_____

_____

_____

_____

_____

_____

_____

_____

Quick review: Describe your progress on the habit you explored at the end of Chapter 3 (page 93).

_____

_____

_____

_____

_____

_____

Quick review: Describe your progress on the habit you explored at the end of Chapter 6 (page 186).

_____

_____

_____

_____

_____

_____

Finally, answer about the following questions before you take these habits into your future.

- Which of the three habits you explored in these exercises have you made the most progress on?

_____

- Which is proving the most difficult for you?

_____

- What positive effects are you experiencing as a result of developing these habits? Name one or more.

_____

_____

_____

_____

- What do you think is, or will be, the most significant change in your life that will come from making the Habits for Success part of your life?

_____

_____

_____

_____

_____

_____

Appendix A

Guide to Library and Internet Research

Research and writing are essential to academic and career success. Through library and Internet research, you collect and analyze information. Through writing, you analyze ideas, think creatively about what they mean, and communicate information and perspectives to others.

Get to Know Your College Library

Although most students start researching with the Internet, the library may be the best place to begin. Instructors who understand the value of library research expect to see library citations in your work.

Start with a Road Map

Sign up for a library orientation session. Familiarize yourself with these library resources to give yourself a head start:

- **Circulation desk.** All publications are checked out at this location.
- **Reference area.** Here you'll find a variety of reference books, computer terminals containing the library catalog and online databases, and information specialists who can direct you to sources.
- **Book area.** Books are generally stored in the area known as the "stacks."
- **Periodicals area.** Here you'll find recent magazines, journals, and newspapers.
- **Audio-visual materials area.** Look here for a variety of non-print materials including video, art and photography, and recorded music collections.
- **Electronic library resources.** Network systems allow access to online materials via computers. If your school has a wireless Wi-Fi system, you can conduct research anywhere on campus.

Conduct an Information Search

Use a practical, step-by-step search method that takes you from general to specific sources:

- *Start with general reference works* (e.g., encyclopedias, almanacs, dictionaries, biographical references).
- *Move to specialized reference works* (e.g., encyclopedias and dictionaries that focus on a narrow field).
- *Browse through relevant books and articles.* Search the library catalog by author, title, or subject to learn where to locate specific books, periodicals, and journals.

IF YOU WANT TO SEARCH...	VISIT THIS INTERNET ADDRESS
Copyrighted books in print	Amazon.com: www.amazon.com Barnes and Noble: www.barnesandnoble.com
Encyclopedia entries	Encarta: http://encarta.msn.com
Print and electronic media	Arts & Letters Daily: http://aldaily.com/ (links to conventional and new media including weblogs)
Magazine and newspaper articles	AJR Newslink: http://newslink.org The Reader's Guide to Periodical Literature: http://www.hwwilson.com/databases/Readersg.htm
Academic publications	Google Scholar: scholar.google.com
Book search	Google Book Search: books.google.com (access to thousands of scanned books)
Weblogs	Quack Track: http://quacktrack.com/
Library of Congress	loc.gov (primary sources in U.S. history, culture, politics) Library of Congress American Memory: http://memory.loc.gov/ammem/
Federal legislation	Thomas, Legislative Information on the Internet: http://thomas/loc.gov
Biographies	Biography.com: www.biography.com/search Biography-Center: www.biography-center.com
Maps	Google Earth: http://earth.google.com Perry-Castañeda Library Map Collection: http://www.lib.utexas.edu/maps/
Country profiles	Atlapedia Online: www.atlapedia.com/online/country_index.htm
U.S. population and economic data	U.S. Census Bureau, U.S. Department of Commerce: http://www.census.gov
U.S. historical documents	The Avalon Project: yale.edu/lawweb/avalon/avalon.htm (documents from colonial period to today)
Company information	Thomas Register: www.thomasregister.com
European primary sources	EuroDocs: http://eudocs.lib.byu.edu/index.php/Main_Page (sources from two dozen European countries)

Ask the Librarian

Librarians can assist you in locating unfamiliar or hard-to-find sources, navigating catalogs and databases, uncovering research shortcuts, and dealing with pesky equipment. Know what you want to accomplish before asking a question. At many schools, you can query a librarian via cell phone, e-mail, and instant messaging. Among the helpful online reference sources they will point to are those listed in Key A.1.

Conduct a Keyword Search

Searching databases requires that you use a *keyword search*—an exploration that uses a topic-related natural-language word or phrase as a point of reference to locate other information. To narrow your topic and reduce the number of "hits" (resources pulled up by your search), add more keywords. For example, instead of searching through the broad category *art*, focus on *French art* or, more specifically, *nineteenth-century French art*. Key A.2 provides tips for using the keyword system to narrow searches with what is called *Boolean logic*.

Key A.2   Perform an effective keyword search with Boolean logic

IF YOU ARE SEARCHING FOR...	DO THIS	EXAMPLE
A word	Type the word normally.	Aid
A phrase	Type the phrase in its normal word order (use regular word spacing) or surround the phrase with quotation marks.	financial aid, or "financial aid"
Two or more keywords without regard to word order	Type the words in any order, surrounding the words with quotation marks. Use *and* to separate the words.	"financial aid" and "scholarships"
Topic A or topic B	Type the words in any order, surrounding the words with quotation marks. Use *or* to separate the words.	"financial aid" or "scholarships"
Topic A but not topic B	Type topic A first within quotation marks, and then topic B within quotation marks. Use *not* to separate the words.	"financial aid" not "scholarships"

Finding What You Need—and What Is Useful—on the Internet

The *Internet*, a worldwide computer network, can connect you to billions of information sources. Unlike your college library collection or databases, Internet resources may not be evaluated by anyone who vouches for their quality. As a result, your research depends on critical thinking (see Key 5.3 on p. 135 in Chapter 5 for information on how to critically evaluate the information you find on the Internet).

Start with Search Engines

Among the most popular and effective search engines are Google (www.google.com) and Yahoo! (www.yahoo.com). Search engines aimed at academic audiences are the Librarian's Index to the Internet (www.lii.org) and INFOMINE (www.infomine.com). The advantage of using academic directories is that you know someone has screened the sites and listed only those sources that have been determined to be reputable and regularly updated.

Use a Search Strategy

The World Wide Web has been called "the world's greatest library, with all its books on the floor." With no librarian in sight, you need to master a practical Internet search strategy.

1. **Think carefully about what you want to locate.** University of Michigan professor Eliot Soloway recommends phrasing your search in the form of a question—for example, What vaccines are given to children before age 5? Then he advises identifying the important words in the question (vaccines, children, before age 5) as well as related words (polio, shot, pediatrics, and so on). This will give you a collection of terms to use in different combinations as you search.[1]

2. **Use a search engine to isolate valuable sites.** Save sites that look useful. Most Internet software programs have a "bookmark" or "favorites" feature for doing this.

3. **Explore these sites to get a general idea of what's out there.** Look for useful keywords and information locations.

4. **Use keywords in a variety of ways to uncover more possibilities.** Vary word order if you are using more than one keyword (for example, search under "*education, college, statistics*" and "*statistics, education, college*"). Use Boolean logic (See Key A.2).

5. **Evaluate the number of links.** If there are too many, try using more, or more specific, keywords. If there are too few, use fewer or different keywords.

6. **When you think you are done, start over.** Choose another search engine, and search again. Different systems access different sites.

Library and Internet research is an important part of many writing assignments and projects. Remember: The success of your work depends on the quality of your research.

Appendix B

Communicating Ideas Through Writing

The Writing Process

Writing a research paper or essay involves *planning*, *drafting*, *revising*, and *editing*.

Planning

The planning process involves six steps that help you think about the assignment:

Pay Attention to Logistics

These practical questions will help you decide on a topic and depth of coverage:

1. **How much depth does my instructor expect, and how long should the paper be?**
2. **How much time do I have?** Consider your other courses and responsibilities.
3. **What kind of research is needed?** Your topic and purpose may determine this.
4. **Is it a team project?** If you are working with others, determine what each person will do.

Brainstorm Topic Ideas

Start the process of choosing a paper topic with *brainstorming*—a creative technique to generate ideas without judging their worth (see Chapter 5):

- Begin by writing down anything on the assigned subject that comes to mind, in no particular order. Tap your multiple intelligences for creative ideas. To jump-start your thoughts, scan your text and notes; check library or Internet references, or meet with your instructor to discuss ideas.
- Next, organize that list into an outline or think link so you can see different possibilities.

Use Prewriting Strategies to Narrow Your Topic

Prewriting strategies, including brainstorming, freewriting, and asking journalists' questions, help you decide which possible topic you would most like to pursue. Use them to narrow your topic, focusing on the specific sub-ideas and examples from your brainstorming session.

- **Brainstorming.** The same creative process you used to generate ideas will help you narrow your topic. Write down your thoughts about the possibilities you have chosen, do some more research, and then organize your thoughts into categories, noticing patterns that appear.

- **Freewriting.** When you *freewrite*, you jot down whatever comes to mind without censoring ideas or worrying about grammar, spelling, punctuation, or organization.
- **Asking journalists' questions.** When journalists start working on a story, they ask Who? What? Where? When? Why? How? Asking these questions will help you choose a specific topic.

Prewriting helps you develop a topic that is broad enough for investigation but narrow enough to handle. Prewriting also helps you identify what you know and what you don't know. If an assignment involves more than you already know, you need to do research.

Conduct Research and Take Notes

Research develops in stages as you narrow and refine your ideas. In the first brainstorming-for-ideas stage, look for an overview that can lead to a working thesis statement. In the second stage, track down information that fills in gaps. Ultimately, you will have a "body" of information that you can evaluate to develop and implement your final thesis.

As you research, create source notes and content notes to organize your work, keep track of your sources, and avoid plagiarism.

- **Source notes,** written on index cards, are preliminary notes that should include the author's name; the title of the work; the edition (if any); the publisher, year, and city of publication; the issue and/or volume number when applicable (such as for a magazine); and page numbers consulted. Notes on Internet sources should reference the website's complete name and address, including the universal resource locator (URL), which is the string of text and numbers that identifies an Internet site. Include a short summary and critical evaluation for each source.
- **Content notes,** written on large index cards, in a notebook, or on your computer, are taken during a thorough reading and provide an in-depth look at sources. Use them to record needed information. To supplement your content notes, make notations—marginal notes, highlighting, and underlining—directly on photocopies of sources.

Write a Working Thesis Statement

Next, organize your research, and write a *thesis statement*—the organizing principle of your paper. Your thesis declares your specific subject and point of view and reflects your writing purpose (to inform or persuade) and audience (your intended readers).

Consider this to be your *working thesis*, since it may change as you continue your research and develop your draft. Be ready and willing to rework your writing—and your thesis—one or more times before you hand in your paper.

Write a Working Outline or Think Link

The final planning step is to create a working outline or think link to guide your writing.

Drafting

You may write many versions of the assignment until you are satisfied. Each version moves you closer to saying exactly what you want in the way you want to say it. The main challenges you face at the first-draft stage are:

- Finalizing your thesis
- Defining an organizational structure
- Integrating source material into the body of your paper to fit your structure
- Finding additional sources to strengthen your presentation
- Choosing the right words, phrases, and tone
- Connecting ideas with logical transitions
- Creating an effective introduction and conclusion
- Checking for plagiarism
- Creating a list of works cited

Don't aim for perfection in a first draft. Trying to get every detail right too early may shut the door on ideas before you even know they are there.

Feewriting Your Draft

Use everything that you developed in the planning stage as the raw material for freewriting a draft. For now, don't think about your introduction, conclusion, or organizational structure. Simply focus on what you want to say. Only after you have thoughts down should you begin to shape your work.

Writing an Introduction

The introduction tells readers what the paper contains and includes a thesis statement, which is often found at the end of the introduction.

Creating the Body of a Paper

The body of the paper contains your central ideas and supporting *evidence*, which underpins your thesis with facts, statistics, examples, and expert opinions. Try to find a structure that helps you organize your ideas and evidence into a clear pattern. Several organizational options are presented in Key B.1.

Writing the Conclusion

A conclusion brings your paper to a natural ending by summarizing your main points, showing the significance of your thesis and how it relates to larger issues, calling the reader to action, or looking to the future. Let the ideas in the body of the paper speak for themselves as you wrap up.

Avoiding Plagiarism: Crediting Authors and Sources

Using another writer's words, content, unique approach, or illustrations without crediting the author is called *plagiarism*, and it is illegal and unethical. The following techniques will help you properly credit sources and avoid plagiarism:

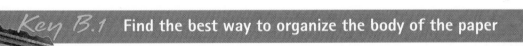

ORGANIZATIONAL STRUCTURE	WHAT TO DO
Arrange ideas by time.	Describe events in order or in reverse order.
Arrange ideas according to importance.	Start with the idea that carries the most weight and move to less important ideas. Or move from the least to the most important ideas.
Arrange ideas by problem and solution.	Start with a problem and then discuss solutions.
Arrange ideas to present an argument.	Present one or both sides of an issue.
Arrange ideas in list form.	Group a series of items.
Arrange ideas according to cause and effect.	Show how events, situations, or ideas cause subsequent events, situations, or ideas.
Arrange ideas through the use of comparisons.	Compare and contrast the characteristics of events, people, situations, or ideas.
Arrange by process.	Go through the steps in a process: a "how-to" approach.
Arrange by category.	Divide topics into categories and analyze each in order.

Make source notes as you go.   Plagiarism often begins accidentally during research. You may forget to include quotation marks around a quotation, or you may intend to cite or paraphrase a source but never do. To avoid forgetting, write detailed source and content notes as you research.

Learn the difference between a quotation and a paraphrase.   A *quotation* repeats a source's exact words and uses quotation marks to set them off from the rest of the text. A *paraphrase*, a restatement of the quotation in your own words, requires that you completely rewrite the idea, not just remove or replace a few words.

Use a citation even for an acceptable paraphrase.   Credit every source that you quote, paraphrase, or use as evidence (except when the material is considered common knowledge). To credit a source, write a footnote or endnote that describes it, using the format preferred by your instructor.

Understand that lifting material off the Internet is plagiarism.   Words in electronic form belong to the writer just as words in print form do. If you cut and paste sections from a source document onto your draft, you are probably committing plagiarism.

Key B.2 will help you identify what instructors regard as plagiarized work.

Instructors consider work to be plagiarized when you:

- Submit a paper from a Web site that sells or gives away research papers.

- Hand in a paper written by a fellow student or family member.

- Copy material in a paper directly from a source without proper quotation marks or source citation.

- Paraphrase material in a paper from a source without proper source citation.

- Submit the same paper in more than one class, even if the classes are in different terms or even different years.

Students who plagiarize place their academic careers at risk, in part because cheating is easy to discover. Increasingly, instructors are using anti-plagiarism software to investigate whether strings of words in student papers match those in a database. Make a commitment to hand in your own work and to uphold the highest standards of academic integrity.

Citing Sources

You may be asked to submit different kinds of source lists when you hand in your paper:

- **A References list,** also called a *List of Works Cited,* includes only the sources you actually cited in your paper.

- **A Bibliography** includes all the sources you consulted, whether or not they were cited in the paper.

- **An Annotated Bibliography** includes all the sources you consulted as well as an explanation or critiques of each source.

Your instructor will tell you which documentation style to use. Among the most common are:

- **The Modern Language Association** (MLA) format is generally used in the humanities, including history, literature, the arts, and philosophy.

- **The American Psychological Association** (APA) style is the appropriate format in psychology, sociology, business, economics, nursing, criminology, and social work.

Consult a college-level writers' handbook for an overview of these documentation styles, or read about them online at www.mla.org and www.apa.org.

Get Feedback

Talk with your instructor about your draft, or ask a study partner to read it and answer specific questions. Be open-minded about the comments you receive. Consider each carefully, and then make a decision about what to change.

Revising

When you *revise*, you critically evaluate the content, organization, word choice, paragraph structure, and style of your first draft. You evaluate the strength of your thesis and whether your evidence proves it, and you look for logical holes. You can do anything you want at this point to change your work. You can turn things around, presenting information from the end of your paper up front, tweak your thesis to reflect the evidence you presented, or choose a different organizational structure.

Engage your critical-thinking skills to evaluate the content and form of your paper. Ask yourself these questions as you revise:

- Does the paper fulfill the requirements of the assignment?
- Do I prove my thesis?
- Is each idea and argument developed, explained, and supported by examples?
- Does the introduction prepare the reader and capture attention?
- Is the body of the paper organized effectively?
- Does each paragraph have a *topic sentence* that is supported by the rest of the paragraph?
- Are my ideas connected to one another through logical transitions?
- Do I have a clear, concise writing style?
- Does the conclusion provide a natural ending without introducing new ideas?

Check for Clarity

Now check for sense, continuity, and clarity. Focus also on tightening your prose and eliminating wordy phrases. Examine once again how paragraphs flow into one another by evaluating the effectiveness of your *transitions*—the words, phrases, or sentences that connect ideas.

Editing

Editing involves correcting technical mistakes in spelling, grammar, and punctuation, as well as checking for consistency in such elements as abbreviations and capitalization. If you use a computer, start with the grammar check and spell check to find mistakes, realizing that you still need to check your work manually. Look also for *sexist language*, which characterizes people according to gender stereotypes and often involves the male pronouns *he* or *his* or *him*.

Proofreading, the last editing stage, involves reading every word for accuracy. Look for technical mistakes, run-on sentences, spelling errors, and sentence fragments. Look for incorrect word usage and unclear references. A great way to check your work is to read it out loud.

Your final paper reflects all the hard work you put in during the writing process. Ideally, when you are finished, you have a piece of work that shows your researching, writing, and thinking ability.

Appendix C

Problem Solving Strategies for Math and Science Courses

Because *word problems* are the most common way you will encounter quantitative thinking throughout your life, being able to solve them is crucial. Word problems can be tough, however, because they force you to translate between two languages—one expressed in words and one expressed in numbers and symbols. Although math is a precise language, English and other living languages tend to leave more room for interpretation. This difference in precision makes the process of translating difficult.

Steps to Solving Word Problems

Translating English or any other language into math takes a lot of practice. George Polya, in his 1945 classic *How to Solve It*, devised a four-step method for attacking word problems.[1] The basic steps reflect the general problem-solving process you explored in Chapter 5, and they will work for any word problem, whether in a math or science course.

1. **Understand the individual elements of the problem.** Read the problem carefully. Understand what it is asking. Know what information you have. Know what information is missing. Draw a picture, if possible. Translate the given information from words into mathematical language (e.g., numbers, symbols, formulas).

2. **Name and explore potential solution paths.** Think about similar problems that you understand and how those were solved. Consider whether this problem is an example of a mathematical idea that you know. In your head, try out different ways to solve the problem to see which may work best.

3. **Choose a solution path and solve the problem.** As you carry out your plan, check the precision of each of your steps.

4. **Review your result.** Check your answer for accuracy, if possible. Make sure you've answered the question the problem is asking. Does your result seem logical in the context of the problem? Are there other ways to do the problem?

Different problem-solving strategies will be useful to you when solving word problems. On a given problem, evaluate which strategy will work best and then apply it. The following section outlines several problem-solving strategies by working through word problem examples.[2]

Problem–Solving Strategies

The following sample problems are designed to give you an overview of problem types and to boost your ability to think critically through some basic math strategies.

Strategy 1. Look for a pattern.

G. H. Hardy (1877–1947), an eminent British mathematician, described mathematicians as makers of patterns and ideas. The search for patterns is one of the best strategies in problem solving. When you look for a pattern, you think inductively, observing a series of examples and determining the general idea that links the examples together.

Example: Find the next three entries in the following:

   a.   1, 2, 4, _____, _____, _____

   b.   O, T, T, F, F, S, S, _____, _____, _____

Solutions to Example:

a.   When identifying patterns, you may find a different pattern than someone else. This doesn't mean yours is wrong. Example *a* actually has several possible answers. Here are two:

   1.   Each succeeding term of the sequence is twice the previous term. In that case, the next three values would be 8, 16, 32.

   2.   The second term is 1 more than the first term, and the third term is 2 more than the second. This might lead you to guess the fourth term is 3 more than the third term, the fifth term is 4 more than the fourth term, and so on. In that case, the next three terms are 7, 11, 16.

b.   Example *b* is a famous pattern that often appears in puzzle magazines. The key to it is that "O" is the first letter of one, "T" is the first letter of two, and so on. Therefore, the next three terms would be E, N, and T for eight, nine, and ten.

Strategy 2. Make a table.

A table can help you organize and summarize information. This may enable you to see how examples form a pattern that leads you to an idea and a solution.

Example: How many ways can you make change for a half dollar using only quarters, dimes, nickels, and pennies?

Solutions to Example:

You might construct several tables and go through every possible case. You could start by seeing how many ways you can make change for a half dollar without using a quarter, which would produce the following tables:

```
Quarters    0   0   0   0   0   0   0   0   0   0   0   0   0   0   0   0   0   0
Dimes       0   0   0   0   0   0   0   0   0   0   0   1   1   1   1   1   1   1
Nickels     0   1   2   3   4   5   6   7   8   9  10   0   1   2   3   4   5   6
Pennies    50  45  40  35  30  25  20  15  10   5   0  40  35  30  25  20  15  10


Quarters    0   0   0   0   0   0   0   0   0   0   0   0   0   0   0   0   0   0
Dimes       1   1   2   2   2   2   2   2   2   3   3   3   3   3   4   4   4   5
Nickels     7   8   0   1   2   3   4   5   6   0   1   2   3   4   0   1   2   0
Pennies     5   0  30  25  20  15  10   5   0  20  15  10   5   0  10   5   0   0
```

There are 36 ways to make change for a half dollar without using a quarter. Using one quarter results in this table:

Quarters	1	1	1	1	1	1	1	1	1	1	1	1
Dimes	0	0	0	0	0	0	1	1	1	1	2	2
Nickels	0	1	2	3	4	5	0	1	2	3	0	1
Pennies	25	20	15	10	5	0	15	10	5	0	5	0

Using one quarter, you get 12 different ways to make change for a half dollar. Lastly, using two quarters, there's only one way to make change for a half dollar. Therefore, the solution to the problem is that there are $36 + 12 + 1 = 49$ ways to make change for a half dollar using only quarters, dimes, nickels, and pennies.

Strategy 3. Identify a subgoal. Breaking the original problem into smaller and possibly easier problems may lead to a solution to the original problem. This is often the case in writing a computer program.

> **Example:** Arrange the nine numbers 1, 2, 3,..., 9 into a square subdivided into nine sections in such a way that the sum of every row, column, and main diagonal is the same. This is called a *magic square*.

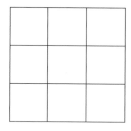

Solution to Example:
The sum of any individual row, column, or main diagonal has to be one-third the sum of all nine numbers (or else they wouldn't be the same). The sum of $1 + 2 + 3 + 4 + 5 + 6 + 7 + 8 + 9 = 45$. Therefore, each row, column, and main diagonal needs to sum to $45 \div 3 = 15$. Now, you need to see how many ways you can add three of the numbers from 1 to 9 and get 15. When you do this, you should get:

$$9 + 1 + 5 = 15 \qquad\qquad 8 + 3 + 4 = 15$$
$$9 + 2 + 4 = 15 \qquad\qquad 7 + 2 + 6 = 15$$
$$8 + 1 + 6 = 15 \qquad\qquad 7 + 3 + 5 = 15$$
$$8 + 2 + 5 = 15 \qquad\qquad 6 + 4 + 5 = 15$$

Now, looking at your magic square, notice that the center position will be part of four sums (a row, a column, and the two main diagonals). Looking back at your sums, you see that 5 appears in four different sums, therefore 5 is in the center square:

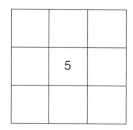

Now, in each corner, the number there appears in three sums (row, column, and a diagonal). Looking through your sums, you find that 2, 4, 6, and 8 each appear in three sums. Now you need to place them in the corners in such a way that your diagonals add up to 15:

2		6
	5	
4		8

Then, to finish, all you need to do is fill in the remaining squares so that 15 is the sum of each row, column, and main diagonal. The completed square is as follows:

2	7	6
9	5	1
4	3	8

Strategy 4. Examine a similar problem.   Sometimes a problem you are working on has similarities to a problem you've already read about or solved. In that case, it is often possible to use a similar approach to solve the new problem.

Example: Find a magic square using the numbers 3, 5, 7, 9, 11, 13, 15, 17, and 19.

Solution to Example: This problem is very similar to the example for Strategy 3. Approaching it in the same fashion, you find that the row, column, and main diagonal sum is 33. Writing down all the possible sums of three numbers to get 33, you find that 11 is the number that appears four times, so it is in the center:

	11	

The numbers that appear three times in the sums and will go in the corners are 5, 9, 13, and 17. This now gives you:

13		17
	11	
5		9

Finally, completing the magic square gives you:

13	3	17
15	11	7
5	19	9

Strategy 5. Work backward.   With some problems, you may find it easier to start with the perceived final result and work backward.

> **Example:** In the game of "Life," Carol had to pay $1,500 when she was married. Then, she lost half the money she had left. Next, she paid half the money she had for a house. Then, the game was stopped, and she had $3,000 left. With how much money did she start?

Solution to Example:
Carol ended up with $3,000. Right before that she paid half her money to buy a house. Because her $3,000 was half of what she had before her purchase, she had 2 X $3,000 = $6,000 before buying the house. Prior to buying the house, Carol lost half her money. This means that the $6,000 is the half she didn't lose. So, before losing half her money, Carol had 2 X $6,000 = $12,000. Prior to losing half her money, Carol had to pay $1,500 to get married. This means she had $12,000 + $1,500 = $13,500 before getting married. Because this was the start of the game, Carol began with $13,500.

Strategy 6. Draw a diagram.   Drawing a picture is often an aid to solving problems, especially for visual learners. Although pictures are especially useful for geometrical problems, they can be helpful for other types of problems as well.

> **Example:** There were 20 women at a round table for dinner. Each woman shook hands with the woman to her immediate right and left. At the end of the dinner, each woman got up and shook hands with everybody except those who sat on her immediate right and left. How many handshakes took place after dinner?

Solution to Example:
To solve this with a diagram, it might be a good idea to examine several simpler cases to see if you can determine a pattern of any kind that might help. Starting with two or three people, you can see there are no handshakes after dinner because everyone is adjacent to everyone else.

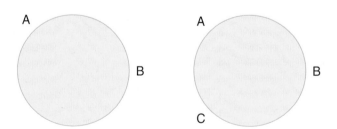

Now, in the case of four people, we get the following diagram, connecting those people who shake hands after dinner:

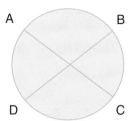

In this situation, you see there are two handshakes after dinner, AC and BD. In the case of five people, you get this picture:

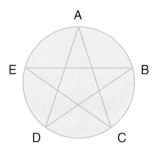

In this case, you have five after-dinner handshakes: AC, AD, BD, BE, and CE. Six people seated around a circle gives the following diagram:

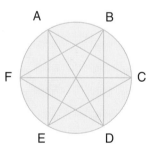

In this diagram, there are now a total of nine after-dinner handshakes: AC, AD, AE, BD, BE, BF, CE, CF, and DF. By studying the diagrams, you realize that if there are N people, each person would shake $N - 3$ people's hands after dinner. (They don't shake their own hands or the hands of the two people adjacent to them.) Because there are N people that would lead to $N(N - 3)$ after-dinner handshakes. However, this would double-count every handshake, because AD would also be counted as DA. Therefore, there are only half as many actual handshakes. So, the correct number of handshakes is $[N(N - 3)] \div 2$. So finally, if there are 20 women, there would be $20(17) \div 2 = 170$ after-dinner handshakes.

Strategy 7. Translate words into an equation.　This strategy is often used in algebra.

Example: A farmer needs to fence a rectangular piece of land. He wants the length of the field to be 80 feet longer than the width. If he has 1,080 feet of fencing available, what should the length and width of the field be?

Solution to Example: The best way to start this problem is to draw a picture of the situation and label the sides:

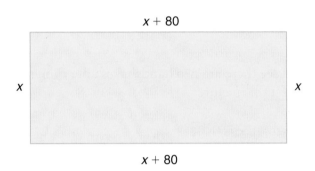

Let x represent the width of the field and $x + 80$ represent the length of the field. The farmer has 1,080 feet of fencing, and he will need $2x + 2(x + 80)$ feet of fencing to fence his field. This gives you the equation: $2x + 2(x + 80) = 1080$

Multiplying out:	$2x + 2x + 160 = 1080$
Simplifying and subtracting 160:	$4x = 920$
Dividing by 4:	$x = 230$
Therefore,	$x + 80 = 310$
As a check, you find that	$2(230) + 2(310) = 1080$

Appendix

Chapter 1

1. Thomas Friedman, *The World Is Flat*, New York: Farrar, Straus & Giroux, 2005, p. 8.
2. Gina Kolata, "A Surprising Secret to a Long Life: Stay in School," *New York Times*, January 3, 2007, (http://www.nytimes.com/2007/01/03/health/03aging.html#).
3. "Attitudes and Characteristics of Freshmen at 4-year Colleges, Fall 2007" *The Chronicle of Higher Education: 2008–9 Almanac*, Volume 55, Issue 1, p.18. Data from: "The American Freshman: National Norms for Fall 2007," Published by University of California at Los Angeles Higher Education Research Institute.
4. Franklin & Marshall College, "Why is Counseling Services Important on Campus," 2009 (http://www.fandm.edu/counselingservices).
5. Elia Powers, "The Non-Monetary Value of a College Degree," September 13, 2007, Inside Higher Ed (http://insidehighered.com/news/2007/09/13/college board).
6. Janet Rae-Dupree, "Can You Become a Creature of New Habits?" *New York Times*, May 4, 2008 (http://www.nytimes.com/2008/05/04/business/04unbox.html?ex=1210651200&en=e84617ddb814d475&ei=5070).
7. Scott Young, "Tips for Breaking Bad Habits and Developing Good Habits," October 16, 2007 (http://www.pickthebrain.com/blog/strategies-for-breaking-bad-habits-and-cultivating-good-ones/).
8. Info for these strategies from Scott Young website and also from http://www.shapefit.com/habits.html.
9. HR.blr.com, "2 in 5 High School Graduates Feel Unprepared," February 8, 2005 (http://hr.blr.com/news.aspx?id=10773).

Chapter 2

1. One such study is K. Warner Schaie, "The Seattle Longitudinal Studies of Adult Intelligence," in *Essential Papers on the Psychology of Aging*, M. Powell Lawton and Timothy A. Salthouse, eds. New York: New York University Press, 1998, pp. 263–271 (http://www.memory-key.com/Seniors/longitudinal_study.htm).
2. Derek V. Price and Angela Bell, *Federal Access Policies and Higher Education for Working Adults*, October 2008 (http://www.americanprogress.org/issues/2008/10/pdf/access_policies.pdf).

3. Howard Gardner, *Multiple Intelligences: New Horizons*, New York: Basic Books, 2006, p. 180.
4. Howard Gardner, *Multiple Intelligences: The Theory in Practice*, New York: Basic Books, 1993, p. 7.
5. Dr. C. George Boeree, "Carl Jung," 2006 (http://webspace.ship.edu/cgboer/jung.html).
6. Derek V. Price and Angela Bell, *Federal Access Policies and Higher Education for Working Adults*.
7. National Center for Learning Disabilities, "LD at a Glance," 2009 (http://www.ncld.org/index.php?option=content&task=view&id=448).
8. National Center for Learning Disabilities, "Adult Learning Disabilities: A Learning Disability Isn't Something You Outgrow. It's Something You Learn to Master" (pamphlet), New York: National Center for Learning Disabilities, 2000.
9. National Center for Learning Disabilities. "LD Advocates Guide," 2009 (http://www.ncld.org/content/view/263/312/).

Chapter 3

1. Jan Graybill, "Will Your Child Finish College in Four Years?" June 2007 (http://www.financial-topics.com/37052/e_article000828981.cfm?x=bdp9nr0,b8ddMsML,w).
2. Cited in Jim Hanson, "Your Money Personality: It's All in Your Head," December 25, 2006, University Credit Union (http://hffo.cuna.org/012433/article/1440/html).
3. "Attitudes and Characteristics of Freshmen at 4-Year Colleges, Fall 2007," *The Chronicle of Higher Education 2008-9 Almanac*, Volume 55, Issue 1, p. 18.
4. Jane B. Burka and Lenora M. Yuen, *Procrastination: Why You Do It, What to Do About It*, Reading, MA: Perseus Books, 1983, pp. 21–22.
5. Jim Hanson, "Your Money Personality: It's All in Your Head."
6. Goldie Blumenstyk, "The $375-Billion Question: Why Does College Cost So Much?" *The Chronicle of Higher Education 2008-9 Almanac*, Volume 55, Issue 6, p. A1.
7. Beckie Supiano, "Many Community College Students Miss Out on Aid—Because They Don't Apply," *The Chronicle of Higher Education*, October 7, 2008 (http://chronicle.com/daily/2008/10/4905n.htm).
8. Information in this paragraph collected from the following articles: Sam Dillon and Tamar Lewin, "Pell Grants Said to Face a Shortfall of $6 Billion," *The New York Times*, September 18, 2008

(http://www.nytimes.com/2008/09/18/education/18grant.html?_r=1&scp=1&sq=Pell%20Grants%20Shortfall&st=cse).
"Downturns, on Wall Street and Beyond, Affect States and their Colleges," *The Chronicle of Higher Education*, September 25, 2008 (http://chronicle.com/daily/2008/09/4745n.htm). Doug Lederman, "Surprising Impact of Student Loan Crunch," *Inside Higher Ed*, October 22, 2008 (http://insidehighered.com/news/2008/10/22/naicu). Jack Stripling, "FAFSA Frenzy," *Inside Higher Ed*, September 18, 2008 (http://insidehighered.com/news/2008/09/18/aid).

9. Beckie Supiano, "Many Community College Students Miss Out on Aid—Because They Don't Apply."

10. Robert Tomsho, "The Best Ways to Get Loans for College Now," *The Wall Street Journal*, August 13, 2008, p. D1.

11. Eric Hoover, "Community College Students Need Better Financial Advising, Survey Finds," *The Chronicle of Higher Education*, November 21, 2008 (http://chronicle.com/weekly/v55/i13/13a01901.htm).

12. Beckie Supiano, "In a Rocky Economy, 10 Steady Tips About Student Aid," *The Chronicle of Higher Education*, November 7, 2008.

Chapter 4

1. Alina Tugend, "Multitasking Can Make You Lose…Um…Focus," *The New York Times*, October 25, 2008 (http://www.nytimes.com/2008/10/25/business/yourmoney/25shortcuts.html?scp=1&sq=Multitasking%20Focus&st=cse).

2. Dr. Marlene Schwartz, Deputy Director of the Rudd Center for Food Policy and Obesity at Yale University.

3. "Help for Sleep-Deprived Students," *CBS News*, April 19, 2004 (www.cbsnews.com/stories/2004/04/19/health/main612476.shtml).

4. Boynton Health Service, "Health and Academic Performance: Minnesota Undergraduate Students," July 2008 (http://www.bhs.umn.edu/reports/HealthAcademicPerformanceReport_2007.pdf).

5. Nicholas Bakalar, "Patterns: Trying to Avoid a Cold? Go Back to Bed," *The New York Times*, January 3, 2009 (http://www.nytimes.com/2009/01/13/health/research/13patt.html).

6. Gregg Jacobs, "Insomnia Corner," Talk About Sleep, 2008 (www.talkaboutsleep.com/sleepdisorders/insomnia_corner.htm); also see Herbert Benson and Eileen M. Stuart, *The Wellness Book*, New York: Simon & Schuster, 1992, p. 292.

7. Joel Seguine, "Students Report Negative Consequences of Binge Drinking in New Survey," *The University Record*, The University of Michigan, October 25, 1999 (http://www.umich.edu/~urecord/9900/Oct25_99/7.htm).

8. Mike Briddon, "Struggling with Sadness: Depression Among College Students Is on the Rise," Stressedoutnurses.com, April 22, 2008 (http://www.stressedoutnurses.com/2008/04/struggling-with-sadness-depression-among-college-students-is-on-the-rise/).

9. The American Psychological Association, "Suicidal Thoughts Among College Students More Common Than Expected," August 17, 2008 (http://www.apa.org/releases/suicideC08.html).

10. Daniel Goleman, *Working with Emotional Intelligence*, New York: Bantam Books, 1998, pp. 26–27.

11. Mark A. King, Anthony Sims, and David Osher, "How Is Cultural Competence Integrated in Education?" n.d., Center for Effective Collaboration and Practice (http://cecp.air.org/cultural/Q_integrated.htm).

12. Louis E. Boone, David L. Kurtz, and Judy R. Block, *Contemporary Business Communication*, Upper Saddle River, NJ: Prentice Hall, 1994, pp. 489–499.

Chapter 5

1. Vincent Ruggiero, *The Art of Thinking*, 2001, quoted in "Critical Thinking," accessed July 2006 from the Web site of Oregon State University, Academic Success Center (http://success.oregonstate.edu/criticalthinking.html).

2. Richard Paul, "The Role of Questions in Thinking, Teaching, and Learning," 1995, accessed April 2004 from the Web site of the Center for Thinking and Learning (http://www.criticalthinking.org/resources/articles/the-role-of-questions.shtml).

3. Lawrence F. Lowery, "The Biological Basis of Thinking and Learning," 1998, accessed April 2004 from the Full Option Science System at the University of California at Berkeley (http://lhsfoss.org/newsletters/archive/pdfs/FOSS_BBTL.pdf).

4. Charles Cave, "Definitions of Creativity," August 1999 (http://members.optusnet.com.au/~charles57/Creative/Basics/definitions.htm).

5. Robert Sternberg, *Successful Intelligence: How Practical and Creative Intelligence Determine Success in Life*, New York: Plume, 1997, p. 189.

6. Lynn Quitman Troyka, *Simon & Schuster Handbook for Writers*, Upper Saddle River, NJ: Prentice Hall, 1996, p. 144.

7. Roger von Oech, *A Kick in the Seat of the Pants*, New York: Harper & Row, 1986, pp. 5–21.

8. Dennis Coon, *Introduction to Psychology: Exploration and Application*, 6th ed., St. Paul: West, 1992, p. 295.

9. Roger von Oech, *A Whack on the Side of the Head*, New York: Warner Books, 1990, pp. 11–168.

10. J. R. Hayes, *Cognitive Psychology: Thinking and Creating*, Homewood, IL: Dorsey, 1978.

11. Sternberg, *Successful Intelligence*, *op. cit.*, p. 219.

12. Adapted from T. Z. Tardif and R. J. Sternberg, "What Do We Know About Creativity?" in *The Nature of Creativity*, R. J. Sternberg, ed., London: Cambridge University Press, 1988.
13. Sternberg, *Successful Intelligence*, *op. cit.*, p. 212.
14. Hayes, *Cognitive Psychology*, *op. cit.*
15. "The Best Innovations Are Those That Come from Smart Questions," *Wall Street Journal*, April 12, 2004, B1.

Chapter 6

1. Quoted in James Freeman, "Raising Bob Costas: Is Memorizing Sports Trivia Good for the Brain?" *The Wall Street Journal*, August 8, 2008, p. A1.
2. University of California–Irvine, "Short-Term Stress Can Affect Learning And Memory," *ScienceDaily* March 13, 2008 (http://www.sciencedaily.com/releases/2008/03/080311182434.htm).
3. Herman Ebbinghaus, *Memory: A Contribution to Experimental Psychology*, trans. by H. A. Ruger and C. E. Bussenius. New York: Teachers College, Columbia University, 1885.
4. Benedict Carey, "H. M., an Unforgettable Amnesiac, Dies at 82," *The New York Times,* December 5, 2008, p. A1; Scott LaFee, "Brain of 'most studied' amnesiac will be evaluated anew at UCSD," *San Diego Union Tribune*, December 6, 2008. (http://www.signonsandiego.com/news/metro/20081206-9999-1n6brain.html); Thomas H. Maugh II, "Henry M. dies at 82; victim of brain surgery accident offered doctors key insights into memory," *Los Angeles Times*, December 9, 2008 (http://www.latimes.com/news/science/la-me-molaison9-2008dec09,0,6956231,full.story).
5. Adapted from the University of Arizona. *The Eight-Day Study Plan.* (http://www.ulc.arizona.edu/documents/8day_074.pdf).
6. "Study Shows How Sleep Improves Memory," *Science Daily*, June 29, 2005 (http://www.sciencedaily.com/releases/2005/06/050629070337.htm).
7. Adam Robinson, *What Smart Students Know: Maximum Grades, Optimum Learning, Minimum Time*, New York: Three Rivers Press, 1993, p. 118.
8. Letter-to-the-editor, *Wall Street Journal*, August 13, 2008.
9. Letter-to-the-editor, *Wall Street Journal*, August 13, 2008.

Chapter 7

1. Francis P. Robinson, *Effective Behavior*, New York: Harper & Row, 1941.
2. John Mack Faragher, Mary Jo Buhle, Daniel Czitrom, and Susan H. Armitage, *Out of Many,* 6th ed., Upper Saddle River, NJ: Prentice Hall, 2009, p. xxix.
3. Charles G. Morris and Albert A. Maisto, *Psychology: An Introduction,* 12th ed., Upper Saddle River, NJ: Prentice Hall, 2005, p. 186.

4. Headings found in John Mack Faragher, Mary Jo Buhle, Daniel Czitrom, and Susan H. Armitage, *Out of Many,* 6th ed., Upper Saddle River, NJ: Prentice Hall, 2009, pp. 264–265.
5. Benjamin S. Bloom, *Taxonomy of Educational Objectives, Handbook I: Cognitive Domain.* New York: Longman, 1956.
6. Ophelia H. Hancock, *Reading Skills for College Students*, 5th ed., Upper Saddle River, NJ: Prentice Hall, 2001, pp. 54–59.
7. Adam Robinson, *What Smart Students Know*, New York: Three Rivers Press, 1993, p. 82.
8. Libby Sander, "For One Transfer Student, the Second Chance Is the Charm," The Chronicle of Higher Education: Community College, October 31, 2008, pp. B18-21 (http://chronicle.com/weekly/v55/i10/10b01801.htm).
9. Pam Belluck, "Another Potential Benefit of Cutting Calories: Better Memory," *The New York Times*, January 27, 2009, p. D3.
10. For more information on digital natives, see John Palfrey and Urs Gasser, *Born Digital: Understanding the First Generation of Digital Natives.* New York: Basic Books, 2008.
11. Mark Bauerlein, "Online Literacy Is a Lesser Kind: Slow Reading Counterbalances Web skimming," *The Chronicle Review*, September 19, 2008.
12. "Universities See Double-Digit Increase in Online Enrollment, Study Finds," *The Chronicle of Higher Education*, November 12, 2008.
13. Nicholas Carr, "Is Google Making Us Stupid?" *The Atlantic,* July/August 2008. (http://www.theatlantic.com/doc/200807/google).
14. Nancy Bunge, "Assign Books, and Students Will Read," *The Chronicle Review*, from the issue dated October 17, 2008 (http://chronicle.com/weekly/v55/i08/08b02401.htm).
15. John J. Macionis, *Sociology*, 6th ed., Upper Saddle River, NJ: Prentice Hall, 1997, p. 174.

Chapter 8

1. Quoted in *Keys to Lifelong Learning Telecourse* (videocassette), directed by Mary Jane Bradbury, Intrepid Films, 2000.
2. Richard T. Wright, *Environmental Science,* 10th edition. Upper Saddle River, NJ: Pearson Education, 2008, p. 466.
3. Adapted from Gina Allred Website, 'Math Anxiety Worksheet,' (http://www.gallred.com/actwork/MathAnxietyWS1.doc/).
4. Anderson, Wilson, & Fielding, 1988 (accessed online at http://www.readfaster.com/education_stats.asp#readingstatistics).
5. "Call to Scientists: 'Dance Your Ph.D.'" *The Chronicle of Higher Education*, November 14, 2008, (http://chronicle.com/news/index.php?id=5494&utm_source=pm&utm_medium=en).

6. "Attitudes and Characteristics of Freshmen at 4-year Colleges, Fall 2007" *The Chronicle of Higher Education: 2008-9 Almanac*, Volume 55, Issue 1, p. 18. Data from: The American Freshman: National norms for fall 2007: Published by University of California at Los Angeles Higher Education Research Institute.

7. Institute of International Education, "Top 2007-8 Destinations for U.S. Students," in Karin Fischer, "For American Students, Study-Abroad Numbers Continue to Climb, but Financial Obstacles Loom," *The Chronicle of Higher Education*, November 21, 2008, p. A24.

8. National Endowment for the Arts, "To Read or Not To Read: A Question of National Consequence,) Research Report #47, Washington, DC: Office of Research and Analysis, NEA, November 2007). (www.nea.gov/research/ToRead.PDF).

9. Aisha Labi, "As World Economies Struggle, Competition Heats Up for Students From Abroad," *Chronicle of Higher Education*, November 21, 2008, p. A22 (Table: "Foreign Students in the U.S. by Region of Origin, 2007–8").

10. Frank Schmalleger, *Criminal Justice Today: An Introductory Text for the 21st Century,* 10th ed. Upper Saddle River, NJ: Pearson Education, 2009, p. 583–584.

11. Charles G. Morris and Albert A. Maisto, *Understanding Psychology,* 8th ed., Upper Saddle River, NJ: Pearson Education, 2008, p. 396.

Chapter 9

1. Ralph G. Nichols, "Do We Know How to Listen? Practical Helps in a Modern Age," *Speech Teacher*, March 1961, pp. 118–124.

2. Alina Tugend, "Multitasking Can Make You Lose … Um … Focus," *The New York Times*, October 25, 2008.

3. Nichols, "Do We Know How to Listen?" *op.cit.*

4. Elia Powers, "The (Non-Monetary) Value of a College Degree," *Inside Higher Ed*, September 13, 2007 (http://insidehighered.com/news/2007/09/13/collegeboard).

5. Lizette Alvarez, "Combat to College," *The New York Times Education Life Supplement*, November 2, 2008, pp. 24–27.

6. Walter Pauk, *How to Study in College*, 7th ed., Boston: Houghton Mifflin, 2001, pp. 236–241.

7. James Deese and Ellin K. Deese, *How to Study and Other Skills for Success in College* 4th ed., New York: McGraw-Hill, 1994, p. 28.

8. John J. Macionis, *Sociology*, 10th ed., Upper Saddle River, NJ: Prentice Hall, 2005, pp. 203–204.

Chapter 10

1. Adapted from Ron Fry, *"Ace" Any Test*, 3rd ed., Franklin Lakes, NJ: Career Press, 1996, pp. 123–24.

2. "Attitudes and Characteristics of Freshmen at 4-year Colleges, Fall 2007" *The Chronicle of Higher Education:*

2008-9 Almanac, Volume 55, Issue 1, p.18. Data from: The American Freshman: National norms for fall 2007: Published by University of California at Los Angeles Higher Education Research Institute.

3. Sandra McCleaster, "Test Anxiety in Students," *Journal for Respiratory Care & Sleep Medicine*, Winter, 2004 (http://findarticles.com/p/articles/mi_hb4758/is_/ai_n 29152568).

4. Carla Baku Living Design Manifesto (http://shortassignments.blogspot.com/2008_04_27_archive.html). Jack Kent Cook Foundation: Current Scholars – Carla Baku (http://www.jkcf.org/our-scholars/current/395-Carla-Baku). Luke Henesy, "The Road Less Traveled," *The Stanford Daily,* October 29, 2007 (http://daily.stanford.edu/article/2007/10/29/theRoadLessTraveled).

5. Gregory Berns, "When Fear Takes Over Our Brains," *The New York Times,* December 7, 2008, p. Business, 2.

Chapter 11

1. Dir. Mary Jane Bradbury, *Keys to Lifelong Learning Telecourse*, Videocassette. Intrepid Films, 2000.

2. Ibid.

3. Tim Jarvis, "Steal These Strategies!" *O, The Oprah Magazine*, January 2009, p. 147.

4. Scott Jaschik, "Mixed Grades for Grads and Assessment," *Inside Higher Ed*, January 23, 2008 (http://insidehighered.com/news/2008/01/23/employers)

Chapter 12

1. Arthur L. Costa, "Habits for Success," in *Developing Minds: A Resource Book for Teaching Thinking*, Arthur L. Costa, ed., Alexandria, VA: Association for Supervision and Curriculum Development, 2001, p. 85.

2. Ibid., p.80.

Appendix A

1. Lori Leibovich, "Choosing Quick Hits Over the Card Catalog," *New York Times*, August 10, 2001, p. 1.

Appendix B

1. Analysis based on Lynn Quitman Troyka, *Simon & Schuster Handbook for Writers,* Upper Saddle River, NJ: Prentice Hall, 1996, pp. 22–23.

Appendix C

1. George Polya, *How to Solve It*, London: Penguin Books, 1990.

2. Rick Billstein, Shlomo Libeskind, and Johnny W. Lott, *A Problem Solving Approach to Mathematics for Elementary School Teachers*, pp. 5–22, 24–26, 28–36. Copyright 2004 Pearson Education, Inc. Reproduced by permission of Pearson Education, Inc. All rights reserved.